THE LONDON
METROBUS

Matthew Wharmby

Ian Allan

Front cover: Fulwell garage operated Metrobuses for the longest period, the type racking up 24 years there between 19 March 1979 and 21 May 2003. Seen in its element on Richmond Bridge is M54 (WYW 54T) during April 1982. *Haydn Davies*

Back cover, top: As the traditional London Transport was compelled to give way to market forces, competitors of varying quality sprang up. Very few had the resources or wherewithal to invest in new vehicles, but Ensignbus cemented its status and its longevity by taking on 24 brand new mkII Metrobuses in 1988, one of which is 284 (F284 NHJ) at Hornchurch on 21 March 1989. The mkII, though evaluated by LT, did not catch on, the only other undertaking to specify the type being the ill-fated Harrow Buses division of London Buses Ltd. Under the guises successively of Ensign Citybus, Capital Citybus and First Capital, these particular Metrobuses lasted until 2002. *Malc McDonald*

Back cover, bottom: London Buses Ltd buckled under competitive pressure and then came apart entirely upon the great sell-off at the end of 1994. Privatisation divided the Metrobus fleet among seven new companies, which quickly clustered in pairs. Cowie Leaside and Cowie South London became Arriva London North and South in 1998, and the former was an extensive user of Metrobuses, inheriting over 300. At the end of their lives surviving Ms found themselves shuffled constantly as short-term stopgaps, the last such task being on the 125 from Edmonton garage. M651 (KYV 651X), a very late repaint and with plain upper-deck front windows, is seen at North Finchley on 1 June 2002. *Author*

Contents

First published 2009

ISBN 978 0 7110 3377 1

© Matthew Wharmby 2009

Published by Ian Allan Publishing

an imprint of Ian Allan Publishing Ltd, Hersham, Surrey, KT12 4RG
Printed in England by Ian Allan Printing Ltd, Hersham, Surrey, KT12 4RG

Code: 0908 / B2

Visit the Ian Allan Publishing website at www.ianallanpublishing.com

Foreword

Unprepossessing, box-like, knockabout even – nobody would really imbue the humble MCW Metrobus with the glamour of the Routemaster or the sophistication of the Titan, but it was cheap, reliable and it lasted a quarter of a century. The M class of 1,440 members, plus two mkIIs taken new, 29 more leased and eventually 14 second-hand examples, would participate in the most desperate upheavals to affect bus operations in London, in the course of which the familiar London Transport was first battered by tendering and then broken up into pieces and sold. London's Ms came out of that débâcle still intact and capable of a further decade's service. It was not until the very end of the century that numbers started dropping as low-floor buses arrived to replace them, and even then scattered examples returned to service with LT contractors not derived from the old LBL, as inexpensive stop-gaps.

Enthusiasts who have come to like the Metrobus appreciate their mellifluous, never predictable sound qualities and their virtual indestructibility in a range of operating conditions, helped along by the great variety of change to occur visually both externally and behind the doors.

I extend my thanks to the range of photographers whose work over the last three decades in all weathers has provided the stock for this book and to the publishers for allowing me to cram such a long story into such a small space. And, lastly, to the Metrobus's creator, MCW, which perished in the upheavals of deregulation but whose products' simplicity and versatility would be much appreciated today.

Matthew Wharmby
Walton-on-Thames
January 2009

Left: London Transport's M class of MCW Metrobuses, in spite of their 'off-the-peg' status, still incorporated enough traditional LT features – comprehensive blinds, proper seating and ventilation and white-on-black numberplates – to make them as valid as any STL, RT or RM. In the quarter-century of their service period, their environment would change utterly. During 1983 Fulwell's M558 (GYE 558W) is seen at East Twickenham. *Haydn Davies*

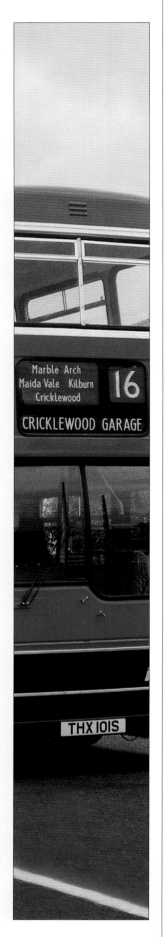

ONE

Initial Experience

London in 1975 was not a happy place. The Reshaping Plan, fashioned by politicians on the pressing need to match falling ridership with declining staff availability, had not met with passenger approval. The mass introduction of self-service OMO buses in replacement of the reliability and supervision afforded by crew operation had driven even more passengers to private cars, never to return. Stripped by the same politicians of the ability to design its own buses to the perceived operating conditions of the capital, London Transport had discovered that its first-generation purchases, the Merlins, Swifts and Fleetlines, were catastrophically unreliable by comparison with their RT and Routemaster predecessors, and could not be adapted to existing maintenance procedures. Spares shortages and one oil crisis after another added to the desperation.

Having swallowed up the majority of firms which had ever built buses for London Transport and its predecessors, Leyland planned to centralise their products into just one – the all-encompassing Titan – but itself fell on hard times, declaring bankruptcy in 1975 and having to be bailed out by central government. Without time to wait until a shortfall of deliveries imperilled its orderly replacement and overhaul programme, London Transport was forced to look abroad for the first time in its history, and one manufacturer to step into the breach was Scania-Vabis. This long-established Swedish truck, bus and aeronautics manufacturer teamed up with a very British bodybuilder, Metro-Cammell-Weymann of Washwood Heath, Birmingham, and together they produced the Metro-Scania single-decker (six of which LT took in 1973 as the MS class, with London Country purchasing four and acquiring two). The Metropolitan double-decker followed. In 1975 London Transport ordered 164 of this new chassis, which it would dub the MD class.

Emboldened by its association with Scania and the successful performance of the Metropolitan, MCW decided to go it alone. Support came from West Midlands County Council, anxious to protect its local industry against what was shaping up to be a joint venture between LT, the NBC and Leyland. Confidence was also assured on MCW's doorstep from West Midlands PTE, which immediately ordered five, taking an option on 20 more. MCW was certainly galvanised by the defection of Leyland's chief sales and marketing officer to take up the same role at Washwood Heath.

In July 1977 London Transport placed an order for five Metrobuses, simultaneously ordering an equivalent number of Titans (as the B15 project was now known). Embarking on a strategy of dual-sourcing, LT was still keen to limit the number of suppliers to avoid overproliferation of types, while ensuring that its chosen manufacturers had sufficient capacity; for this reason contemporary offerings by Foden, Volvo-Ailsa and Dennis were not pursued.

1977 was taken up with Metrobus development; certainly there was less to do than on the comparable Titan. MCW simply carried over its existing body (codenamed Apollo for its application to the Metrobus), in build since 1970 and familiar on the DMS and MD classes. The curious asymmetrical windscreen of the MD class was also perpetuated, but without such a sharp drop on the nearside, and the chrome ostentation was omitted other than a single thin strip around the headlights and frontally-mounted radiator grille. A similar refinement extended the staircase by half a bay to permit every step to have a square edge, an improvement that found great favour in the eyes of the authors of a comparative trial instituted 25 years later.

No moves were made at this stage to invite other bodybuilders to body the chassis, though MCW offered the integral Metrobus with a limited range of powerplant and transmission choices; Gardner 6LXB or Rolls-Royce Eagle engines, mated to Voith D851 gearboxes and with hydraulic brakes similar to those specified on Routemasters (and thus satisfying LT's requirements for familiar, proven technology). Increased saloon space was provided by the specification of somewhat smaller wheels (of a diameter of 22.5") than was familiar on contemporary types. Noise levels were set at 80dB.

An engineering test prototype began trials in October, and in December out came the first prototype, TOJ 592S. Wearing full London Transport livery of red with white upper-deck window surrounds, and unusually a black skirt, this Gardner-engined vehicle was taken into Chiswick for inspection. By contrast with the extensive road trials performed by the two evaluatory Titans between 1976 and 1978, TOJ 592S never turned a wheel in service,

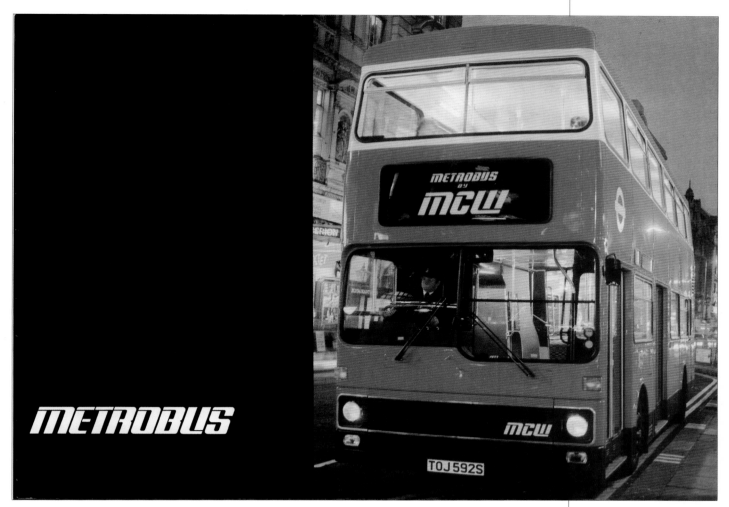

METROBUS

its only foray being to carry GLC officials to view the newly-revamped Heathrow Central Bus Station on 22 December. Still, this experience secured GLC approval for 1978's bus orders, which were announced the following February as fifty of each of Metrobus and Titan. However, GLC advice that up to 450 new buses would be needed to maintain vehicle levels in the face of withdrawals and overhauls prompted this order to be increased by 250 Titans and 200 Metrobuses. All the while LT's own XRM project, enabled by a late change in legislation that allowed LT more leeway in bus-construction specifications, was progressing, the results of which could be expected to take over from these types by the mid-1980s.

The code specified for the Metrobus was MT, and it was in this form that MT1 (THX 101S) was delivered to Chiswick Works in April 1978 (via a handover to the LT Chairman at the Hilton Hotel); two more MTs arrived (in June and July respectively) before the code was simplified to plain M, though at one point it was considered that MC would be the code for crew-operated Metrobuses. This was certainly to be the initial deployment for the class, with the first routes being the crew-operated 16 and 16A pair run by Cricklewood (W). LT's engineering code to begin with was 1M1.

In full LT 'white-top' livery of the day, MT1 added a black skirt, which was not to be perpetuated but which would be associated with this bus for ever

after. Black-on-white numberplates were another modern touch that didn't detract from the general attractiveness of the vehicles, whose essentially square profile, carried over from the DMS, updated that design by including a front-mounted radiator. Unencumbered by exhaust chimneys or cosmetic engine shrouds, the rear aspect featured a generously-sized rear window, with the engine carried within the full-width rearmost sixth panel.

Inside was fitted the orange-based moquette that was intended for LT's abortive 'Speedbus' network and then trialled on DMS2121, with brown walls in the fashion of the day intended to convey a soothing, comforting atmosphere for passengers. Unladen weight was 9833kg (the white labels carried at the bottom of the bay behind the exit door), while the height was 14ft 4¼in (4.374m) and the length 31ft 4⅜in (9.55m). Seating capacity for these crew buses was 71 (H43/28D), plus the legal maximum of five standing.

The Gardner 6LXB/Voith D851 combination, which was to be standard on the vast majority of London Transport Metrobuses, afforded a most unusual set of sounds; at idle the familiar chugging, but at speed set off by an agitated, expectant whine in a key of D, a strange but essentially harmonious crescendo that critics have likened to a hairdryer. The higher the speed, the higher the note, only to be brought to a halt by the application of the brakes with a tremendous whistle as the retarder kicked in. Gearchanges could be somewhat pronounced, especially so the more

Above: On the back of comparative success with the Scania BR111DH-based Metropolitan, 164 of which entered service with London Transport during 1976/7, MCW adapted its angular bodywork superficially to produce the Apollo body for the new Metrobus chassis. A single demonstrator, TOJ 592S, was built for LT in 1977, but this bus, shown off on the front cover of its manufacturer's brochure, never turned a wheel in service. It is still extant today, in the hands of Midland Classic.
MCW / Ian Allan Library

Right: The quintet of evaluatory Metrobuses ordered by London Transport in 1977 exemplified the link between the previous MCW bodies on DMSs in that they had blind boxes capable of taking DMS blinds. During July 1978 MT1 (THX 101S), as it was then known, demonstrates the panels for the Metrobus's first intended route, Cricklewood's 16, at Bollo Lane in Acton, just a short drive from Chiswick Works.
Tony Wilson

elderly the bus; with a great clonk, the bus would thump itself into second gear, rattling the driver's cashbox; and if the brakes were insufficiently lubricated, passengers would hear and feel a groan from the undercarriage. Finally, the application of the handbrake at stops was apt to produce a deafening squawk!

The blind box was a single glass panel masked so that standard-width destinations (code KK, MM and NN) could be carried in the manner of the DMS family; side blinds were a combined unit able to show number and destination (code CC).

The delivery of MT2 in June (as with all new buses prior to allocation, to Aldenham for pre-service checks to be made) allowed MT1 to commence driver training at Cricklewood (after a visit to Showbus at Hillingdon on 25 June). M4 appeared in August and M5 in September, concurrent with the first examples of the 1979 order, headed by M6 (WYW 6T). M4/5 were sent to Fulwell, known to be the first recipient of the first production order, for driver training, and were not present when it was at last decided to place the first three into service at Cricklewood. M3 was the mechanical trainer at Cricklewood.

The last demonstration of the Metrobus prior to squadron entry into service was when M1 (as renumbered from MT1) accompanied T1 to LT's Syon Park gala on 16 September.

Right: The rear of the Metrobus afforded an enormous rear window by comparison with that of previous rear-engined double-deck types, with no need for shrouds, chimneys or other impediments. The unique black skirt and *'METROBUS'* type badge on the back of MT1 (THX 101S) are shown to good advantage during the first Metrobus's spell at Chiswick Works.
Tony Wilson

Into Service

Strangely, no reliable source has ever been able to provide details of exactly when the Metrobus entered traffic on the 16; suffice to say M1-3 slipped out some time in the third week of November 1978, perhaps on Saturday 11th. Appearances, rare at first, picked up to the extent that Cricklewood felt confident in putting them out on the N94, the class's first night route, at the start of the New Year. M4 joined its sisters there in March. Meanwhile, deliveries of M6-55 were causing concern by their sluggishness, in that just ten buses of this batch were in stock by year's end and DMS withdrawals had to begin imminently. Parts shortages meant that buses were having to be assembled without certain components and delivered on the promise of their fitment later. Similar delivery issues were affecting the Titans.

M6 upwards (LT code 2M2) were OMO vehicles seating 67 (H43/24D), the AFC cabinet over the front nearside wheelarch reducing seating capacity downstairs by four; 21 standees were permitted (19 on some buses). The numberplates on these buses were of further note; still black-on-white, the typescript was of a fashionably futuristic style with computer-like square figures. However, after M54 traditional white-on-black LT numberplates were introduced, coinciding with the unfortunate decision not to apply white relief to future deliveries from

Above: At last the M class entered service – quite when, nobody knows – and such would be the manner of the class's exit 26 years later. Working in support of DMs on the 16 and 16A and now with the class code chosen for the type, M2 (THX 102S) works through Marble Arch towards Victoria on 5 June 1980, though as yet without any holders for running-number plates. The 16A had been created in order to bring extra custom to Brent Cross Shopping Centre, opened in 1976 and soon to be a focal point for several Metrobus-operated routes. *Geoff Rixon*

Right: Fulwell was the first London Transport garage to receive the production order for Ms. There were five routes to convert from DMS between March and July 1979, requiring enough vehicles for a PVR of 52. M6-54 stood out for their curious computer-style registration plates, shown off by M17 (WYW 17T) at work on the 270 at Teddington on 26 March, a week after entering service. In their livery of white-topped red with black radiator grille, the Metrobuses represented a considerable improvement aesthetically over the flat-fronted and plain DMS, and the new design of blind boxes permitted a taller and more legible route number. *Geoff Rixon*

Right: One sunny day in June 1979 M51 (WYW 51T) is espied leaving Fulwell garage by the west gates on its way to take up a shortworking on the 267. This former trolleybus route would operate Ms for the longest period, the type only being withdrawn in 2002 after 23 years, longer than the RMs that replaced the trolleys in 1962. Through the entrance doorway, a cord blocks off the automatic fare-collection (AFC) cabinet following an LT instruction to discontinue this unpopular and unsuccessful method of payment. *Geoff Rixon*

Right: Another Fulwell Metrobus in its element is M44 (WYW 44T) on the 90B at Hatton Cross on 5 August 1979. Part of a family of routes bearing southwestward from Hammersmith through Richmond and Twickenham, the 'B'-suffixed variant was as yet the only one to operate double-deckers, though the 90 and 290 would subsequently be converted thus and even the 190, a much later innovation along broadly the same corridor, would see the odd unscheduled M. *Geoff Rixon*

M56; thus M55 was uniquely all-red but with a black numberplate. The blind box was positively gargantuan by contemporary minimalist standards, its single glass panel extending almost across the entire front and approaching the dimensions of the equipment fitted to the RT family. The blinds themselves inaugurated a new standard by combining the number (KK) and via (MM) panels into a new panel (KM), as on RCLs, and permitting the display of a considerably taller route number. Surprisingly, the blind boxes on M1-5 were never altered to match.

In the same month that the M class made its debut, LT asked for GLC authority to purchase a further 450 second-generation buses (again, 250 Ts and 200 Ms) for 1980 at a cost of £22m; one reason was to gain maximum benefit from New Bus Grant before its progressive reduction from 1981, the Government having decided that sufficient OMO vehicles were now in place nationwide. The continuing availability and extent of Bus Grant would be key themes when deciding future orders. Mindful of the experience with the Merlin, Swift and DMS families, the GLC insisted that large-scale testing must precede volume orders, but LT stated that not only could other manufacturers not rise to supplying replacements in sufficient numbers, but that a smooth intake must continue – already, cover was desperately needed while early DMSs were away on their prolonged overhaul cycle and others began suffering CoF expiry.

The conversion of Fulwell's OMO routes to M operation, scheduled to start on 11 December with the 270, was put back to 15 January due to the delivery issues above; this date too slipped but on 19 March the 110 and 270 began taking Metrobuses, the former route receiving an upgrade from LSs and the latter losing its DMSs. The 285 was simultaneously converted from DMS to M, this daily route being completed by 12 April, while the 90B was converted in one go on that day. On the 13th the 281's Sunday OMO complement was also treated. The 267, destined to be the longest-serving host of the class, needed rather more vehicles and was treated between 25 May and 16 June.

Crucially, the abandonment of self-service fare collection took effect from the Spring Bank Holiday weekend (26-28 May) as part of a productivity deal; those Ms with the cabinet fitted had it blocked off with a bar or cord affixed to the doorway stanchion, and beginning in August 1980 (and completed once the batch had fully passed through overhaul mid-decade), M6-205 would have their AFC cabinets removed at Aldenham to bring them up to full capacity, but the machinery fitted new to most of this batch was destined never to be used. Deliveries were picking up by the second half of 1979, enough to commence the conversion of a third garage, Norbiton (NB). Its routes were also treated one by one; first the 211 (15 July, ex-SMS), then the five-bus share of the 213A (16-29 July) and after that the 131 (29 July-27 September). Norbiton's Sunday-only share of the 285 went over on 29 July, making the route wholly-M. The August plate change introduced V-suffixes, beginning with M96 (BYX 96V). A cosmetic change

Deployment of the M class was channelled by the fruition of plans to divide London Transport's bus arm operationally. Its existing structure of four divisions would be replaced by one of eight Districts. As Fulwell fell under Cardinal District, the introduction of Ms to fellow Cardinal garages Norbiton, Southall (HW) and Turnham Green (V) was scheduled to come next, and so did Southall's portfolio of OMO routes start taking their Ms on 17 September. Here ran the 92, 120, 232, 274 and 282, plus the recently-introduced Sunday double-deck allocations on SMS routes 195 and 273, and all DMSs had been swept away by 19 December. On that date the 91 at Turnham Green went over in one go, this conversion also encompassing the garage's minority allocation on the 267 and the N97, the first officially scheduled operation of the M class on a night route. The District structure would dictate both the initial allocation of both M and T classes and subsequent transfers as this structure evolved.

Consternation was the order of the day when the extraordinary announcement was made on 10 September 1979 of the intended closure of Leyland's Park Royal works and the resulting cessation of Titan production. With 300 Titans on order and a looming shortage of vehicles already anticipated, LT was furious. DMS replacement alone would require 2,000 new buses between 1981 and 1984, after which it was hoped that XRM production would begin, but for the moment talks were immediately opened, at the behest of the GLC, with overseas manufacturers. MCW was quick to see an opening, emboldened by the healthy pace of deliveries that had seen the 1979 order fulfilled bang on schedule, followed immediately by the first of the 1980 order. An extra 100 Metrobuses were added to this order to compensate for the reduction of Leyland's 1980 order from 250 Titans to 200. The imminent delivery of 140 Leyland Nationals, ordered earlier in the year and designated to participate also in DMS replacement, would pick up the slack. MCW was assured by LT that orders for the Metrobus would be renewed up to

Above: Southall's five double-deck OMO routes passed through a heavily-populated area that was sure to make great use of them. Beyond their built-up heartland, however, was an oasis of calm at Ruislip Lido, served on summer Sundays by an extension of the 273, which was converted on that day to M operation in lieu of its normal SMSs; M92 (WYW 92T) lays over on 14 October 1979. When the Swifts were disposed of the following year, both the 273 and 195 were double-decked with further new Ms rather than the normal expedient of allocating Leyland Nationals; other single-deck routes would not be so lucky, and indeed other routes would have to drop a deck as their DMSs fell due for replacement and all that was available was LSs. *John Laker*

externally amid the production run saw, from M106, the curved front indicators carried on the front corners give way to a combined indicator/sidelight unit (as on Titans from T7 up).

Left: Hendon's pair of routes, the 143 and 183, received Ms between 10 February and 15 June, the slow pace of conversion resulting from an industrial dispute. M289 (BYX 289V), lacking instructions on whom to pay, was one of this garage's intake, and in July lays over at Brent Cross. *Geoff Rixon*

1984 in quantities that would assure its continued existence, and similar assurance applied to Leyland's Titan once production was transferred to Workington. Intent on keeping hold of the healthy order book which was putting the type into service at West Midlands PTE in the same numbers as at LT, MCW despatched M373 to the Commercial Motor Show at the NEC in Birmingham. Capacity was increased at MCW by halting the building of bodywork for other chassis.

M206-505, the increased 1980 batch of 300 Metrobuses, began arriving in February 1980 and were subtly different again; as well as resuming the H43/28D configuration so as to be capable of crew operation (the intended use of many of this batch), another change now saw a pair of round foglights carried behind a circular cutout, in lieu of the previous lozenge-shaped units and similarly-shaped aperture. The first Metrobus movements of 1980 saw the class strike up a new allocation at Alperton (ON) on 24 January, taking over routes 79, 79A, 92, 182 and 297, plus, on Sundays, the 18 (with conductors) and the 83 (OMO on that day). This garage's conversion was accomplished in tandem with that of Hendon (AE), which had just the 143 and 183 to cover beginning on 10 February, but due to an industrial dispute that suspended new vehicle allocations between 28 February and the first week of June, the conversions were not completed until 15 June (Hendon) and 13 July (Alperton), when members of the 1980 batch were released from storage at Aldenham and AEC. At Hendon the 183 took priority for Ms while mixed-type operation endured. M3 was loaned from Cricklewood to Stonebridge during February for trials on the 18 prior to adoption of the type there.

On 10 May Turnham Green garage closed, but its replacement nearby, Stamford Brook, adopted not only its 'V' code but its entire runout, the M routes comprising the 91, 267 (part) and N97. On 17 May the first route change to affect the class involved a pair of Alperton routes then under conversion to the type; this involved the withdrawal of the 79 between Alperton and Northolt, the resources released being used to engender an extension of the 79A from Alperton Station to Willesden Junction. The first garage to use Ms, Cricklewood, then saw the rug pulled from under its prototypes as the 16 and 16A were converted to RML operation on 24 May. Unable to work these routes any longer, M1-5 (the final two having finally entered service at Cricklewood some months after their siblings) concentrated on the N94, coming out only at night and only unofficially, as crew DMSs were the prescribed type. M1 was loaned to Fulwell in July, taking blinds from an RM to make crew-operated appearances on the 281.

Below: Just one OMO route resided at Turnham Green garage at the end of 1979; the 91, requiring fifteen vehicles. It was converted in one fell swoop on 19 December, but the garage was scheduled for replacement and would close on 10 May 1980; the day before, M148 (BYX 148V) peeps out for one last time. From M96 V-suffix registrations commenced, and from M106 new combined sidelights/indicator units were carried. *John Laker*

Left: Alperton's five DMS routes received Ms between 24 January and 13 July 1980. One such was the 79, which on 5 July was in the hands of M286 (BYX 286V) at Alperton Station. Although on an OMO route, this M has not yet had its 'PLEASE PAY AS YOU ENTER' transfers applied to the front, potentially confusing it with one of the dedicated crew-operated buses from the same batch simultaneously entering service at Stonebridge. Round foglights replaced the lozenge-shaped units on M206 upwards. *Geoff Rixon*

Above: On 8 June 1980 M242 (BYX 242V) leaves Golders Green on the 226, seven days after the conversion of this route had introduced Metrobuses to Willesden garage. On 28 July it would be the first of many to lose its roof underneath a low bridge, this one in particular over Headstone Drive in Wealdstone. *Geoff Rixon*

Right: Crew-operated Metrobuses were at one time intended to be coded MC, but this was dropped and all were Ms. Stonebridge received the first (and only) purely two-man examples for the 18, a route converted to DM in 1976 to offset the growing social problems in this part of north-west London. On 12 June M209 (BYX 209V) is pictured south-east of Wembley; here the plain front is correct and no Almex E ticket-machine baseplate is fitted. For completeness, the Sunday-only Alperton allocation of the 18 was also converted to crew M on 2 June, allowing Stonebridge's surplus to assume a similar role on the 266 on that day of the week. *Geoff Rixon*

Willesden (AC) joined the growing network of M-operating garages when the 226 was converted from DMS on 1 June, and on the next day Stonebridge (SE) put into service its first crew-operated Ms on the 18 (daily) and 266 (on Sundays only), replacing DMs. These Metrobuses could be distinguished by the lack of 'PLEASE PAY AS YOU ENTER' encouragement on the front, but remained coded M. The backlog of new Ms that had been stacking up at Aldenham enabled this conversion to take place over just two weeks. The union agreement of May 1980 that permitted, where necessary, more flexibility of vehicle use, led almost immediately to strange workings, Alperton setting the ball rolling with appearances of its Ms in crew mode on the 83 during weekdays and Stonebridge's DMS-operated 112 (and RM-worked 260) seeing

occasional Ms wandering from the 18. On 5 July Fulwell put spare Metrobuses onto the 90 on Saturdays and Sundays in lieu of LSs, fears that double-deckers would not be able to fit under a 14ft 6in bridge in Staines being proven wrong by the M's slightly lower height (14ft 5in) by comparison with the prohibited DMSs. This would not be the first time the M's comparative compactness enabled double-deckers to return where they were still needed. However, the first London Transport Metrobus to come off worst with a low bridge was Willesden's nearly-new M242, which on 28 July was decapitated under Headstone Drive bridge in Wealdstone. M182 and 202, both Hendon vehicles working the 183 on 10 September, were damaged in an accident also involving two cars.

On 6 July the N94 was formally converted to crew M, as the time had come to replace the garage's B20 DMSs from the 32 and 245; this was done in four days, and more Metrobuses would arrive between the 21st and 31st of that month when the 616 was converted. The opportunity was taken to abandon flat-fare operation on this semi-express route, in favour of conventional OMO with cab door-mounted Almex E ticket machines. 'PAY DRIVER'/'PAY CONDUCTOR' reversible front plates made their first appearance at this point and would be fitted to all subsequent Metrobus (and Titan) deliveries. At Southall, it was the task of a further intake of Ms to replace the garage's last Swifts between 3 and 17 August, thereby restoring an upper deck to the 195 and 273 on weekdays; unofficial M wanderings had

been the case ever since the conversion of the Sunday services the previous autumn.

As the summer progressed, new Ms were temporarily allocated to Southall and Fulwell during August to allow early examples to return to MCW to have their AFC equipment removed and attention given to teething problems. These affected the front axle, engine and gearbox mountings, the cab heating and main cooling systems, while more minor problems concerned door interlocks, pipework layout and retarder operating controls. This delayed the proposed introduction of Metrobuses to Finchley (FY) garage until 25 September, covering the 125 and Finchley's allocation on the 263. On the 27th a route-change scheme implemented in north London made this garage's route 26 the first to be one-manned with

Above: The second week of July 1980 saw brand new Ms pour into Cricklewood for the 32 and 245, joining M1-5. One last DMS route remained here, flat-fare 616 which until conversion to M needed farebox-fitted buses. M327 (EYE 327V), rounding Marble Arch on 24 July, shows the 616's white-on-blue blinds. The route, however, was no match for the 16 and 16A's speedy RMLs and was withdrawn outright on 25 April 1981. *Geoff Rixon*

Left: The allocation of buses to garages did not necessarily have to be by monolithic consecutive blocks of fleetnumbers, and inevitably batches would mix in spite of efforts to concentrate specific mechanical sub-types. Southall, for example, took additional new Ms during August 1980 to double-deck the 195 and 273, and on the 26th of that month at Ealing M334 (EYE 334V) has broadened its scope to the rest of Southall's routes, this one being the 274. A new feature is the 'PAY DRIVER' plate, which when turned over read 'PAY CONDUCTOR' in white on blue. *Geoff Rixon*

Above: By 1980 Finchley's route 26 was a shadow of its former self, having been reduced from a partner to the trunk 2 group to a local service emanating from Golders Green. On 27 September it became the first service to assume OMO with Ms, and was extended to Brent Cross to increase its sagging viability. M350 (GYE 350W) is seen on 4 October at Finchley. *Geoff Rixon*

Ms. It was simultaneously extended from Golders Green to Brent Cross and from New Barnet to Barnet, Chesterfield Road. At Fulwell, the Monday to Friday service on the 90 was converted to M operation on 27 September, the weekend service having taken them earlier in the year. The 270 was extended both from Fulwell garage to a new development at Hampton, Nurserylands, and at the other end beyond Richmond Station to Dee Road, the whole route being introduced on Saturdays. The withdrawal of Merton's allocation from the 131 on weekdays allowed Norbiton to add some new Ms from the current batch.

Perhaps the greatest vindication of the Metrobus so far came in October when LT announced the shelving

of the XRM project in favour of continuing orders of what it considered the broadly satisfactory Metrobus and Titan – in the case of the M, May had seen another 300 examples (M506-805) ordered for 1981 delivery as against 200 Titans (total cost £30m). This stance also allowed MCW to look further ahead, to the generation that would succeed the Ms and Ts once production wound down in 1984 or so. The company was already investigating an evolution of the Metrobus model, but already it was becoming clear that the M was proving cheaper to rectify than the T, owing to easier access to the affected parts. Fuel economy at 6.5mpg was, however, slightly less than the 6.8mpg recorded by Titans at this point.

Coming rather ahead of schedule was the allocation of Ms to Edgware (EW) on 22 October, an advance guard taking over the 292 from DMSs on that day and allowing the Fleetlines to cover for failing SMSs on the 142, 186 and 286. Between 7 November and 8 December a further intake of Ms swept away Swifts and Fleetlines alike, taking over the 205, 240 and 288 as well and assisted by the stopgap Ms at Fulwell transferring to Edgware once their original early Ms returned from MCW. Stonebridge's Sunday allocation on the 260 was converted from RM to crew M on 26 October, on an unofficial basis but reflecting the social problems to be found in that area of town. Further Metrobuses into Finchley ejected the garage's last DMSs between 1 and 7 November with the conversion of that garage's share of the 221. On 4 December the Cricklewood share of the 240 was also converted from SMS to M, by the expedient of fitting M1-5 with Almex baseplates to enable dual-purpose crew and OMO operation. Perhaps anxious to remain on the familiar Edgware Road, they were more often seen on the 616.

Right: The innings of London Transport's Swifts was at an end by 1980, the class concentrating at Edgware in some numbers by that year, but the coming of the Metrobus eclipsed both the SMSs and their putative replacements, the DMSs. Ms arrived at Edgware on 22 October and took over the 292 first, allowing its Fleetlines to eject some Swifts from the other six routes at the garage; then, in November, Edgware's entire OMO complement gained or regained an upper deck when the garage's Swifts were all swept away by Ms. M461 (GYE 461W) is seen in Edgware on 30 November. *Geoff Rixon*

Left: The 221 was Finchley's last DMS route and this garage's third of it was officially converted in the first week of December 1980, exemplified by M402 (GYE 402W) passing Mill Hill Broadway station. Wood Green's 14-strong complement would have to wait another six months. *Geoff Rixon*

The final change of 1980 introduced a new innovation – Airbus. In spite of the success of the Piccadilly Line's Heathrow extension, which had first condemned British Airways' Routemaster-operated service in 1979 and, after service on 14 November, the airline's latter service to Victoria Air Terminal, a need was still seen for a service of this nature. M431-446, allocated new to Stamford Brook, were fitted out specially by having the entire lower deck (save the back row and the seats over the rear wheelarches) given over to luggage racks, making them H43/9D in capacity. The racks could be labelled for each of the three Heathrow terminals. Emblazoned with bold white AIRBUS logos, the sixteen Ms commenced two services on 15 November; route A1 to Victoria and route A2 to Paddington, both routes taking the M4 motorway.

Left and above: The service to Heathrow always did require a different level of sophistication, and the luggage-carrying capacity of new Airbus routes A1 and A2 made them a credible alternative to the Piccadilly Line. Outside the new Stamford Brook garage M433 (GYE 433W) is ready to go, showing off its luggage racks and remaining seats, while under cover M445 has just been delivered and is as yet without blinds. The Airbus Ms wore their giant between-decks signwriting with pride, plus a more discreet logo on the top half of the folding engine cover. Not long after entering service M444 (GYE 444W) lays over at the Paddington terminus of the A1. *Geoff Rixon (left); Chris Evans (above)*

Right and below: Routes E1 and E2 were particularly unhappy hosts of MBSs, having received the type in 1969 under Reshaping. The Merlins gave way to DMSs, but in 1980 Ms reached Hanwell, where flat-fare equipment was installed. In January 1981 M499 (GYE 499W) works through Brentford. The low bridge in Acton Lane, however, ruled out DMSs on the E3, but Ms could fit under it, thus 26 new examples into Hanwell and further Ms for Stamford Brook completed the set. Based at the former, M486 (GYE 486W), is seen at Ealing on 19 January 1981. Both: *Geoff Rixon*

1981 commenced with the first farebox-operated Ms entering service, starting a new allocation at Hanwell (HL) on the E1 and E2 in replacement of DMSs. The E3 had been restricted to single-deck operation (latterly LSs) due to a low bridge at Acton Lane, but Metrobuses could clear it so took over this route too. There were not enough buses left from the 1980 order to complete Hanwell, so the E1 and E2 had to remain partially-DMS for the moment. The 1981 order for Ms commenced delivery in May, a decision having been made to delay construction so that the last 75 vehicles could spill over into 1982. During that interim crew-operated examples supplanted RMLs on Willesden's night route N91 on 30 March. A programme of 25 April saw changes to the Edgware Road corridor. The 32 gained a spur taking it off this thoroughfare at Burnt Oak over a withdrawn section of the 266 to Mill Hill. The 616 was withdrawn, its one-time flat-fare OMO remit being replaced by a diversion of RML-operated 16A to Oxford Circus and the Ms transferred to complete the E3 at Hanwell. On 30 April the Stamford Brook allocation of this route was upgraded from LS to M operation, and on

Right: Airbus grew so successful so quickly that during 1981 it was given a summer timetable needing six more buses; these were drawn from surrounding garages and were not always fitted out with luggage racks. M401 (GYE 401W) came from Alperton, and while on attachment to Stamford Brook is seen at Hyde Park Corner on 16 April 1981. *Geoff Rixon*

9 May the one-Metrobus 205 at Edgware was withdrawn. The Airbus network, particularly the A1, had proven so popular that a five-bus supplementary schedule was introduced on the A1 between 16 May and 31 October. Ms 86, 211, 343, 374, 401 and 478 were fitted out with simplified luggage racks for use on the A2 as spare vehicles to release others to the A1. Summer augmentation of this nature would be the case for the next decade. The Wimbledon tennis service, mounted for the first time in 1981, featured a Norbiton complement with Ms.

After all the work MCW had done single-handedly to ensure the input of new vehicles into London Transport amid Leyland's troubles, it was rewarded in May by the announcement of the 1982 orders – 275 Titans and no Metrobuses! Although the reduction of Bus Grant had prompted a general cutback in spending and any reduction in Titan orders threatened the future of the model itself, MCW understandably felt hard done by. Meanwhile, the time-honoured overhauling system was about to be applied to the Metrobus, M44 being taken into Aldenham in May as a pilot example for the class.

The first deployment of the 1981 order was to another trio of flat-fare routes; the W2 and W3 at Wood Green (WN) from 4 June and the W7 at Muswell Hill (MH) from 11 June, both conversions introducing the M class at their respective garages and both being completed by 15 August. Between 15 July and 10 September Uxbridge (UX) received Ms for the 222 and 223, but these were earlier Ms displaced from Finchley by new buses due to the perceived need to concentrate within Leaside District M506 upwards, which featured significant mechanical differences and thus had different stores requirements. Uxbridge put out its Ms occasionally on the 98 and 204 and with conductors on the 207, recently converted from DM to Routemaster operation.

The early 1980s saw an extensive programme of new garage construction which, in the sectors of town operating Metrobuses, saw Stonebridge and Middle Row closed on 15 August and their services reallocated to new Westbourne Park (X). The closure of Stonebridge saw both the 260 and 266 lose their crew-M aspects, while the 112 was reallocated to Cricklewood and traded its DMSs for Ms (ex-Finchley displaced by new examples), but the fact that the new Westbourne Park was part of Abbey District meant that Ms were as yet unfamiliar there. Thus a three-way swap was instituted whereby the 18 was converted from crew M to B20 DM, Westbourne Park taking the Fleetlines from Brixton's 109 and 133; these gained RMs from Fulwell, which in turn took on the Metrobuses from Stonebridge for the conversion of the 33 and 281 to crew M. Fulwell's Sunday share of the 27 also adopted crew Ms.

The 1981 order continued to pour in, all buses into Leaside District staging through Finchley for pre-service checks before allocation. After several weeks of type training, the conversion from DMS of the 34 and 121 at Palmers Green (AD) commenced on

19 September, Wood Green receiving additional Ms on the same date for its share of the 144, 221 and 298, all conventional OMO services. The concurrent conversion of Walthamstow to Ts meant Metrobuses and Titans appearing together for the first time on the 34 and 144. M606 upwards had red-painted radiator grilles following a money-saving edict issued by London Transport in April, while routine repaints to black-fronted examples saw this feature begin to disappear over time, the Airbus versions taking precedence.

After several months' lull, the final DMSs at Hanwell were replaced between 23 October and 23 November when enough of Finchley's original Ms were gathered to finish off the E1 and E2. On 19 November, by which date Palmers Green and Wood Green had lost their last DMSs, Potters Bar (PB) began taking Ms, covering the 84 and 242 and completing the 298. As the year closed, Enfield (E) commenced M operation on the 107, 135, 191, 217, 217B and 231 from 30 December. Enfield's vehicles were prepared at Edmonton rather than Finchley. The conversions at Potters Bar and Enfield dragged out into 1982,

Left: After Wood Green and Muswell Hill, Palmers Green was the next Leaside District garage to convert to M. Here the 34 and 121 had B20 DMSs to replace, and in April 1982 M560 (GYE 560W) is seen heading south from Enfield Town towards Winchmore Hill. *Tony Wilson*

Left: The northernmost 'red bus' garage, Potters Bar lay some distance beyond the GLC border; this made no difference at the moment as Ms arrived during November 1981 for the 84 and 242, but would become critical at the end of the decade. The rural backdrop to M689 (KYV 689X) belies the location on 2 March 1982; it's South Mimms, not far from where the M25 motorway, a later symbolic border of London, was under construction. From M606 a red-painted front had been specified, which could hardly have saved much money at the expense of attractiveness; this would spread to earlier members of the class following routine repaints. *Tony Wilson*

Left: On 30 December 1981 Enfield took its first Metrobuses for the conversion from B20 DMS of routes 107, 135, 191, 217, 217B and 231. The lot of the 217 and 231 was to trundle up and down the Great Cambridge Road before branching off in separate directions to the north, while the 217B was only loosely related to the former by disappearing off into Essex beyond GLC territory at Waltham Cross. On 24 April 1982 brand new M700 (KYV 700X) enjoys spring sunshine within sight of St Paul's Church at Enfield Town. *Geoff Rixon*

the latter's intake including the first examples with a revised radiator grille again, implemented from M706 upwards. Still surmounted by the chrome beading, the grille was now a mesh unit covering the offside two-thirds (allowing space for the MCW badge) and itself divided into three portions; it brought some maturity to the Metrobus's face and was said to be easier to repair; certainly, the barred grilles of earlier Ms tended to warp with heat and did not take kindly to impacts. As the chrome detailing started to disintegrate and fall off, or when touching up was required, the front of Ms started appearing in all combinations of colours and undercoats. M125 at Southall was the first officially to receive a red front, in January 1982. M706 onwards also received a second grille at the rear of each side, carried lower.

Boxing Day saw Wood Green's allocation on both the 29 and 141 all crew-M, while wanderings of the class away from their scheduled routes by this time saw crew Ms on the 13 (Finchley), 134 (Potters Bar) and 279 (Enfield), while an advance preview saw the odd M turn out on the 202 from Fulwell. Tachographs made their first appearance on Ms from the latter garage and from Stamford Brook at the turn of 1981/2, permitting increased private-hire use.

The year 1982 was to prove harsh for London Transport, but for the M class it was a quiet one. Potters Bar's conversion from M was completed on 19 January and Enfield on 22 March, the 24th of the latter month seeing Edmonton (EM) gain the class through the conversion of its share of routes 191 and 259. Three more routes were introduced to the class as winter wound down; the Saturday workings of the 244 from Muswell Hill on 30 January, the 202 at Fulwell receiving an upgrade from BL on 8 March and new night route N29 making its bow from 27 February, with crew Ms from Wood Green. The A1 and A2 received re-routeings in central London

Left: Muswell Hill was a flat-fare operator, but on 30 January 1982 the Saturday allocation of its LS-operated 244 was converted to M operation using four buses fitted with Almex baseplates. M545 (GYE 545W) passes Bounds Green station on 27 March. This was six days after the 100% fares increase had been introduced in the post-Fares Fair era, and custom for all routes would slump to such an extent that the 244 would be withdrawn outright as early as 24 May. *Colin Stannard*

designed to bring them closer to potential custom, the former serving Sloane Square from 30 January and the latter redirected through Kensington on 3 April. 1982's Airbus augmentations comprised M212, 264 and 380, while Ms 401, 447 and 478 became permanent Airbuses in April, the luggage racks being installed at Chiswick.

The outlawing of Fares Fair had grave repercussions on London Transport's provision of routes; cross-border services were pruned first, on 24 April. In this scheme the 84 was given over to London Country in exchange for the 313, most of which ran within the GLC boundary and took on the Potters Bar Ms made spare. The London portion of the 84 became new route 84A, also with Potters Bar Ms, running between Arnos Grove and Barnet Church. The 244, flagged in a 1981 study as one of several chronically loss-making routes, was withdrawn entirely in spite of its conversion from LS to M on Saturdays earlier in the year. Four of the otherwise flat-fare Ms at Muswell Hill (M511/37/9/45) had received Almex baseplates to enable them to turn out on this route.

Above right: The need to make drastic cuts following the debacle of Fares Fair saw attention visited on the outskirts of LT's bus operations; deals were cut with neighbouring county councils to have several outer routes transferred to London Country, whose level of sophistication was lesser and thus demanded a lower level of subsidy. On 24 April 1982 the 84 passed to London Country and was pulled back to New Barnet, the GLC roads being taken over by new Potters Bar-operated route 84A (Barnet Church-Arnos Grove). On 1 May M668 (KYV 668X) is in charge between those termini, but opportunity would soon beckon for expansion at both ends. Ironically, the 84 would return in 1986 as a 'red bus' route and stay that way! *Geoff Rixon*

Right: At the time Ms arrived at Stamford Hill, the 67 was its only OMO service, requiring ten buses for its journey between Wood Green and Wapping. M780-90 were allocated in April/May 1982, and the following January M782 (KYV 782X) is seen arriving at Wood Green from the south, blinds already set for the return journey. *Geoff Rixon*

The final examples of the 1981 order were delivered in March 1982, again sidestepping the continuing reduction in Bus Grant rates (this year's reduction applying from 1 April) in that several arrived incompletely finished – this strategy saved £7,000 per bus! Edmonton's conversion from DMS to M was completed with the flat-fare W8 between 9 April and 24 June, the lag owing to an industrial dispute involving ferry drivers and the overtime accrued from this work; between 3 and 22 June Stamford Hill (SF) took Ms for the 67, also introducing them officially (if not that often in practice) to the N83 with conductors. On Sundays the 67 was operated by Tottenham (AR), which received Ms between 17 and 28 June; on weekdays they took over (and completed) the 259. Just six Ms remained of the 1981 order to be

deployed, and the choice raised eyebrows when M800-5 accompanied an equivalent number of Titans to Sidcup (SP), far out of Metrobuses' possible range for allocations. The reason was to compare the two types side-by-side (and with the outgoing DMSs) to determine future ordering policies, especially important when budgeting was likely to be sharply curtailed. Placed on specific duties on the 51, the six Ms entered service from 12 July (the experiment lasting until 1 November), but even before the conclusion of the trials turned out regularly on the 21A and 228 (and the 229 from 4 September). Even more unusually, they stayed put, even when more Titans arrived to replace the garage's DMSs in accordance with Selkent District's choice of second-generation vehicle.

Left: Another OMO conversion on 4 September 1982 was Fulwell's 281, seen in the hands of M660 (KYV 660X) in Surbiton that month. This bus was one transferred from Wood Green (as evinced by the 'WN' code still just about extant on its side), allowing Fulwell to displace earlier examples elsewhere, notably to Hounslow where the conversion of the 202 from LS brought the garage its first Ms. *Geoff Rixon*

In August 1982 B20 DMS overhauls were terminated to allow Metrobuses and Titans to enter Aldenham. Legislation had obliged the revision of the system whereby a Works Annual Service Programme (WASP) would take place at four-year intervals, broken by a GASP (Garage Annual Service Programme) each year. For Metrobuses, the latter process had commenced earlier in the year, the former Turnham Green garage being used for this purpose. Overhauls would ensure that stock numbers would start becoming thoroughly mixed up, batches based since delivery being broken up due to the roughly four months it took to overhaul an M (no body lifting or identity changes taking place on these integral buses). The first float cover was provided by spare Ms in the 500s and 600s, which following the 4 September changes drifted into Fulwell. The white-windowed livery was thus set to dwindle, but Fulwell's M35 became the only example to combine this feature with a red-repainted grille, plus a traditional black-on-white numberplate. Unlucky M610 of Palmers Green suffered two accidents in its first six months, while similarly-affected M502 returned from repair to serve as an experimental testbed at Chiswick. M376 was also assigned here on skid bus duty during August.

Reflecting reduced expectations in the face of the doubling of fares, followed by a sharp drop in demand, LT's order for 1983 (placed in May) numbered just 360 vehicles; 210 Ts and 150 Ms. Having fought against the expected massive reductions to services, London Transport bit the bullet and took 13% off the runout on 4 September. Starting with Cardinal District and proceeding in a clockwise direction, the changes to Metrobus operations were as follows:

The 27 and 33 were altered beyond Richmond, the 27 being withdrawn south-west of that point (and losing its Fulwell crew M allocation), to allow the diversion of the 33 to Fulwell. This garage, taking on a number of new X-registered Ms to displace earlier examples, undertook the OMO conversion of the 281, which had had Ms in place for over a year, but lost the 90 (withdrawn entirely) and the 202 (reallocated to Hounslow (AV), bringing that garage its first Ms and allowing them to drift in due course to routes 116, 117, 203 and 257). Ms into Hounslow also upgraded the 111 from LS operation. Having undergone changes to its termini, the 270's spine was rerouted this time, now omitting Teddington. The 290 was reallocated from Riverside to Fulwell and converted from BL to M operation, being extended from Richmond to Staines to replace the 90. Part of the 85 was transferred from Putney to Norbiton, bringing Ms onto six of the 11 workings, Norbiton withdrew from the 285 on Sundays and Stamford Brook renounced its participation from the 267.

At Alperton, the 83 was converted from RM to crew M, but the level of crew operation actually rose with the introduction of a Monday to Saturday crew-M allocation on the 18. To accommodate this, the garage withdrew from the 92, transferred the 297 to Alperton and pulled the 182 back from Finchley to Brent Cross. The reconfiguration of the 187 as a substantially shorter M OMO route removed the last RMs from the garage and made it 100%-Metrobus. Southall also assumed total M operation through the conversion of

Below: Upon its one-manning, the 187 lost its Westbourne Park share and section east of Kilburn Park to become an all-Alperton route. M282 (BYX 282V), freshly repainted with red front, works through Kensal Rise on 18 September. With the simultaneous conversion to crew M of the 83, Alperton became 100% Metrobus-operated, managing to retain conductors on its just-introduced daily share of the 18 until 1 February 1986. *Geoff Rixon*

Above: Wending its peaceful way across much of north London, the 102 under Palmers Green accepted OMO without complaint; Ms were now the complement and would remain so for 19 years. M690 (KYV 690X) was a transfer from Potters Bar on 4 September and in November is seen in the 102's dedicated stand at Golders Green. *Geoff Rixon*

route 105 from RM to crew M, presaging future plans, while its 195's forays as far south as Perivale were weakened and the 273 was withdrawn between Ruislip and Hayes. Hanwell's E-routes were subtly altered, an independent schoolday bifurcation introduced on the E2 and the Chiswick end of the E3 localised. It also received the N89 on transfer from Riverside, as an OMO service. Hendon's cuts withdrew most of the 183 west of Pinner and shrunk the 143 throughout. The Cricklewood share of the 240 was withdrawn other than on Saturdays, and Finchley's 125 was compelled to fall back from Hendon to North Finchley. Two schoolday duties on the 98 at Uxbridge received Ms, but LSs returned in December and Metrobus appearances on the 98 thereafter would only be as strange workings. The 224 was partially double-decked on Saturdays.

At Palmers Green, the 102 was converted to OMO and the 34 withdrawn between Whipps Cross and Leytonstone. Enfield garage underwent surgery to its routes, the 135 being withdrawn and the 107's eastern end rerouted to replace it to Brimsdown. Instead of going to Chingford, the 121 (which dropped its weekend Palmers Green participation to be transferred daily to Enfield) was rerouted to replace the 107 to Enfield Lock and the gap across the Lea Valley Reservoir was filled by extending the 313 to Chingford. The 191, also withdrawn from points east of the Lea Valley Reservoir, was pushed at the western end to Carterhatch to replace the other end of the 135. Enfield also abandoned Upshire by retracting the 217 and 217B back to Waltham Cross. The 259's Edmonton allocation was withdrawn, removing the possibility of garage journeys beyond Lower Edmonton Station. The 144 was withdrawn between Turnpike Lane and Muswell Hill Broadway, the Wood Green allocation coming off to form new route 144A heading as far east as Edmonton and then turning left to reach Lower Edmonton Station. Wood Green and Potters Bar altered their formerly daily allocations on the 298, the former now covering weekdays and the latter Sundays. Finally for this area, the W2 was projected between the peaks from Turnpike Lane Station to Wood Green.

Sidcup's route 51, deep in its Metrobus/Titan comparison trial, found itself withdrawn between Orpington Station and Green Street Green, that section passing to a one-manned 229 (and thus allowing M800-5 to appear).

With such tremendous upheaval, subsequent changes for 1982 numbered just one; on 28 October the 202 was rerouted within Heathrow Airport away from the Cargo Tunnel. Operational considerations saw a number of Ms appearing on the 29 at Palmers Green over Christmas (officially at weekends from 18 December), as well as on the 279 from both its garages.

1983 marked fifty years since the formation of London Transport, and Jubilee celebrations were commissioned in spite of continuing cuts. On 29 January economies were made across the border into Surrey, Norbiton's 211 being withdrawn outright so that cheaper London Country services could replace it to points west. At Tottenham the 76 was one-manned on Sundays, using Ms spare from the 67 and 259. Stamford Brook's allocation on the 27 had been scheduled to include one crew-operated M on Saturdays since 4 September 1982; this change was belatedly implemented on 5 February.

Having been the first Metrobus into overhaul, M44 was the first outshopped, leaving works on 12 January for its new deployment at Cricklewood, and the programme was in full swing by April. Before passing through overhaul, Fulwell's M7 was sent to Chiswick for the experimental fitting of hard-backed fibreglass anti-vandal seats throughout the upper deck. Removal of AFC cabinets and the consequent upseating to H43/28D was carried out on M6-205 as they passed through works.

In January M806, the first of 1983's order for 150 Metrobuses (M806-955), commenced delivery; this batch's engine note sounded perceptibly different from that of its predecessors. With such mechanical differences in mind, again a buffer shed was needed where it would be economical to hold spares for more than one sub-classification, and Fulwell was chosen. Most of its new intake replaced the W- and X-registered stopgaps, which were earmarked for Harrow Weald (HD) for the proposed OMO conversion of the 140, while M420 and 479 were displaced to Airbus work (without downseating). The bulk of the 1983 intake, however, was for Abbey District, and on 25 February Putney (AF) became this district's first recipient, taking M810/1/4/8-20/45/8/50-4 for the 85 and 264. Underscoring continuing difficulties with the union over the correct display of 'CC'-code side blinds and remuneration for the same, Putney's Ms had their overpainted black so just the route number at left showed through. M819 suffered an accident early in its career, necessitating the return of a single DMS, which was not to depart Putney until 8 July.

A substantial programme of one-manning was implemented on 23 April. The aforementioned 140, having phased in crew Ms from the 14th, was treated (exchanging its eastern section to Mill Hill with that of the 114 and now terminating at Harrow Weald garage), as well as two routes that had already had crew Ms pre-positioned since 4 September 1982, Alperton's 83 and Southall's 105. The latter two changes made these all-Metrobus garages 100%

OMO, and Alperton was rendered daily on the 182. This garage's route 79 was extended to replace the 79A between Alperton and Willesden Junction. To the north, out-county cuts took Potters Bar's 242 off between the station and South Mimms and the 313 altogether on Sundays, while its 84A was transferred to Wood Green and extended not only from Barnet to Arkley to support the 107, but also from Arnos Grove southeastward to Turnpike Lane. In its place came the 263, which lost its Holloway DMSs and Wood Green Ms and everything south of Archway Station; instead it was projected northwards from Barnet Church to Potters Bar Garage over the 134. Potters Bar also collected from Wood Green the weekday workings of the 298, while Palmers Green gained Saturday work on the 121. The two Airbus routes spawned a third

Above: The 1983 order for 150 Ms began to arrive in January, and as with the previous denizens of revised mechanical specification, these were put into Fulwell to allow predecessors to depart. On 9 April at Twickenham we are afforded two consecutively-numbered examples laying over, M833 (OJD 833Y) and M834 (OJD 834Y). The W- and X-registered Ms displaced by the mass entry of this batch into Fulwell supplied Harrow Weald with the stock it needed to convert the busy 140 to OMO on 23 April. *Geoff Rixon*

Left: Putney garage was the first Abbey District garage to introduce the M, putting them on the 264 and its share of the 85. The 264 had been introduced in 1981 as a six-bus OMO adjunct to RML-operated trunk route 74, but the latter had failed to take the hint and continued to operate through to Roehampton. On 9 June M820 (OJD 820Y) is seen in Danebury Avenue, Roehampton. *Colin Stannard*

(albeit before 14.30), the A3 to Euston, while the A2 regained its former routeing into town via Holland Park Avenue.

May saw Battersea (B) receive Ms 846/7/9/5-60/5-9 for the 39, displacing DMSs between the 6th and 22nd of that month, while the latter date introduced the Travelcard to London's bus and tube passengers, in tandem with a welcome fares cut implemented under the banner of 'Just the Ticket'. Flat-fare operation was abandoned on routes W2, W3, W7 and W8 on 22 May.

Harrow Weald's M stock soon began to wander from the 140 to the 114, and the route was officially converted on Sundays from 19 June, though turning and parking problems at the garage caused the cancellation of this move on 3 July. The 209 and 258 joined the 114 as Harrow Weald LS routes seeing occasional M augmentation, with one most unofficial appearance on the 136 by M625 on 2 August; double-deck operation was otherwise precluded by

overhanging trees. Hounslow Ms, meanwhile, started popping up on the 81, Muswell Hill Ms with conductors on the 43 and 134 and Finchley likewise on the 43. Conversely, a move to standardise took the Saturday crew M off the 27 on 25 June. This latter date saw the closure of Mortlake garage and, amongst other reallocations, the absorption by Fulwell of its half of the 33, rendering this route wholly crew-M. The Stamford Brook allocation on the E3 was withdrawn, eight Ms passing to Hanwell. At Potters Bar, a staff night route was livened up as new route N80, operating a circular configuration over 298, 84, 107, 125, 26 and 263 to and from the garage. On the 26th the Chelsea Flower Show perennial, route 137A, saw its first Ms with the introduction of a Battersea allocation. Other one-offs in this half of the year brought Norbiton Ms to the Wimbledon tennis run and Metrobuses from four local garages to cover the construction of the Piccadilly Line extension to Heathrow Terminal 4.

Left: The year 1983 marked the fiftieth anniversary of London Transport's formation, and despite ominous forebodings for the future of the organisation all the stops were pulled out to ensure a memorable Golden Jubilee year. Part of the celebrations involved the repaint of examples of modern classes into a livery approximating that of 1933, and for M57 (WYW 57T) the effect was spectacular. Named *Aldenham Aristocrat,* the Metrobus returned to Norbiton where it worked routes 72, 85, 131 and 213A between July 1983 and February 1984. The nearside treatment is seen on 13 August, a day when it was at work on the 131 through Kingston. *Geoff Rixon*

The Golden Jubilee celebrations spawned undoubtedly the best livery ever to appear on a London Transport Metrobus – the 1933-style colour scheme applied to M57, then in overhaul, by coachpainters at Aldenham. Named *Aldenham Aristocrat* and fitted with RM seat moquette, M57 was handed over to Cardinal District at the Chiswick Open Day on 2 July, and then went into service at Norbiton from the 8th, chiefly on the 131 but also making regular appearances on the 72, 85 and 213A. The companion Titan was T66 (*Aldenham Diplomat*), allocated later that month to Hornchurch. In July M359 was also painted in 1933 livery, with significant differences in application from its Norbiton counterpart, as a retirement present from a coachpainter; it made its service debut in the last week of July. Later in the year the frontal treatment was revised. Not a showbus as such, M6 was distinguished by the re-application of white upper-deck window relief following its outshopping from overhaul in July, the bus (with red grille) returning to Fulwell. For all Aldenham's heroics this Jubilee Year, a review carried out in October cast serious doubt upon its continued viability.

Above right: The offside profile of M57 (WYW 57T) can be seen at Putney Station when in action on the 85 three days later. Hopes were high that it would resume this livery sometime in the future, and it did in 2000 when with White Rose Travel. Most unfortunately, the next owner but one has gone over the 1933 colours in two hideous shades of green! *Mike Harris*

Right: M57 wasn't the only Metrobus to take on the colours of Pick and Ashfield's London Transport; local initiative at Southall accorded M359 (GYE 359W) the same treatment, though the front was different. On 15 August the bus is seen in the Wembley Trading Estate area. A little later its grille was altered to increase the proportion of black, staying in this condition until repaint in February 1984. *Geoff Rixon*

On 28 June vehicle orders were approved for the next two years; 1984 would bring 240 Titans (T886-1125) and 150 Metrobuses (M956-1105), and for 1985, to offset the cessation of Titan production, 335 Metrobuses (M1106-1440). London Transport's insistence on standardisation kept the mkI Metrobus in production, while other operators (particularly West Midlands PTE) had now standardised on the mkII model. What would follow these types was already under discussion, and to this end orders were placed in July for three examples each of four current chassis, one of which was the mkII Metrobus. As well as evaluating the chassis themselves, LT would be trying out various gearbox and powerplant combinations, with what was to be numbered M1441-3 involving a Cummins L10 engine, a Maxwell gearbox and an air-cooled engine of unspecified provenance. Plans to use a Cardinal District route as a testbed were replaced by one with experience of neither M nor T so far, the 170 from Wandle District's Stockwell garage.

The conversion to M of Abbey District's Fleetline-operated routes continued with the treatment from 27 June of the 18 at Westbourne Park (X), but a twist here saw six Titans join 14 Ms in crew mode to replicate the 51's experiment of the previous summer, only in more congested conditions. M872/3 were loaned first to Harrow Weald and then to Alperton, while six others (plus these two) received Fred Perry adverts in order to be seconded temporarily to Norbiton for the Wimbledon tennis service. Two Westbourne Park DMs lingered until 20 September, by which time the conversion of Shepherd's Bush (S) had commenced; between 31 August and 23 November the 72, 220 and 283 received their Ms. Among these were the first A-registered examples, commencing from M892. Not long after their introduction they started turning up on the 88, as had their DMS predecessors.

Wood Green's Ms operated to the unlikely target of Romford Market when a Christmas service was mounted on 15 October, while custom on the Airbus A3 was sufficient to prompt its introduction all day

from the 22nd. From the 29th the Norbiton allocation on the 72, introduced only to keep the former route 211 and 219's drivers in work after 29 January and requiring a lengthy extension from Tolworth to Kingston, began to receive Ms to replace its LSs, the type having made appearances since the early summer. These were early examples displaced from Fulwell by new A-registered Ms. 29 October also saw the E1, E2 and E3 converted from flat-fare to conventional OMO, while that night saw Saturday night/Sunday morning services introduced to the N91 and N94. During November crew Ms gained in strength on the officially RM-operated N83, and on the 23rd of that month Wandsworth (WD) began the DMS-to-M conversion of the 44, 295 and its vestigial Sunday share of the 220, together with the N68 and N88 (both crew-operated) at night. On Boxing Day the 28's Westbourne Park allocation was crew M (and one crew T), after which followed further Sunday appearances of Metrobuses on this route as well as the odd strange working since the 18's conversion. Examples from the next 150-strong order followed shortly on the heels of the 1983 orders, and contributed to the completion of Wandsworth by 21 March 1984. Uxbridge garage moved location on 3 December, retaining its code, buses and routes but now sited right next to the Underground station. Two of Sidcup's Ms wandered during December, M801 to Muswell Hill and M804 to Palmers Green, but both returned in January. Rarer were crew Ms on the 207, both at Hanwell and Uxbridge, while Stamford Hill started putting out crew Ms on the 149 and 253 and Edmonton used examples on the 149 and 279A, the latter in some strength on Sundays.

In the face of subsidy reductions mandated following the Conservative return of 1983, London Transport applied economy measures to its operational structure from 2 January 1984, reducing its eight Districts to six by eliminating Watling and Tower. Of Watling's garages, Willesden, Alperton and

Cricklewood joined Cardinal, while Harrow Weald, Edgware and Hendon were absorbed by an enlarged Leaside. Former Tower District garages Clapton and Ash Grove were appended to Abbey, which meant that in order to ensure standardisation of vehicle types, Ms would need to replace Ts. To make room at Abbey, Stockwell was transferred to Wandle, removing it from consideration where M deployments were concerned; the decision to retain B20 DMSs led to their effective concentration there.

Kingston garage closed on 14 January 1984; where Metrobuses were concerned, the 71, which had been operated by Norbiton alone on Sundays was converted from LS to M on that day of the week; clearance problems forced an accompanying diversion northbound away from Kings Road. Another loss to the Kingston area involved the repaint of M57 back into red during February; in its last months as the *Aldenham Aristocrat* the side adverts had been amended to omit any reference to Aldenham's coachpainters having done the work; portentously, as it turned out. Somehow, it also acquired wings with round foglight holes, though the RM seat moquette was retained. M359 was also repainted red, being taken into works on 13 February. The future of Aldenham Works was contingent upon it being able to carry out work at lower prices than potential competitors; certainly it helped when three outside sources that were approached turned down potential overhauling contracts late in 1983. Still, quotes were obtained and Midland Red took on a deal to overhaul ten Ms at its Carlyle works, accepting Ms 85, 103/36/9/71, 204/5/15 between 16 January and 3 February. The process, however, took so long (some examples being away for over eight months, and returned to a perceived lower standard) that a repeat option was not pursued, a plan being implemented instead to reduce Aldenham's workforce by 40% of its 1983 numbers and dividing the business into four sectors.

Above: Norbiton was revitalised twofold on 14 January 1984 with the input of the closed Kingston garage's two RM routes plus the majority of the 213A, which now dropped its suffix to accompany reconfiguration to an unprecedented four-terminus format. Having spent its first four years at Southall, M123 (BYX 123V) was overhauled between November 1983 and January 1984 and outshopped to Norbiton; on 26 June it is descending Kingston Hill towards Kingston. *Colin Stannard*

The 4 February programme transformed the 213A into plain 213, altering the Sutton and Norbiton proportions in favour of the latter by withdrawing Norbiton's allocation from the 72 (and retracting it back to Tolworth). Unusually, the 213's eastern end proceeded in a choice of *four* different directions – first its normal terminus at Sutton Garage, now joined by a projection over new ground to St Helier Station, while retaining the peak-hour and midday bifurcation to Belmont Station, and on Sundays extended over routes 151 and 154 to West Croydon! M964 and 965 joined Norbiton new, M956-63 going into Shepherds Bush for the increased 72. From this year's batch, the driver could change both sets of blinds from the cab. Sidcup's six Ms had stayed put despite the loan of two mentioned earlier, and their remit now extended to new Sunday-only route 299, commissioned from 4 February to link the 228 and 229 but which in the event lasted only until 27 October.

On 8 February the evening and Sunday workings of the 266 at Cricklewood were unofficially converted to crew M. The input of four new Ms allowed Uxbridge to partially double-deck the 98 plus the 224 on Saturdays from the 18th, while an occurrence that month with greater ramifications was the diversion of the 72 away from Hammersmith Bridge from 25 February after the crossing by an overloaded HGV had weakened the structure sufficiently for the council to impose a weight limit. It took the long way round, via Fulham Palace Road, Putney Bridge and Lower Richmond Road, while 33s would terminate at either side of the bridge, disgorging their passengers to cross on foot. Another partial conversion involved Harrow Weald, which had also been taking in small numbers of new Ms (including M1000), and which from 8 March added them to the 114, 136 and 209. On Saturdays the 114 and 258 went fully double-deck. Shepherd's Bush's 283 route was diverted on 31 March to reach West Brompton rather than Fulham Broadway. Hounslow and Alperton received a new M each to cover for buses going away for overhaul, while this year's Airbus extras comprised Ms 211/32/3/56, 372, 401/20/78/9; of these, M233, 372, 401/20/79 (which operated until 8 October) lacked the rear wheelarch seats for a capacity of H43/5D. New Bus Grant ended for good on 29 February; again, savings were made by accepting several Metrobuses and Titans unfinished.

Above left: Since the input of Metrobuses into Uxbridge in July 1981 the garage had moved location, though retaining the name and code. Four more Ms were added to the allocation in February 1984 to add capacity to the LS-operated 98, which otherwise hadn't seen double-deckers since its conversion from RT to SMS a decade previously. On 17 April M975 (A975 SYF) lays over at Ruislip Station. *John Laker*

Left: Comparatively few London Transport bus classes have reached a thousand stock numbers, but both the M and T classes crossed that line early in 1984. M1000 (A700 THV), already claimed by Harrow Weald and seen there on 7 April, was the subject of a ceremony at Covent Garden on 10 May. Harrow Weald, like Uxbridge, required some double-deck stiffening of hard-pressed LS routes like the 114. *Tony Wilson*

Consultation had uncovered considerable demand for expanded night services, and a comprehensive revision to the network was undertaken on 13/14 April under the banner of 'Buses for Night Owls'. New routes numbered to approximate their daytime equivalents were N13 and N21 (both Finchley-operated and terminating at North Finchley, the latter replacing the night service on the 221), N14 (Putney, to Roehampton), N18 (Willesden, to Sudbury) and N27 (Stamford Brook, commencing at Liverpool Street before joining the 27 to Richmond). Extensions to existing M-operated night routes took Stamford Hill's N83 from Tottenham (Swan) over the 243 to Wood Green (also adding a Tottenham share), the N89 at Hanwell from Southall over the 207 to Uxbridge and the N90 over the 279 from Waltham Cross to Hammond Street; this last-mentioned route lost its Tottenham allocation to Enfield and Edmonton nightly. Cricklewood's N94 was projected from the garage to Edgware via the 32. The N68, N83, N88, N90, N91 and N94 were all converted to OPO (as OMO was now generally referred to); just one crew-operated night bus remained, the N29 at Wood Green.

Over a thousand Ms were now in stock; the registrations A500-555 SYL, booked in September, had been hurriedly voided when the DVLC decided to withdraw potentially objectionable combinations from this year letter (those in the 550s being most suspect!) and the buses entered service carrying A700-755 THV instead. M1000 was the subject of an official handover of 'LT's 1,000th Metrobus' at Covent Garden on 10 May, after which it was allocated to Harrow Weald, while M919 was loaned to Ogle Designs in connection with studies aimed at designing 'The London Bus of the Future'. The 1984 order included three batches of distinctive Ms, the

first being 24 (M1006-29) to upgrade the Airbus services at Stamford Brook from April; differences here included front doors opening to either side and, for enhanced luxury, coach seats and carpeting upstairs. The Ms released, plus their peripatetic reinforcements, were upseated to standard capacity and sent mostly to Willesden for the conversion to crew M of the 260, begun tentatively on 13 March and made official from 17 May, the process lasting until 12 July. In the interim the conversion of the 22A and 277 at Clapton (CT) from T to M commenced when M991 was sighted on 14 April, but this conversion was to drag out for many months as other Abbey garages took priority. On 28 April a single Enfield M commenced a new Monday to Saturday route numbered 192, linking Lower Edmonton and a new Tesco at Turnford, north of Flamstead End.

Abbey District garages remaining to have their DMSs replaced by Ms included Chalk Farm, but its conversion was postponed when the trainer sent there grounded at the garage entrance, and instead Holloway (HT) was tackled, its first Ms appearing on 8 May to cover routes 104, 214 and 271, plus night routes N92 (OPO) and N93 (one of just two still crew-operated). Holloway added to its roster on 2 June with the introduction of new route 153, restoring buses to the Barnsbury estate in its progress between Archway and the Angel. That date also saw new route 265 make its debut with M1036/40 from Putney; its one-way circular aspect was based on Putney Bridge Station and served Queen Mary's Hospital in Roehampton before returning via the 264. A third new route was the 205, the second incarnation of this number to feature Ms, and it was a one-bus Cricklewood venture linking Willesden Garage and St Raphael's Estate in Neasden. Finally, the E3's

localised service to Chiswick, Grove Park was split off as new Stamford Brook-run E4, which then proceeded north to Park Royal ASDA. In the debits column, the 273 was withdrawn, to be replaced towards Ruislip (and including the summer-Sunday Lido projections) by an extension of the E2 from Greenford, and on Sundays being covered by an ambitious extension of the 79 from the Alperton direction. The 297 also broke new ground beyond Perivale with its own extension to Ealing Broadway.

On 29 June London Transport was transferred from the GLC to Government control under the London Regional Transport Act and rechristened London Regional Transport (LRT), buses' legal lettering being amended accordingly but still with the 55 Broadway address. This was just the first of several step changes which would fundamentally alter the structure of London's bus operations during the decade.

M1039/43 were despatched to Norbiton to form this year's Wimbledon Tennis complement in the last fortnight of June, supported by Sutton DMSs, while the second tranche of unusual Ms took over the Round London Sightseeing Tour between 4 July and 4 August. M1044-55 had special signwriting and were equipped with internal PA systems and tachographs for this Victoria-based tour, which was beginning to see serious competition from the likes of London Pride and Culture Bus. At night, from 12/13 July, the new Ms took over the N2 and N11 from the outgoing B20 Fleetlines, and soon wandered to the 2B. From 30 July Battersea joined in on the RLST's London By Night sightseeing tour. The 1 August registration change occurred at M1056 (B56 WUL), booked marks A56-75 TJD being outpaced and thus voided. B-WUL combinations would appear on 250 Ms.

From 28 August the Metrobus complement was added to the AVE trials that had opened on 26 March when the three Ls had entered service on Stockwell's 170 (plus 44 on Sundays and N87 at night), to be followed in June by two of the Vs. Only two mkII Ms existed at this time; M1441/2 had been delivered in June carrying A101/2 SYH, the marks meant for the delayed three Hs, but had been corrected to A441/2 UUV by the time they were sent to Stockwell for driver familiarisation on 9 July. M1441 mated Gardner 6LXB power with Voith D851 transmission, but M1442 combined the Cummins L10 engine with a Maxwell gearbox, generating an aggressive snarling sound. The look was certainly more simplified, with 60% fewer parts and die-stamped sections creating greater gaps between the windows, while at the rear of both decks, the windows were even bigger than on the mkI. Gone also was the characteristic asymmetrical windscreen, but LT chose to have the registration number in the middle rather than offset to the nearside as on mkIIs generally. Three taller 'M', 'C' and 'W' letters constituted the vehicle's manufacturer identity. M1443, the third evaluatory Metrobus ordered, was to be powered by a Gardner 5LXCT engine while incorporating styling and engineering differences significant enough to render it a mkIII (LT code 7M8), and its delivery was awaited (B443 WUC now being reserved in lieu of A443 UUV). Further power/transmission experiments envisaged the conversion of six Ms to Maxwell gearboxes and the fitment of a Metrobus with a Deutz engine (the air-cooled unit mentioned earlier); in the event, only the latter option would reach fruition.

A new route to see M incursions was the 216; following isolated appearances since August, a schoolday-only diagram was allocated from 14 September on the independent Kingston-Tolworth section, which descended from the 211. The 279A's Edmonton allocation, meanwhile, was wholly crew M for some Sundays during mid-1984. Notting Hill Carnival augmentations saw the 28's Wandsworth share predominantly crew M. The Thames Barrier, opened earlier in 1984 to some popularity at first, saw excursions to it from far and wide, the likes of Edmonton, Potters Bar, Wood Green and Edgware supplying Ms for four weekends in August. Private-hire work was increasingly recognised as good business, and by August a dozen further Ms had been fitted with tachographs for this purpose. Normal services saw, from the autumn, the progressive replacement of side blinds, which had rarely been used properly, with panels carrying just the route number in the middle.

On 30 August Chalk Farm (CF) commenced M operation, the site's road-camber problems having been sorted out, and despite neither Clapton nor Holloway being anywhere close to completion, the 46 only needed twelve buses and all were in place by 27 October, just in time for the route to suffer reductions at its western end. Ash Grove (AG) simultaneously took its turn, its first Ms commencing on the 106 on 18 October and again not managing to oust the garage's Titans by year's end. A small programme on 29 September saw the 79 withdrawn outright in spite of its recent Sunday projection; instead, and not to great acclaim, the 226 was extended all the way over this route (and adding its Alperton share) to Burnt Oak,

Left: 1984's most important event was the commencement of the Alternative Vehicle Evaluation (AVE) trials, by which three examples of contemporary chassis would battle it out over the 170 road to see which type LT would order after M production finished; Titans were already in their last months of delivery by the time the L-class Leyland Olympians began running on 25 March. Here at Chiswick Works on 5 July is M1442, here erroneously carrying A102 SYH, the registration meant for the second Dennis Dominator. The simpler and perhaps less elegant construction is evident; as well as the physical differences explained in the text, the entrance doors were different in that they opened independently to each side rather than folding over each other. The Cummins badge denoting its engine type did not survive into service. *John Laker*

Above: The mkII Ms, of which there were only two at the moment pending further developments to be announced, entered service on the 170 on 28 August and here at Roehampton is M1442 again one day short of three months later, now registered with the correct A442 UUV. *Geoff Rixon*

producing a circuitously U-shaped route. The 297 was introduced on Sundays, terminating at Wembley Arena on this day rather than the normal Wembley Central Station.

Further additions to the night bus network were introduced overnight on 26/27 October; Holloway gained a share of the N2, which was extended at either end (southwards to Crystal Palace over the 2B and northwards to North Finchley, while gaining a spur from Victoria to Pimlico, replacing the N92 to that point), and its N93 was one-manned to accompany twin extensions, at one end to Hammersmith over the 9, and at the other in a circle to and from Hampstead Heath. The N91 was withdrawn, the N13 was extended from North

Finchley to Barnet Church and the N87 was cut slightly, falling back to Streatham, St Leonard's Church. To cover this sliver, new route N60 was introduced as another livening up of a staff bus, operating a loop from Clapham Common via Brixton, Streatham, Croydon and Thornton Heath back to Clapham Common. It introduced Ms to Wandle District at Clapham (CA, but, as Streatham's crews were based there from 27 October while their own garage was rebuilt, buses actually carried AK). By day they took over the 249 on transfer from Streatham. Victoria's Ms forsook their occasional forays to the 2B with the transfer out of its allocation but with the introduction of a Victoria allocation on the 2 started appearing on that route instead.

500 VICTORIA STATION & OXFORD STREET
via Park Lane

PAY CONDUCTOR

mcw

GYE 401W

VICTORIA & OXFORD CIR

500

In Selkent District, Sidcup's sextet of Ms abandoned the 21A and 299 (both withdrawn) but added new route 233, a re-routeing (via Avery Hill) of the former. At Leaside, the 34 was pruned at its eastern extremity, losing its section beyond Whipps Cross to Leytonstone, while the 144A gained Wood Green workings on Saturdays and Wood Green drivers were further employed by the OPO conversion of the 141's Sunday service. The W2 was projected from Wood Green along the 29 to Enfield to support that service. A week later a small but significant cut to the 195 withdrew it between Southall Garage and Ealing Hospital, and on 24 November the 153 was extended from the Angel to Tottenham Court Road Station.

Unusual batch number three comprised M1084-1105, 22 Cummins L10-engined Metrobuses. Thoughts of putting them into Hendon (which had 22 workings at the time) or Fulwell were dropped, and they entered service at another new garage, Brixton (BN) from 19 November. Although the 50, 95 and N78 were converted as planned by 12 December, their DMSs were retained to edge RMs off the 133; with plans to convert large percentages of the LT

network to OPO during 1985, doored buses were at a premium. From time to time the Ms would pop up with conductors on the 109, 133 and 159 – save for M1102, which was seriously damaged in an accident on 17 December, its first day in service. A particularly unusual visit on that day was of Holloway's M1060 to the C11; this route had started with Ford Transits, although only the southernmost section into town could cope with double-deckers, and would entertain the odd M for some years thereafter.

The most eye-opening event of 1984 was the emergency appearance of Victoria's newish Ms in crew mode on Red Arrow route 500 between 26 November and 21 December, following a fire at Oxford Circus Underground station on 23 November. Three of the former Airbus-augmentation Ms were allocated temporarily to Victoria for this. Even more unusually, RMs appeared on this service too! Shoppers' services in the runup to Christmas brought Muswell Hill Ms to Milton Keynes, Wood Green and Harrow Weald Ms to Romford and Southall Ms to Park Royal ASDA. Boxing Day saw crew Ms on the 28 (Wandsworth) and 207 (Hanwell).

Above: So much for the Red Arrow routes being designed for multiple-standee OMO – an emergency occasioned by a fire at Oxford Circus Underground station on 23 November 1984 necessitated the borrowing of three peripatetic Airbus Metrobuses in crew format. M401 (GYE 401W) is seen at Victoria towards the end of the emergency M operation of the 500, and remarkably, an old SMS blind panel has been unearthed from Victoria's stores to fit to it. *Haydn Davies*

THREE

Mainstay of the Fleet

After a nearly two-year lull, OPO conversions resumed with a vengeance in 1985, four large programmes during the year causing the withdrawal of 300 RMs. The first such was on 2 February, which increased the proportion of OPO from 52% to 56%; one-manned with existing Ms in place were routes 33 (Fulwell) and 260 (Willesden), though the 4 (Holloway), 76 (Tottenham) and 141 (Wood Green) were all straight RM-to-M changeovers, with only a few crew Ms practising on the 76 and 141 and none on the 4. Thanks to a surge in deliveries over the turn of the year, these three conversions had all the Metrobuses they needed in good time. The 141's southern half already had New Cross crew Ts in position; only on Saturdays was through working the case, and even then Wood Green

Ms would reach no further south than Catford Garage. The 260 upon OPO conversion suffered with a withdrawal between Willesden Garage and Hammersmith; the largely parallel 266 picked up a Willesden crew M allocation to compensate, its existing Cricklewood allocation itself commencing conversion to crew M with new vehicles (and allowing the class to make return appearances on the 16 and 16A after some five years. Sidcup's 161 was also one-manned, allowing M visits.

The 195, cut back in November, was extended from Southall once again, this time to Hanwell Garage to accompany its reallocation there from 2 February. Transferred in the other direction was the N89. The last crew-operated night route, Wood Green's N29, was converted to OPO. Minor alterations saw the 33's

Above: One of the more entertaining aspects of observing the M class in the field was seeing how the frontal treatment varied as repaints came due or panels were replaced. M498 (GYE 498W), transferred from Hanwell to Southall in August 1984 and seen at Uxbridge on the similarly transferred N89 night route on 22 April 1985, has had its wings repainted (or replaced) but grille panels left alone, producing a spats-like effect. Other buses would have just one segment done, or run about with panels in undercoat. The imminent end of overhauling meant that general presentation would decline to a considerably worse state than on this bus, and as it happened M498 was not overhauled at Aldenham, but by MCW itself. *Malc McDonald*

Clifford Avenue school bifurcation come off, the 76 rerouted in town via Horseferry Road, the 226 lose its Alperton share on Mondays to Fridays and the 224 withdrawn on Sundays.

The renewed need for doored buses forced a rethink in overhaul policy that led to a number of DMSs being sent out to some of LRT's outside contractors for treatment. To release them, a dozen Ms were allocated to Croydon (TC) from 14 February purely as overhaul cover; affected were routes 127/127A, 130, 130B, 157, 166, 190 and 197, with the 130 pair taking priority and the 234 omitted due to its impending withdrawal. By the time the DMSs had come back from overhaul and been allocated, LRT had changed its mind again, but the DMS/M mix at Croydon persisted. More Ms would arrive in the spring. Metrobuses had already been studied by mechanics at various unfamilar garages in the interests of being able to tackle problems arising to any vehicle at any time; a similar exercise had seen M479 allocated to Sutton for picking over by its engineers, just in case Norbiton's Ms on the shared 213 should require assistance. Ticket-collection training during February was carried out at Finchley, Norwood and Chiswick Works using handfuls of new Ms before they were allocated for service. This year (and for the next three) the Airbus reinforcements were new buses – M1184/5/7/8/90/1, just M1191 being to standard capacity; during the off-season they received their seats back and worked on normal routes. The upseating of M6-205, having commenced in March 1984 with vehicles treated at Aldenham, was completed in March 1985; overhauls stepped up. By April over 65 Ms were tachograph-equipped for excursion work, many M-operating garages able to field three or four so-equipped buses each.

Although the Golden Jubilee-liveried Ms were a memory and all-over ads had been banned once

again after bad experience with lurid green-and-yellow RML2492, two Ms received partial adverts during 1985. January saw M327 gain white between decks, surmounted by multicoloured horizontal stripes all in the aim of promoting System Text, a Hammersmith-based company (for which the bus was outshopped to Fulwell on 13 February and officially rostered on the 33). Either side of the blind box, it carried the cheerful rejoinder 'I'm Stripey!' In July Brixton's M1104 also gained a white midriff, the signwriting therein and down the staircase promoting Cummins, with whose L10 it was engined – and an extra 'C'-in-square' badge appeared ahead of the MCW badge on the radiator grille.

Holloway's conversion to M was finally completed on 21 March after a solid intake spanning the first

Above: One quirk of the overhauling system in its latter days was the constant changing of mind; the decision not to do the Merlins and Swifts had expedited their withdrawal, and in 1985 DMS overhauls, discontinued three years earlier, began again. This led to the input of Ms into Croydon during February to release pilot examples to Aldenham, and in April brand new M1164 (B164 WUL) is captured swinging into the recently-rebuilt West Croydon Bus Station with a more usual inhabitant of the 130/130B pair looking on. After only a handful of Fleetlines were overhauled, their cycle was cancelled again but the Ms stayed put at Croydon. *Chris Evans*

Left: All-over advertising had petered out after its 1970s heyday, modern types not being felt recognisable enough to do the job. Still, two wrap-around adverts appeared on Ms during 1985, the most cheerful of which trumpeted the wares of System Text of Hammersmith to the area served by Fulwell's 33 route, one of the large number of services converted to OPO on 2 February. With 'I'm Stripey' declaration either side of the blind box, M327 (EYE 327V) works through High Street Kensington on 20 August. *Malc McDonald*

Left: OPO reached the fairly quiet inner-suburban route 118 on 27 April 1985, 16 Ms going into Brixton. However, blinds were not yet ready so the new buses had to start with side blinds purloined from the outgoing RMs. M1228 (B228 WUL), at Mitcham on the first day, shows that they just about fit and indeed carry quite a bit more information! *Malc McDonald*

Right: On 27 April 1985 Norwood was allocated its first OPO route, the 196 transferred from Camberwell and thereby converted from T to M. Making the left turn into Herne Hill station's forecourt on its way southbound to Norwood Junction on 31 May is M1182 (B182 WUL). *Colin Stannard*

three months of the year, but even by now neither Clapton nor Ash Grove could muster ten between them. Straight allocations of new Ms to the latter pair replaced a more complicated plan to cascade buses via Finchley, Hendon and Cricklewood, but Finchley still served as pre-service base for buses going into Wood Green.

LRT's first Business Plan, issued at the beginning of 1985, decreed that operations be split into separate, wholly-owned subsidiary companies, and thus was London Buses Ltd (LBL) born from 1 April, to accompany London Underground Ltd (LUL) and Bus Engineering Ltd (BEL). Legal lettering thus had to be changed all over again, after less than one year. On the cards, ominously, was the institution of competitive tendering, the first 13 routes having been offered out the previous autumn and awarded on 11 April (LRT retaining just six), with many more to follow.

Night Bus changes on 26/27 April rerouted the N2 intermediately via Pimlico, extended the N14 to Kingston over the 85 and the N11 to Hackney over the 253; both N68 and N88 were projected from Wandsworth to Sutton, the former via Wimbledon and the latter via Mitcham (allowing, after a month's respite, the withdrawal of the night service on the 220), while the N18 was extended from Sudbury to Edgware via Harrow Weald. The N27 was withdrawn, but three new routes covered bits of this, the Inter-Station Night Bus and Red Arrow 556. Broadly the N56 proceeded to Heathrow, the N50 to Ladbroke Grove and Shepherd's Bush (this number used outward) and N51 identifying the return journey over the same roads. Ash Grove Ms and Ts worked the N56, while the N50 and N51 were shared between Shepherd's Bush Ms and New Cross Ts.

The main 27 April programme involved another RM-to-M OPO conversion, that of the 118 at Brixton. Its new Ms had to work with cut-up RM blinds for the first week or so, while the increased width of the new buses by comparison with the outgoing RMs necessitated 'hesitation points' being set up along Commonside East in Mitcham. To the south, Croydon's route 234 was withdrawn, but not before

Left: Ash Grove's conversion from T to M, begun the previous October due to the need to standardise OPO types in this newly-Abbey District garage, proceeded with painful slowness, only ones and twos being allocated throughout 1985. Their daytime route 106 was joined on 27 April by new night route N56, taking passengers all the way to Heathrow Airport. In the wee small hours of 19 April 1986 M1211 (B211 WUL) is seen at Paddington. *Malc McDonald*

Left: The M class began going into Aldenham for overhaul in August 1982, following the successful example set by M44. In works, the process kept chassis and body united so that the bus that went in was numerically the same one that came out. M256 (BYX 256V) was taken in during December 1984 from Willesden, and on 30 May 1985 is seen in the throes of major repair work, enough to necessitate prising most of the front off. Once finished, it was outshopped to Edgware in October. *John Laker*

M1200, with blinds crafted from DMS panels, was put out on its last day; in replacement the 127 was extended from Purley to Selsdon. Norwood (N) received its first Ms when the 196 was transferred in from Camberwell. The 2 lost its Victoria share and the possibility of Ms, having seen one RLST example turn out all day on occasion during March. Not to be beaten, they began appearing on the 11! Reductions to the 220 south of Wandsworth allowed Shepherd's Bush to release four Ms to Ash Grove and three to Clapton.

At Harrow Weald, the 140 began growing again when it was extended on Sundays to Edgware over the 286, which was withdrawn on that day of the week. The 205 at Cricklewood was revised to omit its Harlesden-Willesden end. Protests over the withdrawal of the 224 on Sundays led to the alteration of the 222 on that day to double-run via Stockley Estate from 18 May. Passengers had not taken to Enfield's 192, and it was withdrawn.

Ash Grove used its growing complement of Ms on a new weekend route dubbed 'Touristlink' from 4 May. From 25 May the 72's summer-Sunday projections beyond Tolworth Broadway to Chessington Zoo were reintroduced, while on 4 June the 205 was further altered to bring it past the Tesco superstore at Brent Park.

Overhauls had by mid-1985 encompassed the majority of Ms up to M505, with examples from the 1981 batch of M506-805 beginning to enter works in May. For the most part the subclassifications remained segregated, garages receiving non-standard examples (like Putney with M370 and 417) soon passing them on; only Wood Green and Fulwell were operating vehicles of both types, the former having received some V-registered examples to bolster the 141's OPO conversion. M193 and 254 somehow managed to be overhauled twice! On new Ms, one final aesthetic change occurred within 170 units of the cessation of production; from M1279, fronts now omitted the chrome beading and the traditional

badge was gone, to be replaced by three individual 'M' 'C' 'W' letters cut out of metal to a very angular design. Very soon they began to fall off, buses turning out with all sorts of combinations of the three, while in the case of M1296 wags at Holloway rearranged the letters to read 'M' 'U' 'M'! The engine cover's badge was also revised to read 'METROBUS' in separate letters of the same design.

Tendering was now upon us; the possibility of Hounslow M appearances on the 81 was extinguished with the transfer of the route to London Buslines on 13 July; the 313 returned to London Country on the same date. Both routes would regain M appearances towards the end of their lives as tenders changed and changed again.

Below: Route 104 (see page 31) was replaced under the 3 August 1985 programme by new route 17, which then covered the withdrawal of the 18 (still crew M even by now) from the roads beyond Farringdon Street to London Bridge. M1136 (B136 WUL), new in February for the 4's one-manning, is at Archway on the first day. *Malc McDonald*

The third OPO-conversion scheme of 1985 took place on 3 August; at Norbiton the 71 was one-manned with new Ms (which had been run in on the Wimbledon tennis service of 24 June-7 July), additionally being re-routed to follow daily the Metrobus-friendly streets of its Sunday service). Brand new Ms also took over the 243 and Sunday 243A at Tottenham, replacing RMLs, while a Sunday conversion encompassed the 74. This route was cut back to West Brompton to allow the 264 to be extended up from Putney Bridge Station to South Kensington as a partial one-manning, and to furnish it six new Ms (1301/2/4/5/11/5) were put into Putney. The 85 was rerouted cumbersomely round the Alton East Estate on its way to Kingston, necessitating a black-on-yellow ultimate for that direction. The Alton East Estate was also the new terminus for the 265, its circular remit reconfigured into a regular service now introducing buses to Mill Hill Road East.

At Holloway, the 104 was withdrawn, to be replaced at the Archway end by a reincarnation of the 17 number, which at its central London end operated to London Bridge, allowing the 18 (still crew-M) to fall back to King's Cross (with peak-hour projections retained only as far as Farringdon Street). On Sundays, however, the 17 did not run; to ensure a service from Archway to the Petticoat Lane-area markets, Sunday-only route 263A was commissioned, again from Holloway. The 4 was tasked with a partial one-manning of the 19's northernmost end by assuming its regular service beyond Finsbury Park to Archway, and at Norwood a quintet of Ms was added so that the route could cover for at least some of the 172's withdrawal through an extension from Brixton to Kennington (and in early mornings, all the way into town as far as Islington High Street).

More partial one-manning took off the 279 and 279A's out-county section north of Waltham Cross and replaced them with a daily extension of the 259 (previously Mon-Sat only) to Hammond Street; this latter route received an Edmonton allocation daily with new Ms. Further north, a Potters Bar allocation was introduced on the W8 to offset the 313's earlier loss on tender. Finally, the Saturday-only Cricklewood share of the 240 was withdrawn, taking with it garage journeys beyond Golders Green.

The closure of the LRT canteen at Liverpool Street and its replacement by an existing facility at Waterloo caused the rerouting or curtailment of six M-operated night routes from 9/10 August; the N14, N18, N68, N88, N89 and N94. This year's incarnation of the Notting Hill Carnival saw Willesden press Ms into service on the 52 on both the Saturday and Sunday, and the first Ms on the 12 from Shepherd's Bush. Further unusual appearances this summer included a Norwood M on the 68, a Holloway M on a weekday 74, occasional Brixton Ms on the 109 and 133, Victoria Ms on the 11 and Ms returning to the 16 and 16A out of Cricklewood. To cover for accident damage to M1051, standard M1306 (otherwise of Clapton) filled in on the Round London Sightseeing Tour during October.

The Deutz air-cooled engine mentioned earlier was fitted to M205 at Chiswick in August, making its debut at the Chiswick Open Day on 11 August. Not only was this engine's pipework in bright orange, but due to the presence of cooling fins, it was slightly too long for the engine bay, a cover with a pronounced bustle having to be fitted to accommodate it. M205 was deployed to Brixton from September, joining what had become a miscellany of unusual Ms (and similarly experimental DMSs!). Advert frames made their first appearance during 1985; T-shaped frames on the offside and rectangular ones on the nearside were designed so that sections of adverts glued to cardboard could be slotted into the plastic frames without risking paintwork damage when removed, as happened with the old pasted panels. At the rear, however, the time-honoured panels pasted either side of the blind box were replaced by one rectangular frame above the rear blind box and one on the top half of the folding engine cover (on Ms so fitted). Renewed attempts at economy saw Ms 405/13/5/25/41/3/54/67/74/6/98, 504 pulled from the overhaul programme to receive GASPs instead, in theory delaying their input into works by a year and helping ease a backlog. A contract was now placed with MCW for overhaul of some Ms, M488 being the first to go in September, followed in October by M462/6 and November by M441/67/76, in which month M488 was returned. An experimental heating system was fitted to M300 in October by the experimental shop at Chiswick.

As MCW resumed business after the August works holiday and C-registrations followed B-registrations at M1306 (C306 BUV), the last hundred Ms continued their deployment, first displacing earlier examples that had been filling in for garages left short by 3 August (like Putney and Tottenham), and then taking over two crew routes. From 27 September the 41 at Wood Green began receiving new examples (most of which had already been delivered but run in on the 29 pending a route survey along the 41), but the introduction of Ms to the 65 at Norbiton from 5 October underscored the fact that not even the busiest of suburban trunk routes were immune from the march of cost-cutting. To that end, 2 November heralded the fourth and last of 1985's big one-manning programmes. The 41 (losing its Tottenham participation) was duly converted to OPO, as was the 266 at Cricklewood and Willesden, but the 133, which was expecting new Ms, had to go over with its existing DMS complement at Brixton, supported by wanderings from the 50, 95 and 118. The 95 was cut down heavily to become a peak-hour-only service going no further south than Brixton Garage; the 133 took over its service to Tooting Broadway. The remaining Putney Sunday OPO share of the 74 was withdrawn, removing the possibility of garage journeys. All M appearances on the 114 ceased by this date, allowing the displaced Metrobuses to effect the formal double-decking of the 209 despite the transfer of its peak-hour Northwick Park projection to the 136 (but needs forced the Saturday service on the 114 to regain a proportion of Ms after just six weeks). The 76 was rerouted in town via Lambeth Bridge rather than Westminster Bridge, while the recently one-manned 243 was altered with the addition of three Stamford Hill Ms on Mondays to Fridays.

A partial one-manning severed the off-peak service on the 113 between Mill Hill (Apex Corner) and Edgware, this section being appended to the 186 as an extension south from Edgware to Brent Cross. The balance of work at Hendon was maintained by giving this garage part of the 186, plus a portion of the 240 on Sundays. Fellow Edgware route 286 was withdrawn entirely, the 140 taking over as a self-contained section and now gaining an Edgware share to join Harrow Weald's Ms.

To the north, Enfield-operated route 231 transferred its Carterhatch-Brimsdown section to an extension of the 191, while to the east Clapton gained nine new Ms for the 277, whose Poplar allocation was taken off upon the closure of that garage. Another closure on 2 November was Battersea, whose 39 was reallocated into Victoria with its Ms, ejecting the RLST and its dozen PA-fitted Ms to Stockwell. On Sundays, however, Putney took up the 39, allowing drivers there to recoup their losses from the 74. Victoria

Above: Standards may have been slipping with the outsourcing of blind manufacture, but the Johnston font itself was continuing to evolve; the '4' on this blind is of a most unusual style that was only printed on a handful of blinds for Wood Green (including route 41) and Holloway (including route 4) late in 1985. The 41 commenced conversion to crew-M on 27 September 1985 ahead of its one-manning on 2 November, and on 27 October M328 (EYE 328V), a low number by Wood Green's standards and devoid of chrome beading around its radiator, is about to ascend the hilly terrain north of Hornsey Rise. *Malc McDonald*

Left: Norbiton had already lost the 71 to OPO on 3 August 1985 and from 5 October it was the 65's turn to take on Metrobuses in preparation for OPO conversion in the New Year. M1340 (C340 BUV), crossing Kingston in October, demonstrates the final aesthetic alteration to the mkI Metrobus's front, with three die-cut letters replacing the MCW badge and the chrome beading omitted altogether; the effect wasn't terribly becoming. *Geoff Rixon*

Left: Clapton was the other former Tower District garage transferred to Abbey on 2 January 1984 and thus requiring Ms to replace its Ts; like Ash Grove nearby, the conversion of the 22A and 277 had dragged out for over a year but on 2 November 1985 Poplar closed and its share of the 277 was swallowed up by Clapton. M1360 (C360 BUV) was one of nine new Ms to go in for this purpose and is seen in Hackney on 9 December. *Malc McDonald*

Below left: Surprises continued to come thick and fast in the last months of M deliveries; in order to help release Ts to furnish a hefty package of changes in Selkent District from 2 November, additional Ms were allocated to Sidcup, which had held onto M800-5 long after the route 51 trials had concluded in 1982, and immediately after that its route 21 was converted to doored crew operation with further new Ms. On 8 April 1986 M1394 (C394 BUV) is seen in Sidcup, not long before moving on. *Malc McDonald*

received a Sunday share of the 52, which was one-manned on Sundays and additionally covered for the 52A's withdrawal on that day of the week. At night, the N50 and N51 were altered to extend them to and from Greenford, each adding an Ash Grove allocation, while the N56 was projected to Heathrow.

An announcement was made on 15 November confirming the run-down of Aldenham as an overhauling site, this work to be carried out principally by garages with just heavy repair done at Aldenham. M606 was the last Metrobus taken in. MCW continued to undertake contract overhauls, and had nine Ms in works by the end of 1985. Unfortunately, the pressure on garages to carry out FFD work as well as running a service led to immediate shortages on the road by the end of the year, Tottenham, Edmonton and Stamford Hill Ms being particularly badly affected. Vehicle appearance began to decline dramatically, underscoring deep division within the industry as staff went on strike repeatedly in an attempt to face down massive job cuts and reductions to working conditions.

Right: The other wrap-around advert M of 1985 was Brixton's M1104 (B104 WUL); if potential customers hadn't already got a good idea of what was under the bonnet from the oncoming Cummins snarl, the advert soon set them straight! The 133 was another route given doored buses before one-manning on 2 November, but these were predominantly DMSs which had stayed behind after their replacement from the 50 and 95 by Ms and M1104 was thus an interloper. From 2 November it would be diverted away from the Streatham terminus seen on the blind to take over much of the 95 to Tooting Broadway. *Malc McDonald*

Left: Catastrophe struck Southall garage on Christmas Day 1985 when a fire raged through the fuelling bay. M71 (WYW 71T) never stood a chance and was burned to the ground along with several other Ms. *John Laker*

Below: The charred remains of the Southall fire victims were towed to the nearby former AEC site pending a decision over which of them could be rebuilt – plainly, not the unidentifiable wreck on the right. M103 (BYX 103V), with severe frontal damage, did manage to survive, returning to service in April 1987, while those at left, M153 (BYX 153V) and M175 (BYX 175V), were also salvageable despite damage further down their bodies. *John Laker*

With the production run of Ms nearly done, there still remained the possibility of surprises, and none was more so thanwhen additional Metrobuses started pouring into Sidcup. Thanks to the garage's familiarity with the type and the lack of spare Titans at the moment, ten new Ms displaced an equivalent number of Ts indirectly to Peckham for the 70's double-decking on 2 November, and more followed when the 21 fell next on the list to be converted to doored crew operation (officially from the 5th with the first Ms sighted on the 13th). The New Cross minority on this trunk route was treated by acquiring the six evaluatory Ts out of Westbourne Park, which were replaced on the 18 with M1376-8/80/2 plus M1364 ex Clapton. M1387 was allocated new to Victoria so that the garage didn't keep having to take Chalk Farm buses on loan at weekends. Thus was 1985 completed, or so it looked until a fire broke out at Southall garage on Christmas Day, the one day of the year when the entire allocation was within the garage. Starting on or around M23 and spreading to the fuelling bay along the west side of the garage, the fire wrought devastating results; four Ms (M23, 116/52, 253) were completely destroyed, M71 and 104 were later judged to be damaged beyond economical repair and a further 14 (M53/81, 103/34/7/8/53/75/88, 200/35/47, 360/473) incurred heavy damage. Immediately contingency plans were mounted; with Hanwell stepping in to fuel Southall's runout, Ms were taken on loan from adjacent garages (Hanwell, Alperton, Shepherd's Bush and Westbourne Park) while ten of the new Ms destined for Brixton's 133 were rushed into service at Southall. It was feared that at least one OPO conversion planned for 1 February 1986 would not be able to go ahead, as ten RMs were plucked from sales stock and put into traffic on the 65 at Norbiton to enable the loan of further Metrobuses. The fire prevented the M class from assuming its maximum amount in stock, even though from 2 November numbers had surpassed that of the fast-depleting RM class, rendering the M the mainstay of the fleet.

Right: The scrambling into service of several new Ms at Southall following the Christmas Day fire put back the full conversion of the 133 to M; M1407 (C407 BUV) was one of those plucked from the reception line at Aldenham on 30 December and only reached Brixton in February; the route was completed using the last sixteen Ms. *John Laker*

Another Southall bus, M359, had already lost its top deck in a fire on 22 December and Ms 110 and 259 were damaged by fire in separate incidents again!

Finally, as 1986 bowed, the last Ms were delivered, the last sixteen heading to Brixton as planned for the 133; together with the return of the loans from Southall enabling the removal of DMSs from that garage. Most of this final two dozen were delivered without the fussy 'M' 'C' 'W' badging. M1440 was taken into stock on 15 January and allocated to Brixton on the 29th, and that was the end of mkI Metrobus production, the model having been taken by London Transport alone for over three years. M1443, meanwhile, was nowhere to be found.

Economy measures over and above OPO conversions began to accelerate; Edmonton closed its doors from 1 February 1986, passing M-operated 144A to Wood Green, W8 to Potters Bar and 259 and N90 to Enfield with the appropriate vehicle transfers. This date also saw the 21 one-manned, as well as the 65. The conversion of this latter route was executed through the transfer of a handful of Ms from Hounslow, whose route 202 was partially converted to LS. Finally losing its conductors after close to a decade with doored crew buses was the 18; its Westbourne Park share came off on Sundays to allow the OPO conversion of the 7 on that day. The 171, already operating in two overlapping sections, was split to allow the northern half to assume OPO as new route 171A, with Tottenham Ms.

The last Metrobus to emerge from Aldenham overhaul was M606 on 14 March, after which a repaint programme commenced; but the lesser nature of this work called Aldenham's viability into question once again. The first of the month saw another Metrobus casualty, M759, which was damaged by arson on Enfield garage's exposed forecourt. 22 March was the date Titans began returning to Ash Grove, displaced from Plumstead by new Ls and intended to ease RMs off the 35 prior to its OPO conversion; standardisation in Abbey District be damned. That day also saw the reconfiguration of the RLST as the Original London Sightseeing Tour, with Routemasters; for the moment, nine of the PA-equipped Ms (minus M1051, victim of a second accident, and M1045/50 which went to Clapham for route 37 familiarisation work) joined the RMs and RCLs at Battersea (reopened to house this much-expanded tour). Touristlink route T1 also commenced on 22 March, shared for the summer between Ash Grove and Clapton, while Victoria's M1172, Holloway's M1035 and Westbourne Park's M1350 combined to furnish the T2. Croydon's 127 and 127A, occasionally host to Ms, were lost to London Country. Although the input of 1985's five extra Airbuses had stabilised that fleet (the buses staying put to work normal Stamford Brook services during the winter), M583 was fitted out as H43/5D during March. After some time languishing at AEC or Aldenham, Southall fire victims M53, 103/34/53/75/88, 200/35/59 were sent to MCW for repair; just M53 was additionally struck off stock, due to a fire at MCW in December 1987.

Tendering losses cost LBL the 195, which passed to London Buslines on 12 April, but LBL retained the 79A and 125; the latter received a Sunday extension from Winchmore Hill to Enfield Town. This date also saw the opening of Heathrow Airport's Terminal Four with extensions or diversions to local M-operated routes. Airbus A2 was rerouted to Victoria rather than Paddington, allowing the A3 to be withdrawn. An unprecedented fifth terminus was taken up by the 213 on 21 April when one schoolday journey was diverted at St Helier to serve Love Lane; the concept of separate schoolday augmentations had effectively been introduced on 10 March when a single route 266 journey was projected from Brent Cross to Finchley, Manor Cottage Tavern, and such curios would characterise the latter days of the M class's career in particular.

Repaints officially ceased at Aldenham after 6 May, not long after the announcement of the inevitable closure of the works, but buses continued to receive treatment both here and at garages; for example M6 lost its unique white relief that month. The concept of overhauling too was at an end, M405 returning from MCW on the 8th.

Vehicle orders for 1986 comprised 260 Ls, this first of the AVE classes having taken precedence for an interim order without necessarily having 'won' the trials, which concluded on 31 December 1985 with the vehicles remaining in place for the moment on the 170. Future interior layouts were still under investigation, while LBL had not given up hope that M1443 would eventually make its appearance. What would come next, in the event, would be overridden by the desperate need to save money in the face of tendering, and in the end no more double-deckers at all were ordered. LBL would have to make do with what it had, and to that end niceties like standard vehicle types for each garage would have to be forgotten. When the time came to allocate doored buses to Clapham for the 37, it was accomplished by taking Ms from Brixton and returning DMSs to that garage after just five weeks! The conversion commenced on 28 April, Brixton being partially compensated by the allocation of some of the former RLST Ms released from Battersea by the increased number of Routemasters; Hounslow's allocation on the 37 was tackled from 30 May with the deployment

of some of the last overhauled Ms. Another example of declining standards involved the continuation of mixed-type working at Sidcup when half the minority complement of Ms was replaced there by an equivalent number of incoming new Ls during May and reallocated to Muswell Hill for the 134, another busy RM-operated trunk route. The conversion took from 10-19 May. Changes to the 22A from 17 May saw an evening extension from Clapton Pond to Lee Valley Ice Centre.

The tendering losses that forced the closure of Loughton garage on 24 May also cost LBL the 217B (to Sampsons), six Ms leaving Enfield mostly for Finchley. To keep itself viable, Potters Bar's 242 abandoned its path between Waltham Abbey and Chingford, denuding the roads as far as Yardley Lane of buses entirely. A week later the 283 was lost, Shepherd's Bush Ms giving way to weird-looking Jonckheere-bodied Scania K92s operated by Scancoaches, but 21 June marked the date of another large programme. Today the 37 was one-manned, its Clapham majority being stiffened by the input of the last remaining Sidcup Ms, but the Hounslow-operated section was withdrawn between Clapham Junction and Clapham Common (or Brixton in peaks)

Above: Even though the supply of Ms had run dry, OPO conversions still needed stock, and where the 37 was concerned its buses were supplied by pulling Ms out of Brixton and replacing them with DMSs, thus reversing its modernisation! M1074 (B74 WUL), however, was one of Clapham's indigenous batch and on 26 May, three weeks after the conversion from RML to crew-M had begun on this garage's allocation, is seen at Barnes, Red Rover. One-manning was implemented on 21 June. *Malc McDonald*

Right: Also losing its conductors on 21 June 1986 was the 35, another route where an established type conversion had to be thrown into reverse due to the lack of new buses, refuting any lofty aims towards standardisation. M922 (A922 SUL), seen at the Elephant on 4 July, was now in the minority at Ash Grove, a flood of Titans having come back to furnish this route. *Malc McDonald*

Left: Busy central-London route 134 was one-manned on 21 June 1986, its Muswell Hill garage taking Ms from Sidcup (where new Ls from the only batch ordered replaced them) and from Edgware, which ceded the 142 to London Country under tender. M402 (GYE 402W), seen at Highgate in crew mode on 8 June, had already been transferred the previous November, from Cricklewood. *Malc McDonald*

Below left: Norwood received the 2 from Stockwell to accompany its one-manning on 21 June, and on a sunny 1 October M1213 (B213 WUL) begins the stiff climb up Knights Hill towards Crown Point in Norwood. *Malc McDonald*

to allow the extension of the 35 from the other direction. This route lost its conductors, but Ash Grove was still able to commit Ms alongside a large number of Ts; the other garage on the route, Camberwell, used solely Ts. The 134 was also converted to OPO, additional Ms coming from Edgware, which was compelled to release the 142 to London Country under tender. Extraordinarily, the vicissitudes of tendering brought 'home' the 84, which resumed Potters Bar M operation but now as a Hertfordshire County Council contract; slipboards to this effect were designed to be carried within brackets fitted over the nearside of buses' radiators. In order to let the 84 take the main effort between Barnet and Potters Bar (via Hadley Highstone rather than South Mimms), the 263 was reduced north of the border, several journeys now terminating at Barnet General Hospital. Another Potters Bar route, the 298, departed for London Country. Foreshadowing its future direction, the 113 was treated to weekday crew-M workings as a cross-working from another Hendon route.

The 2 group's corridor was affected by the conversion to OPO of the 2 and its reallocation from Stockwell to Norwood (which received eight ex-Brixton Ms), plus the withdrawal of the 2B north of Baker Street, to be replaced by new Finchley M-operated route 82 (Victoria-Golders Green, or Barnet on Sundays over the 26). Holloway passed the 214 to Chalk Farm, while the 221 lost its Finchley buses and gained some from Edgware instead. At Tottenham the 76 was withdrawn on Sundays and lost its off-peak service beyond Waterloo to Victoria, but the 171A was introduced on Sundays, taking on the 76's roads to Northumberland Park on that day.

Left: Another Metrobus with a piebald front following repairs or repaints, M569 (GYE 569W) is also different from fellows by virtue of its Wayfarer ticket machine, at the time under evaluation at Finchley but soon selected to be fitted to all London Buses Ltd OPO vehicles. The 82 was created to serve as the one-manning of the 2B's northern section to Golders Green, and on Sundays it incorporated the 26's service to Barnet; it is to this destination that M569 is bound when captured setting off from Victoria on 22 June. *Malc McDonald*

Finally, at night the N50/N51 pair were renumbered plain N50, gaining an extension to Ruislip and a Westbourne Park M share. This garage also received part of the N18 on Friday/Saturday nights. Potters Bar's N80 was withdrawn, but incorporated into the N92 as an extension north from Archway and then via either Hadley Highstone or South Mimms. New route N59, shared between Hendon and Edgware, made its debut, probing northwest from Victoria along routes 11, 59, 113, 240, 140 and 142 to Watford Junction (pencilled in earlier in the year as N58).

Ash Grove's M-to-T conversion already having been thrown into reverse, it was now Clapton's turn to gain back Titans when several arrived from Sidcup on 16 May; the Ms released helped convert the 52A to crew M at Victoria.

Having wandered since their displacement from the OLST, M1044-55 found an interesting interlude when, shared between Brixton, Norwood and Stockwell, they assisted on the Wimbledon tennis service between 21 June and 5 July. Less auspicious was the mass delicensing of M1275-83/5-97, forcing Tottenham to call in loans from far and wide. This had knock-on effects, with Harrow Weald having to use surplus LSs to release four Ms to Tottenham.

Advance warning of future one-manning came in the conversion of the Stamford Brook allocation of the 27 to crew M from 2 July (including the garage's Saturday 237s, the conversion taking until the 19th) and of increasing numbers of Ms on Croydon's portion of the 68 from the 9th. The 16th saw the 52A converted to crew M at Victoria, and from 9 August Croydon Ms no longer needed after the 197's loss to London Country stayed behind to displace RMs from its allocation on the 68.

Below: When the time came for the conversion to crew-M of the Croydon allocation of the 68 in August 1986, M1164 (B164 WUL) was still based there, though its frontal condition had altered somewhat since featuring on page 37. Ms would not last much longer at Croydon, Ls being scheduled to replace them (but not all the accompanying DMSs) by year's end. The full sickly horror of the design of West Croydon bus station's exterior is the backdrop for this 1 October 1986 photograph, the building being somewhat toned down in later years. *Malc McDonald*

Left: The lunge towards full OPO continued without pity as 1986 rolled on; not even routes battling through the increasingly-congested West End were spared. The 52 and 52A were converted to crew M during the summer, the latter being selected for tourist-oriented branding despite the reduced appeal of OPO buses as compared to Routemasters. One of the features was a 'Route 52A' blind panel in yellow on black which was, unfortunately, neither attractive nor particularly visible! M946 (A946 SUL) was ousted from Clapton garage by a returning Titan in August and on 30 September is well bedded in at Victoria when caught in Kensington. *Malc McDonald*

Above: Already used to Metrobuses since the year-long stint of Fulwell Ms on a since-abandoned section beyond Richmond, the 27 was another route earmarked for OPO with the 25 October 1986 programme and Ms began to be phased in during the summer. Seen at Notting Hill on 1 October, Stamford Brook's M1177 (B177 WUL) had hitherto eked out its summers as an extra on the Airbus routes, this group of five or six sometimes receiving luggage racks, sometimes not. *Malc McDonald*

Right: The AVE trials had concluded on 31 December 1985 without a clear winner among the four types other than the order for 260 Ls. Eventually the buses began moving on from Stockwell, the two mkII Metrobuses going into Brixton in August 1986 and exemplified here by M1441 (A441 UUV) on the 118 outside its home garage on 17 September.
Malc McDonald

Southall garage now closed, after service on 8 August – the fire had brought its closure forward by several months. Its routes were distributed between Hanwell (92, 105, 274, 282 and N89), Hounslow (120 and 232) and Alperton (part of the 92). Garage journeys to their new homes were added to the 92 and 232. At night the N11 was rerouted at Shepherd's Bush to reach Turnham Green Church rather than Acton Tram Depot.

Over July and August the cab doors of all OPO buses were fitted with perspex anti-assault screens, but the standard design adopted for Ms and Ts could not be fitted to the AVE trials buses still in service at Stockwell, so after 31 August they were stood down, the 170, 44 on Sundays and N87 nightly regaining full-time DMS operation. M1441/2 found themselves transferred to Brixton, where, despite the renewed threat by DMSs, they settled in nicely alongside their mkI counterparts, plus Deutz-engined M205 (deployed from September) and M597 (with a Maxwell gearbox, from November). It was at about this time that the mkIII version was cancelled; now that Leyland had stepped into the breach by taking what turned out to be the last yearly order, MCW was not prepared to risk further development without a solid order, and the underframe of M1443 was broken up without having been used. Stockwell continued to see the odd M, despite being some years away from the replacement of its DMSs, when M1046/95 were loaned from Brixton to work on the 77A. During Carnival the 88 and 12's Shepherd's Bush allocations were predominantly crew M, the latter including buses loaned from Putney. Three one-off night routes were commissioned, of which the N12 included Shepherd's Bush Ms and the N73 was M-worked by Wood Green. The expansion of Night Buses prompted the supply of a spare pair if anything transpired to affect any other route during the course of any night; these were two Victoria Ms.

From time to time London Transport would send buses on various goodwill tours to foreign countries, but this practice had tailed off since the end of Routemaster production, subsequent vehicles lacking the international appeal of that type; however, from 13 September until 6 October M1387 embarked for a trip to Berlin in connection with the Berlin National Festival. An additional revival was of the showbus concept, Enfield's M714 receiving locally-applied accoutrements (including a silver-painted grille and a computer-style numberplate) during October.

Tendering split the 107, London's longest daytime bus route, into two from 27 September. To allow the eastern portion to pass to Eastern National as the 307, the route was reallocated from Enfield to Edgware and withdrawn east of New Barnet Station. The Ms needed at Edgware were some of Wood Green's earliest examples received at overhaul but non-standard at the garage.

On 25 October a very large swathe of one-manning brought OPO buses to central London streets thought previously to be too much for the mode to handle. At Chalk Farm the 24 lost its RMLs and conductors, but its Ms had been joined from 9 October by large numbers of Ts, the 46 and 214 having seen Ts since 23 September. The 68 lost its Chalk Farm share upon OPO conversion but this became new route 168, accompanying the 68 between Waterloo and Euston (where the 68 was curtailed), and beyond the former Chalk Farm Station terminus of the 68 covering new ground up to Hampstead Heath. At the other end of the 68, both the Norwood and Croydon allocations were still able to field Ms as part of their OPO contingent, though Ls were arriving in force at the former and DMSs remained by far the majority at the latter, just two Ms remaining available after 25 October following the exit of the rest into Norwood (though loans persisted until 31 January 1987). Croydon lost its share of the 157, and thus the possibility of Ms on that route. The closure of Elmers End garage saw its DMSs move into Brixton, expelling most of the newest Ms to Willesden to one-man the 52. The 52A at Victoria was also converted to OPO, while the 27, already with crew Ms at Stamford Brook, was one-manned, Ms for the Holloway

allocation coming from Chalk Farm where Ts replaced them (but not all, as Titan unreliability necessitated extensive M loans from fellow Abbey sheds Victoria, Holloway, Wandsworth and Shepherd's Bush to assist officially-reallocated holdout M1065). Hendon lost its last conductors with the one-manning of the 113, Ms for the route coming from spare stock at Wood Green and Enfield. Hendon thus withdrew from the 186 on Saturdays and 240 on Sundays.

The 12, since the split of the 107 London's longest route, was subjected to curtailment, its western end to Willesden Junction being curtailed at East Acton and that section given over to new OPO M route 255 from Shepherd's Bush; Chalk Farm supplied seven Ms it didn't need any more. Another long route was split, but due to tendering; after little more than a year taking passengers beyond the GLC border to Hammond Street, the 259 was now cut back to Ponders End to accommodate new London Country (North East)-operated route 359. Its Saturday service withdrawn entirely, the 259 operated two distinct service patterns – Ponders End to Holborn Circus on Mondays to Fridays (operated by Enfield), and

Waltham Cross to Finsbury Park on Sundays (operated by Tottenham). Stamford Hill withdrew from the 243 and Stamford Brook from the 267.

Unnoticed by London, which had troubles of its own, deregulation was implemented across the rest of the UK from 26 October. At least the garages on the borders perceived opportunity as well as retrenchment, and it was Potters Bar which took the lead, commencing a 310A between Enfield Town and Hertford from the 27th, in direct competition with London Country (North East), one of four firms created upon the split of London Country from 7 September. Ms formed the 310A's Saturday complement on an otherwise LS-operated service. While commercial ventures were being explored, one traditional aspect of London bus operations bit the dust on 16 November when Aldenham finally closed – at its end it had been reduced to just accident repair, and its effect was much missed when looking at the condition of London's buses when deprived of an overhaul. M99 was the last Metrobus to undergo repaint there. The only consolation was that Chiswick had been upgraded to serve as something of a successor, and to that end body repairs began taking

Right: From Ford Transits to Metrobuses in 14 years! The C11 had begun as a backstreets route only, but in 1981 had had the York Road section of the old 239 appended to it, bringing it into King's Cross and widening its commuter appeal. Holloway's normal allocation on the C11 was BLs, but every so often an M would turn out on the double-deck-navigable King's Cross-Archway portion, and at King's Cross on 22 December 1986 here is M1038 (A738 THV). *Malc McDonald*

Below: More reliable than its considerable length would imply, the 113 was on its own along the dual-carriageway Hendon Way for the northernmost part of its journey to and from Oxford Circus. After a backdoor attempt to one-man part of it during 1985 by extending the 186 from Edgware to Brent Cross, the whole route inevitably fell due for OPO and Ms replaced RMLs at Hendon on 25 October 1986. M312 (BYX 312V), already based at Hendon since October 1984, flies through Swiss Cottage on 14 March 1987. This is another early M with replacement mesh grille and no adornments. *Colin Stannard*

place there during December. Still, competitors were awakening, Gatwick Engineering being quick off the mark to take accident-damaged buses (including Ms) early in the New Year. Not among them were M71 and 104, the remains of which were disposed of in January.

Only one Routemaster-operated route remained at Hounslow, the 237, and this began converting to crew M from 26 November, its vehicles supplied by Metrobuses coming out of Norwood following their replacement by Ls. Ash Grove too lost its last Ms at the end of this month, swapping them for Titans from Clapton, which after a process spanning nearly two

years and interrupted by intakes of Ts, was finally fully M by the same point, its last three Ts departing by year's end. Even then stragglers would make return appearances and Ts would start pouring back into Clapton during 1987 as further OPO loomed. The supreme irony was that Abbey District too was about to be deleted, rendering all this type standardisation pointless. In an era where cuts were so savage that no new vehicles could be counted on at all to help improve age profiles, garages had to make do with what they had got. And Clapton, in the last insult, was scheduled for closure during 1987.

Below right: Anything to save that little bit of money while capitulating to traffic congestion – as well as straight OPO conversions, sections of longer routes were lopped off under different numbers, and thus did the 12's leg west of East Acton become new Shepherd's Bush M-operated 255 on 25 October 1986. M843 (OJD 843Y) demonstrates on 8 November, but the route wasn't viable on its own and was soon appended to the 260, another route to have suffered a recent cutback. *Colin Stannard*

Right: A particularly severe programme of OPO conversions on 7 February 1987 struck right at the heart of the West End. To make the concept pay, some of these routes had to be cut back, like the 30, which fell back to West Brompton to pass the section beyond to the 74, which was also one-manned on this day. On the 16th Clapton's M1360 (C360 BUV), not to last much longer at this garage, is seen approaching the Angel, where it will be turned short. *Malc McDonald*

The year 1987 was to prove one of the hardest in a generation. The first occurrence to Ms this year was a tendering loss which cost Fulwell the 110 on 24 January in favour of London Country South West's ex-Greater Manchester Atlanteans; the Ms moved to Hounslow for the 237, the OPO conversion of which took off the Saturday-only Stamford Brook allocation. With weeks to spare, the 149 at Enfield and Stamford Hill had started converting to crew M from mid-December, taking vehicles from Norwood; more followed upon its OPO conversion alongside four other routes on 7 February 1987. The one-manning of the 30 saw Clapton's Ms (now joined by three dozen early Ts ex-Plumstead) swallow up Putney's allocation with the route's curtailment at West Brompton; in its place came a return of the 74 all the way to Roehampton with Putney Ms, thus obviating the need for the 264. Putney's latest intake comprised C-registered examples displaced by the closure of Clapham following the completion of Streatham's rebuilding, plus five from Brixton and Norwood's last three (for the moment). The 74 lost its Holloway share other than on Sundays, but the drivers were switched to new route 14A (also using ex-Clapham Ms), which was introduced between Piccadilly Circus and Turnpike Lane as an OPO conversion of the 14's northern end, plus a bit added on beyond Hornsey Rise. On Sundays the 14 remained a through service, but was converted to OPO on that day with Holloway and Putney Ms, not only being projected to Turnpike Lane but even up the High Road to Wood Green for midday meal reliefs at the garage. Sunday OPO conversion, the latest in cost-cutting wheezes, also encompassed the 22, with Putney Ms and Clapton (for now) mixing Ms and Ts, the 29 (with Wood Green and Palmers Green Ms), the 13 (with Finchley Ms), the 88 (sharing Stockwell DMSs and Shepherd's Bush Ms) and the 137 (Streatham L and Brixton DMS/M).

Above right: Another partial OPO conversion cut the 14 in half on 7 February 1987, its northern, Holloway-operated section becoming new route 14A. Transferred from the closed Clapham to Holloway for this role, M1074 (B74 WUL) is heading south from the Nag's Head. *Malc McDonald*

Right: M1360 (C360 BUV) was a busy Metrobus in its short four months at Clapton, not only adding to the 277 (see page 42) and one-manning the 30 (see top picture) but, from 8 February 1987, turned also to work the 22 on Sundays in OPO format; on 29 March it is rounding Sloane Square on its way to Putney Common. The Helvetica-lettered ultimate blinds spreading like wildfire do look awkward and out of place. *Malc McDonald*

Right: The 137, still stretching from Archway to Crystal Palace through the heart of the West End, was one-manned on Sundays with the 7 February programme. Owing to the closure of Clapham garage, the route weas reallocated to Streatham and Brixton; only the latter used Metrobuses, like M1100 (B100 WUL) at Crystal Palace on 26 April. *Malc McDonald*

Just before Clapham's closure it had been treated to an influx of Ls, not only training drivers for their 7 February move (back) to Streatham, but also preparing Ms for their transfer to Putney. Thus the new Streatham garage was allocated the 249 (from Clapham) and the 50 and 118 from Brixton, all three services losing Ms for L operation. The routeings of the 118 and 137 were transposed between Clapham and Streatham Hill to allow the latter to pass its new base at Brixton (ex-Clapham). In the same region the 109 was converted to OPO, but Brixton's share was taken off (other than on Saturdays) to add a supporting element to the 59, which was extended from Brixton to Farringdon Street on Mondays to Fridays. Norwood lost the 196 to Cityrama under tender, the Ms released also heading to Putney or Holloway, and finally the 237 was one-manned, costing Hounslow crew operation. Norwood and Croydon thus relinquished M operation through the transfer to Hounslow of their last Metrobuses. Norwood, having gained M1201 in mid-February as cover for accident-damaged Ls, lost it after 15 March, while Croydon's last straggler (M1199), having been supported briefly by M1438 on loan, last operated on the same day, though both sheds were to regain the type later in their career. So too would Clapton, which lost its Ms (barring dogged holdouts M1211/358 until 2 April, replaced until 22 April by M806/922 from Uxbridge) when the conversion of the 173 to LS at West Ham (on 28 February) provided enough Ts to eject the Metrobuses. These passed mostly to Wandsworth, which released Y- and A-registration Ms to Fulwell so that earlier-numbered Ms still could be prepared for Hanwell and Uxbridge. Here the 207's OPO conversion (originally set for 7 February with the 30, 74, 109, 149 and 237) slipped repeatedly due to there simply not being enough vehicles available owing to the lack of a solid order for new buses; crew Ms began to appear on 14 March.

Preparation for a tendering scheme in which a whole town's routes would be offered as a network was carried out in Kingston on 7 February; trunk route 65 was recast to only work south of Kingston

on Sundays, the service otherwise being transferred to the 71 (which was accordingly rerouted via Copt Gilders Estate around Chessington North and South). Already discontent was simmering, both Norbiton and Clapton working to rule and repeated strike action becoming commonplace at other garages threatened by network tendering.

The beginnings of technological upgrades to the Metrobus family could be said to have begun on 31 January when Tottenham, Enfield, Wood Green and Stamford Hill undertook a swap of several of their Ms; this was so that the higher-numbered ones could be concentrated at the latter pair in the interests of converting an initial total of 100 to air braking at a cost of £340,000, the work carried out by SBG Engineering at Kilmarnock. Also in Leaside District, Enfield's M1253 received a black skirt and a thin white cantrail band during January; the latter feature was liked enough that it was soon widened, producing a bold new livery that was undoubtedly an improvement on LBL's dull all-red. Epitomising aspirations towards autonomy even within sections of LBL, Leaside District adopted this livery as standard for its OPO buses, sending five Stamford Hill Ms to Gatwick Engineering and three Wood Green Ms to BEL. Garages began to apply the black skirts over existing paintwork and also applied the embellishments without a full repaint. In spite of all this the 'London Transport' identity was beginning to creep back into official parlance, 'LRT' not having stuck. A new roundel was commissioned for this purpose, being 'LONDON BUSES' in red on a yellow roundel with red crossbar, on a white background to contrast with buses' red paint. Leaside also distinguished itself by reintroducing upper-case lettering on its via blinds, an aesthetic improvement which was not to find official favour and which was thus declared outlaw by September.

The OPO conversion of the 207 was only accomplished on 28 March by the uncomfortable expedient of using the large surfeit of LSs to demote several double-deck routes and thus release the Ms needed. These were Cricklewood's 112 and 245 on

14 March, which together with Uxbridge's 98 and 224 from 28 March released enough Ms to tackle the 207's 54-bus PVR in replacement of RMLs. Already weakened by the input of LSs and the withdrawal of much of its Twickenham-Richmond section (from 7 February), the 202 withered further by being withdrawn on Sundays from 28 March. A Hounslow allocation was added to the 98, nominally LS but capable of producing Ms.

In March Maxwell gearbox-equipped M597 transferred from Brixton to Norbiton, soon to move on to Stamford Brook. Presaging the surveillance society yet to come but for now on staff safety grounds in the face of an increase in assaults, Fulwell's M877 was fitted with a camera in the cab. Also during March a programme commenced to fit the exit doorways of the M1006-29 batch of Airbus Metrobuses with wheelchair lifts; this modification (carried out by MCW) required the fitment of four-leaf door units; the backup quintet varied in capacity as different seating layouts and luggage-rack combinations were fitted during the 1987 summer season. Tottenham's M1401 was heavily damaged on 24 April while on the 243, striking a tree in Gray's Inn Road, while Wood Green M1325 was deroofed under Finsbury Park station bridge on 16 May while diverting off the N29 and M1069 was set alight outside Shepherd's Bush garage on 11 May, the date of a fleetwide strike against the current practices and programmes.

The Sunday services on the 253 and 279A assumed crew-M operation during April, while on the 4th of that month the 153 was another route lost to tender, passing to London Country North West with minibuses, its mooted conversion to LS on 7 February having been abandoned. The 223 did, however, gain back its Ms on Sundays. Clapton finally expelled its last Metrobus on 22 April, and for its final three months worked entirely with Ts. During April the M1044-55 batch was split up so that various M operators could each have a private-hire vehicle. On 23 May further advances of a Night Bus route brought

the N88 to East Croydon via St Helier in replacement of the N54; that route's Sutton DMSs now joined the Wandsworth Ms. 27 May saw Brixton's increasingly eclectic fleet afforded further variety with the arrival of the three Hs.

LBL's refusal to place an order for new buses was now beginning to impact on existing stock, and from the beginning of 1987 the extraordinary decision was taken to acquire second-hand vehicles in some quantity. Hundreds of surplus double-deckers were becoming available through the enormous drop in patronage caused by the imposition of deregulation outside London the previous 26 October. Metrobuses were at the forefront of this exercise, and in May nine were procured through Ensign. M1443-7 (GBU 1/4/5/7/9V) were nine-year-old examples from Greater Manchester Buses, broadly compatible with existing early-model Ms despite their single-door configuration and local blind boxes (the latter feature being replaced by standard KM/NN equipment). Together with four even more unusual examples, Alexander-bodied M1448/9 (UWW 518/9X) ex-West Yorkshire PTE and mkIIs M1450/1 (CUB 539/40Y) from the same source, plus twelve Van Hool-McArdle-bodied Volvo Ailsas bartered with South Yorkshire PTE for nine surplus LSs, they were allocated to Potters Bar, which by virtue of a local agreement ensuring more autonomy could get away with operating such non-standard buses. The swift treatment of most of them to Leaside livery reinforced their standing out. To allay passengers' confusion about non-red buses operating on provincial routes and *vice versa* from Potters Bar and Edgware, brackets were fitted across the nearside of Metrobus grilles to carry slipboards denoting either 'London Regional Transport Bus Service' or 'Hertfordshire County Council Bus Service'. Tenders like this had been required to use Wayfarer computerised ticket machines, but since the beginning of 1987 LBL's own buses began re-equipping with them, this model having triumphed in evaluations that also included Timtronic and Farestream machinery.

Below: The vehicle availability situation had grown so grave due to the lack of a 1987 order for buses that LBL was forced to the most undignified option of purchasing second-hand buses, just like the independent operators that were undercutting it steadily out of existence. Thankfully the MCW Metrobus proved a solid option, no matter if those chosen were a little careworn and thoroughly non-standard by accepted criteria. M1445 (GBU 5V), turning at New Barnet in August 1987, was formerly Greater Manchester PTE 5005 and was delivered in May 1987 for Potters Bar. This bus was one of the first recipients of the striking Leaside livery of black skirt and thick white band, which really did improve the lines of the undeniably boxy Metrobus. The 84 had been taken back the previous year but now as a Hertfordshire County Council contract, hence the slipboard in the tough-looking GM-spec radiator grille. *Tony Wilson*

Above: Even stranger were the two Alexander-bodied Metrobuses taken from a large batch new to West Yorkshire PTE; these became M1448/9 and the former (UWW 518X) is pictured opposite its home garage on 21 August 1987. Completing the improved ambience offered by the Leaside livery are blinds in upper-case lettering, an aesthetic upgrade which was, unfortunately, not to last long, and only Leaside District had them. *Mike Harris*

Right: LBL may not have taken any more mkII Metrobuses after the AVE pair – and M1443 never did manifest itself – but M1450/1 arrived instead, again from West Yorkshire PTE. On 2 August M1450 (CUB 539Y) is three or four stops into a route W8 journey to Potters Bar, a garage journey livened up when this shed took over after Edmonton's closure in 1986. *Malc McDonald*

Garage closures continued to press, and Hendon was the latest victim on 6 June. The 113 and 186 passed to Edgware, the 183 to Harrow Weald, the 143 to Holloway and the N59 to Muswell Hill. Finchley helped out Holloway by assuming a partial allocation on the 17 on Mondays to Fridays, while Edgware made room by abandoning its share of the 221 as well as the 292, which was lost on tender to London Country North East; the 107 passed to Potters Bar, allowing its madcap collection of second-hand buses to spread their wings. The 143 was withdrawn on Sundays in favour of projecting the 271 along its entirety all the way to Hendon Central Station. Further economies on that day of the week took off the 191, the 217 (to be replaced by an extension of the 231 to Waltham Cross), and saw OPO now reach the Sunday service on the 19 (though an industrial dispute at Holloway meant no service until 14 July). An important change in central London affecting routes 1 and 176 saw their cross-town remit severed and new route 172 commissioned to link at least part of the 176's leg to Willesden, but starting only as far into town as Euston. Willesden Ms were in charge.

Tendering had now advanced sufficiently for the planners to consider subjecting whole towns to the process, rather than the ragbag hitherto of isolated and unremunerative routes. However, the choice of the Kingston area for a network of this nature was accompanied by swingeing cuts in wages and increases in working hours, alienating Norbiton garage's existing workforce to such an extent that they went on strike repeatedly and, after the changes to employment conditions were proven to be lawful in a High Court judgment, transferred away *en masse*. Key among this extreme cost-cutting was an extraordinary plan to resuscitate 35 ageing DMSs from the training fleet and return them to service, forgetting quite why they were culled in the first place! The first of these began drifting into Norbiton in time for the commencement of the programme on 27 June. This involved further fixing the 65 and 71 so that the former worked no further south than Kingston, while the 85 lost its Putney allocation and the 213 its Sutton buses. While mixed DMS and M operation prevailed on the 71, 85 and 213, the 65 remained wholly M due to the official inability of the Fleetlines to get beneath the entrance doorway of Kingston garage, which was reopened under the Westlink banner to operate two minibus routes. This revamped pair of K1 and K2 cost the 216 its M-capable Kingston-Tolworth section, while the 131 was

lost outright, taking up with London Country South West. The revamped K1 and K2 also replaced the 281's Chessington Industrial Estate leg and finally, the 285's remit east of Kingston was weakened to peaks only. Norbiton's first Ms to leave were C-registered examples (to Willesden for the 172), older vehicles departing in July to Brixton (displacing DMSs to top up elsewhere) and to Alperton, allowing Muswell Hill to take on some unusually early examples from that garage in advance of the 43's forthcoming one-manning).

Further gloom followed that summer with the closure of two garages, the first of which was Wandsworth on 11 July. The 44 lost Ms entirely with its transfer to Merton (Mon-Sat) and Sutton (Sundays), while Putney picked up the 39 and Sunday 22; Shepherd's Bush absorbed the rest of the 220 on Sundays and Westbourne Park acquired the 295. Ms also left night routes N68 and N88 with their move to Sutton under DMSs. This was also the date of two major OPO conversions, by necessity deferred by six weeks: the 43 (RML to M at Muswell Hill) and 49, but while Shepherd's Bush's RMs were replaced by Ms, the other garage on the route, Streatham, now had to take on Ms of its own as the lack of any more Olympians meant there weren't enough Ls to go around. Thus did M operation return to the 50, 118 and 249 as fit. M1230 (allocated on 14 May as a type trainer) had started the process rolling with its first appearance in service on 10 June, but the requirement was achieved by splitting Wandsworth's Ms between Shepherd's Bush and Streatham, the rest passing to Westbourne Park.

Above: Wandsworth garage closed on 11 July 1987. As Sutton was the recipient of the N68 and N88, both routes lost Ms for DMSs and thus the visit of buses like M1356 (C356 BUV) to South Wimbledon on 2 June would not be the case for much longer. This bus moved on to Shepherd's Bush and remained there for the rest of its life. *Malc McDonald*

Left: Another former Wandsworth Metrobus to leave on 11 July 1987 was M1359 (C359 BUV), like M1356 new as a Clapton bus. However this one was transferred to Streatham, which shared the newly one-manned 49 with Shepherd's Bush; due to the lack of Ls available to support the allocation it received upon opening, a number of Ms had to be introduced, forming an untidily mixed allocation in contravention of all preceding standardisation aims. On 11 August it splashes through an un-summery Kensington. *Malc McDonald*

The 11 July programme also saw Sunday OPO come to the 159, Streatham supplying Ls and Ms by taking its participation off the 137. The 28 was also one-manned on Sundays, with Westbourne Park Ms, but neither Tottenham nor Muswell Hill could supply enough Ms for a similar change to the 73, so the route was transferred on that day to Shepherd's Bush and Stamford Hill. To clear space, the latter handed the 149 and 67 to Tottenham on Sundays, which garage also absorbed Wood Green's Sunday participation on the 67. On 15 August Clapton garage closed, but its Ms had already gone.

As part of progressive reduction in staff numbers, Abbey District was disbanded on 15 August; Putney and Stockwell were transferred to Wandle, Shepherd's Bush and Westbourne Park to Cardinal and Holloway and Chalk Farm to Leaside. Further dismemberment envisaged the splitting of the districts themselves into smaller units, with the centre withering to the bare minimum other than the introduction of a Central Traffic Unit to supervise routes rather than garages.

The appearance of former West Midlands Volvo Ailsas at Potters Bar during the summer released enough Ms to begin the conversion of the 279 and 279A to crew M at Enfield during July; these routes lost their conductors on 26 September. To help out struggling independent Sampson's, both services were projected at night over the 317 (as the 217B had been renumbered since its loss) to Upshire. The receipt of Vs prompted Potters Bar to transfer M1443-6 to Wood Green, where despite their single-door configuration, soon wandered from their intended 84A to the garage's other services, even to the 29 into central London. 26 September also saw the night routes in north-west London shuffled, Edgware losing the N59 to Westbourne Park but gaining that garage's N18, Harrow Weald also withdrawing from the N59 and Muswell Hill joining forces with Victoria on the N2. Off came the 259's Sunday service.

Harrow Weald took the other half of the ex-West Midlands Volvo Ailsa intake, which began filtering into service from 28 September. This released enough Ms to tackle the 16 and 16A, which began losing their RMLs from 2 October, but Harrow Weald was not able to collect enough buses in time for the introduction of its ill-starred Harrow Buses network on 14 November. While 27 new mkII Metrobuses were awaited on lease, a wretched collection of exhausted Daimler Fleetlines unwanted by GM Buses, the aforementioned Volvos and some surplus repainted LSs had to bed the new network in. Route changes saw the 140 split again, the eastern leg to Edgware now taking the number 340, while the inevitable minibus encroachments cost the 183 much of its path west of Pinner and reduced the 136 and 209 to peak-hour remnants. Edgware was compensated for the loss of its part of the 140 by taking on the 143 from Holloway.

The Harrow scheme, together with the concurrent loss of Finchley's 125 to Grey-Green and Alperton's 79A to London Buslines, had also provided enough Ms to tackle the most controversial OPO conversion of all under the political climate of the time;

Left: As the districts of LBL saw stark change on the horizon, they realised that to stamp their mark in an uncertain future, commercially-based innovation would be required. Leaside, already having got off the blocks first with its elegant new livery, formed a private-hire division and detached the first two of what would be many Ms to furnish it. The epitome of 'cool' in 1987 was a 'cherished' registration number transferred from a departing RM, and the re-registration of M1437 from C437 BUV to VLT 12 also started a trend that would eventually see nearly thirty Ms wearing Routemaster marks. The one-manning of the 253 on 21 November 1987 required 58 buses, 37 of which were Stamford Hill Ms, and on 24 June 1988 M1437 has been pressed into service, an eventuality which, due to the vulnerability of the plush seating to the increasingly uncontrollable spread of vandalism, would be short-lived. *Malc McDonald*

the extremely busy 253, which needed close to sixty buses. When the route was one-manned on 21 November in spite of a vociferous local campaign, its Stamford Hill majority share required 37 Ms, Ash Grove taking on the rest with 21 Ts. The 16 and 16A were duly converted to OPO, costing Cricklewood its last conductors, while a partial one-manning retracted the 7's weekday service from Acton to Wormwood Scrubs so that the 52A could be extended from Ladbroke Grove to replace it. Westbourne Park gained a share of the 52A while Victoria withdrew from the 52 on Sundays and Alperton took its Ms off the 18, putting them on the 92 and 226 instead; Hanwell came off the 92. After just four months on the 295 (which on 21 November was extended full-time to Westbourne Park Station), Westbourne Park had no room left for it and handed it to Shepherd's Bush, restoring its balance after the two-year-old 255 was declared a failure and withdrawn; this service was replaced by an extension of the 260 to Shepherd's Bush. The 9 was one-manned on Sundays with Ms (from Stamford Brook) and the 137 was withdrawn daily north of Oxford Circus, but for the moment its replacement over that section, new route 135, used RMs. At Hounslow, the 120 was extended round the Beavers Farm Estate to replace route 257.

'Harrowing Buses', as the Harrow network was unkindly dubbed, was without Metrobuses for just two days (barring loans taken until mid-December), for while its originals had all gone by 21 November, the 24th saw the entry into service of the first examples of M1452-78 (Birmingham-registered E452-78 SON). Factory models in all aspects save the seat

moquette (orange-based as on all other Ms), these attractively-liveried single-doored mkIIs gradually expelled the weary Fleetlines from Harrow Weald's double-deck services, which comprised routes 114, 136, 140, 183, 209, 258 and 340. To furnish a schedules revision which required two more buses, similar M1479/80 (E479/80 UOF) arrived in April 1988 after being diverted from an order for ten cancelled by East Kent. Finally, numbers were brought to M1485 between February and April by five more second-hand acquisitions; VRG 415-9T came from Busways (better known as Tyne & Wear PTE) and as M1481-5 joined their fellow odds and sods at Potters Bar. These second-hand curios were the only Metrobuses left there, though the last standards did not leave until 21 April and examples continued to be loaned from adjacent garages, often in some quantity due to failures of the older vehicles.

Right: The Harrow Buses network of 14 November 1987 was the second of three self-contained tendering schemes that plumbed new depths of staff unrest and vehicle quality; only the 29 mkII Metrobuses leased for three years brought some measure of honour back to a unit that started with decrepit ex-GM Buses Fleetlines and superannuated West Midlands PTE Volvo Ailsas. M1465 (E465 SON), seen in June 1988 in the appealing red and cream Harrow Buses livery, shows that the 140 had been split again, the eastern section (previously known as 286) now becoming the 340. *Haydn Davies*

The practice of re-registering modern buses with marks from departing Routemasters had begun early in 1987 and on 28 October reached its first Metrobus, M1437, which was allocated VLT 12. This bus, together with M1045 and 1398, had been fitted with four-speed gearboxes during the summer, giving them power enough to tackle more challenging work like Milton Keynes shoppers' service 744. Their increased performance was apt to shake the advert frames loose, so these were removed. MCW converted six more in January, numbering M1248, 1367/79/92/3/6. M1379 was re-registered VLT 88 on 24 February 1988, plans to take ALM 2B from RM2002 being dropped.

Emboldened by the Leaside livery, LT itself adapted it on T917 and M515 during November with an interest to improving the appeal of the increasingly weary-looking fleet as a whole. The black skirt was altered to grey and the white band reduced to 2in wide, applied with tape rather than paint; while not anywhere near as eye-catching as the Leaside livery, the new 'tapegrey' scheme was surely better than all-red and acquitted itself by appearing quickly following its official adoption early in 1988, repaints being stepped up via increased outside contracts as well as at garages; Frontsource (the new owner for BEL at Chiswick) and Gatwick Engineering did some of the Ms. M1421, in this new livery, was the cover star for the London Bus Map from the summer of 1988, replacing all-red M1387. Still the showbus concept persisted; M1104 at Brixton lost its Cummins wraparound ad during 1987 but M1440, the last M delivered, took its place, having its badges repositioned (plus an extra 'GARDNER POWER' device across the front) and 'BRIXTON' applied vertically down the pillar behind the driver's cab and ahead of the exit door, a feature also adopted by Ms 124 and 205. Reflective registration plates were another modern touch that jarred a little against traditional practices; Holloway's M1059 gained a set upon accident damage repair in December 1987, while at least two different Helvetica-based typefaces began to appear on existing plates as stocks wore out and were not replaced. Blinds with upper-case lettering had been declared outlaw by the time Chiswick blind shop closed at the end of 1988.

The immediate aftermath of the King's Cross fire saw Victoria Ms appearing on the 500 again.

Strike action at London Country North East was punished by the removal by LRT of the company's contracts on routes 292, 298 and 313; after three days of emergency work, Grey-Green was awarded six-month contracts on the latter pair from 22 February. This long-established coach company chose to acquire ten single-doored Metrobuses spare from deregulation-related reductions at South Yorkshire PTE; Nos 450-7/60/5, registered EWF 450-7/60/5V) entered service during March. Initially in SYPTE livery, they soon started visiting the 125, 173 and later the 179, this latter otherwise a Lynx-operated contract. Initial repaints into company white, orange and brown ceased when in May 455 received a new livery of grey and green, to match the company name; a revised version (including an orange band), which was to become standard, was applied to 450 in July. These buses were acquired through Ensignbus, which during May set aside five more ex-SYPTE Metrobuses for its own use; these dual-doored examples were given the numbers 295-9 (JWF 495-9W) and entered service alongside its DMSs from 16 July onwards. Further interest was heralded with the company's announcement in July of an order for new dual-doored mkII Metrobuses for its win of the 165 and 365 due in September. Of the oddities at Potters Bar, M1447 moved to Wood Green on 26 March, joining its four single-doored fellows.

Right: The first year and a half of outside operations gnawing into the flanks of LBL had brought with it mostly Atlanteans and Fleetlines cast off by the PTEs as their custom drained away following deregulation. Grey-Green, however, a very long-established coaching firm, managed to inject much more professionalism into its tendered operations than some companies that could be mentioned, and profited accordingly. This company took a liking to Metrobuses, and ten were acquired from SYPTE. The split-step entrance on 460 (EWF 460V), seen on 9 April 1988 in Enfield, was an SYPTE innovation long before it was thought of by LBL, and the exit door was a little further forward than on LT's mkIs.
Malc McDonald

Right: Passengers did wonder why the Metrobuses marketed as 'Grey-Green' were orange, white and brown, but Grey-Green soon developed a livery to match and 455 (EWF 455V), pictured at South Mimms, was the first to carry it. Routes 298 and 313 were rescued from a miserable innings with strike-plagued London Country North East and formed the bedrock of continuous expansion. *Tony Wilson*

During February 'KINGSTON BUS' vinyls, with red text over a yellow base outlined in white, began appearing on Norbiton's Ms and DMSs in place of the London Buses roundels. On certain Leaside-liveried buses the black skirts were repainted grey, leaving the thick white band alone, while it was at the contractor's or garage's discretion whether the grey skirt was also applied to the bottom of the doors. M597 lost its Maxwell gearbox in February for a three-speed Voith unit, while another development during April saw seven Hounslow Ms fitted with fluorescent lighting tubing upstairs, three more following in May.

On 27 February the Brixton participation of the 59 was extended from its home base to Streatham Garage, while the opening of the new Sainsbury's superstore at Ladbroke Grove prompted the diversion via this point of the 52, 52A and 295. Crew operation in London was almost finished – on Sundays, that is – and the treatment of the 11 on 26 March (Victoria with Ms) left just the 12. The 9 on that day of the week ceded its Victoria allocation to make room. However, one recent scheme was pegged back a bit when the 14A (and 14 on Sundays) were withdrawn between Crouch End and Turnpike Lane, traffic on the latter corridor proving too much for Holloway's valiant Ms. In town, the 14A was also cut between Tottenham Court Road and Piccadilly Circus. Evening services suffered cutbacks, the 46, 83,

Below: South Yorkshire PTE was also the source for Metrobuses going to Ensignbus after its supply of DMSs had started to run dry. 297 (JWF 497W), captured at Redbridge on 24 June 1988, shows off the terrific livery of blue and silver, complete with blind boxes to London Transport standard, a thoughtful and unilateral decision that undescored Ensign's quality by comparison with many of its competitors. The 145 had been its first acquisition but the 62 followed it in 1987 and both quickly became host to all five of these initially Purfleet-based vehicles. *Malc McDonald*

Above: Less loved was Kingston Bus, the unfortunate remnants of Norbiton garage's runout following the Kingston-area tendering programme of 27 June 1987. It was lucky that Norbiton managed to retain any Ms at all, otherwise being forced to re-equip with resuscitated DMSs, and in 1988 a half-hearted attempt was made to freshen them up by adding a black skirt and a dedicated logo – carrying both in July 1989 as it passes through Kingston, M1262 (B262 WUL) unfortunately looks a mess. *Geoff Rixon*

Above: Some of the early tendered operators were so bad that even LT had to put its foot down and remove them. Sampson's of Hoddesdon had taken over Enfield's 217B in 1986 with blue-and-red ex-DMSs, but had performed so poorly that on 2 July 1988 the route (renumbered 317 during that company's tenure) was reassigned to LBL, whose Enfield garage resumed control. On 6 August M569 (GYE 569W) in full Leaside livery and with Waltham Abbey looming in the background, presents a stunning sight.
Malc McDonald

172 and 274 all being pruned; the 172 was repositioned altogether to remove its path between Kilburn Park and Euston in favour of a projection north from Willesden Garage to Brent Cross; further alteration from 2 July took it off the main drag to bring first-time buses to Brondesbury Road in Kilburn. Shepherd's Bush gained a share of the N97 at weekends from 23 April, this being the most successful of the night routes to date.

Two more Ms were struck off charge when an arson attack on Enfield's forecourt on 16 April destroyed Ms 735 and 986, the remains being broken up on site by contractors during June. A spate of deroofings affected Palmers Green's M651 (Stroud Green, 26 May), and Brixton's M1440 (in Hastings while on a private hire, 19 June), while on 23 May M892 was crashed into a shop while working on the N59, Wood Green's M534 sustained rear-end fire damage, deliberately inflicted, on 30 June, and Streatham's M290 was damaged in a collision with a lorry on 7 July in Thornton Heath. M1461 became the first mkII to strike the low bridge in Wealdstone Lane on 11 July while moving to take up the 140.

A scheme in south London juggled Streatham's routes from 14 May. The 50 was withdrawn between

Streatham Garage and Stockwell Station but extended southwards over the 190 to Old Coulsdon, while the opportunity was taken to snip off the southernmost piece of the 159 beyond Streatham High Road (Green Lane) by creating new route 250 (Brixton Station-Croydon) for Streatham's Ms and Ls.

Chelsea Flower Show perennial route 137A was this year operated by M66, 124 and 233 from Brixton and M983 from Streatham, running as GM1-4. This pair also provided Ms for the Derby Day service at the beginning of June and for the Wimbledon Tennis service in the last week of that month, though for the latter event Metrobuses were borrowed from Fulwell, Shepherd's Bush, Holloway, Westbourne Park and from even as far away as Uxbridge, Stamford Hill and Wood Green! Similar special services also introduced Stamford Hill's M1000 to Lea Valley Leisure Bus 318 and the occasion of the Pinner Fair caused Harrow Weald to take five standard Ms on loan, three coming from Stamford Hill to assist on the 183 and two from Holloway for the 209. Ms 1379/98 received radio equipment during April, set to broadcast Capital Radio as part of a successful recruitment campaign, while in July M1437, already adorned with VLT 12, was further enhanced for its dedicated private-hire work by a repaint (at Edgware) into red with full white midriff and black skirt, after which it was sent to Hants & Dorset, which fitted it with high-back seats during the middle portion of August. M1045 followed, returning to service at Holloway in September.

Modifications to existing Ms had seen 115 Leaside District Ms converted to air braking by mid-1988; from this point Bendix systems were specified in lieu of the former Clayton systems, Holloway's M1136 being sent to MCW in July as the pilot. 'DRIVER SERVICE' stickers replaced the flip-over plates on a couple of Edgware Ms, but did not spread.

London Buses Ltd had shrunk considerably as tendering worried at its flanks, but the inadequacy of several of its fledgling competitors led to opportunities here and there; on 2 July Enfield regained the 317 from Sampson's, which had disgraced itself with its elderly ex-DMSs and similar unreliable veterans. An unusual Sunday extension from the 9th took 33s to Hampton, Nurserylands, over the 270. Between 10 July and its loss to Pan Atlas on the 30th, the 112 at Cricklewood reverted to M operation due to the spiriting away of its LSs to Kingston for new commercial route K10.

Traffic considerations were now such a problem in central London that time-honoured through routes were suffering; on 13 August the 73 was split to address this. Instead of Hammersmith, its central London terminus was now Victoria, and the Shepherd's Bush allocation vanished to take up much the same role on new route 10 (Hammersmith-King's Cross). The 88 was also split, but as yet without any number changes; the western section (with Shepherd's Bush Ms on Sundays) was projected to Acton Green. All of the 10, 73 and 88 saw frequent crew-M operation, in the case of Shepherd's Bush as cover for RMLs going away for repaint.

After many years of progressive reduction, the 189 bit the dust in favour of two new minibus routes (G1 and G2) on 6 August, but was revived on 6 September as a school route, this time with Ms (and DMSs, and Hs) from Brixton. A single schoolday journey (one morning, one afternoon) was attached to the 317, taking it as far south as Palmers Green; this would settle and transmute through many forms in the years to come.

As LBL dwindled in the east, perhaps its most dynamic competitor grew and grew. This was Ensignbus, which was the major benefactor from the tendering scheme which forced the closure of Hornchurch on 24 September. Now with enough backing to purchase brand new buses, the company's choice for the 165 and 365 was mk II Metrobuses, 16 of which were delivered between 28 October and mid-November as 279-94 (F279-94 NHJ). Barely known in this part of London, the chassis would become familiar, though differences saw the use of South Yorkshire-style split-step entrance doorways and the exit door (covering a three-step exit) positioned slightly further forward than on comparable models, requiring a quarter window downstairs. Blue handrails and a new blue-based seat moquette, together with LBL-standard KM/NN blind boxes at the front and the truly superb blue and silver livery, made for a refreshing sight; the positive aspects of tendering were at last beginning to make themselves felt after three years of substandard second-hand cast-offs. Ensignbus practised considerably more flexibility, however, than LBL, and the type could soon be encountered alongside the company's inaugural DMSs on both this tranche's acquisitions (routes 246 and 446) and existing conquests (the 62, 62A and 145).

Where one set of Metrobuses was bedding itself in, another was dissolving; the large surplus of Titans released by the closure of Hornchurch had provided enough to convert another Leaside District garage

from M, and from 8 October the 43, 134, W7 and N2 at Muswell Hill started losing their Metrobuses. Most headed to Holloway, Palmers Green and Wood Green for the 5 November scheme, but the earliest dozen included members that spread the Leaside livery to faraway Streatham, allowing an equivalent number of Ls to depart for Croydon to displace DMSs to Sutton for the Suttonbus programme. Despite the influx of Titans, Muswell Hill's drivers cherished their two four-speed Metrobuses, M1393/6, and held on to them for dear life; thus the conversion was

Above: The Leaside livery was developed by LBL into a new corporate livery of its own, albeit rather watered down with a grey (rather than black) skirt and a thin relief band applied with tape rather than having to spend money on proper paint.
On 7 September 1988 Brixton's foglight-less M66 (WYW 66T), gained indirectly from Norbiton following the latter garage's part-conversion to DMS a year earlier, demonstrates on route 189, which had declined to the status of just a schoolday route and now come under Brixton's *aegis. Colin Stannard*

Left: Cementing its status as the premier post-LBL operator in the tendering arena, Ensignbus invested in 16 new mkII Metrobuses for its win of route 165 and 365. 291 (F291 NHJ) was one of them, delivered to Purfleet in November 1988 and seen the following June in the Rainham area. *Haydn Davies*

never completed. Towards year's end some of Putney's and Victoria's Ms were fitted with air brakes by Dennis in Guildford rather than by SBG.

Innovations in routes involved the commercial service (a Saturday 310B between Enfield Town and Harlow commencing from 8 October with Potters Bar Ms), the limited-stop express (29 October seeing new with-the-flow peak-hour route X71 commence under Norbiton Ms, linking Hook and Ham (British Aerospace's plant) broadly over the 71) and the county council contract (part of London Country North East route 360, awarded to Potters Bar during weekday evenings from 29 October). The month also saw the official formalisation of Grey-Green on routes 313 (from the 1st) and 298 (on the 8th) and a minor alteration to the A2, which on the 8th was repositioned in central London to terminate at Russell Square via Euston (instead of via Oxford Street) in the interests of circumventing the traffic plaguing the latter thoroughfare. The implementation on 29 October of what portions of the Suttonbus network

were not held up by pay-related strike action affected Metrobuses only with the rerouteing of the 213's Sunday service via Carshalton Beeches rather than Hackbridge and the removal of its weekday spur to St Helier. Finally for October, Cricklewood's 205 gained an experimental Sunday service from the 29th with the remit to serve the extensive Sunday markets at Wembley.

After a bitter half-decade of OPO conversions, which had, just as feared, brought central London's congested streets to near-gridlock, LBL called a moratorium on the practice; but tendering losses could still supply buses for scattered one-manning and thus fell the 29 and 135 on 5 November. These were brought about by the loss of the 24, the most prestigious central London route yet to undergo the tendering process, to Grey-Green; the threat of closure hanging over Chalk Farm was averted by giving the garage and its Titans a majority share of the 29; Palmers Green provided 20 Ms. Wood Green and Holloway withdrew, the former to take over the W2

Left: The 135, introduced only on 21 November 1987 as a localisation of the 137's northern end, was also one-manned on 5 November, and with the 29, was the last route converted to OPO for the time being, following a rethink on the success of the policy of the last few years. Holloway's M667 (KYV 667X), received in October from Muswell Hill after the latter's conversion from M to T, loads up on the first day at Oxford Circus. Holloway also took delivery of a batch of upper-case blinds, after which no more were specified. *Malc McDonald*

from Palmers Green and the latter to convert the 135 from RML and regain part of the 41. All the Ms needed for this conversion were released from Muswell Hill by the influx of Ts.

5 November also heralded the start of a two-stage process by which several routes operating across the Leaside/Forest district boundary (fixed at the Lea Valley Reservoir) were rationalised into their separate districts. This involved much needless splitting of routes hitherto operated by two garages in the realisation that the forthcoming split of LBL's five-District structure into eleven pre-privatisation subsidiaries (under the provisions of April's Business Plan for 1988/89) would make it difficult to apportion revenue. Additionally the Office of Fair Trading had notified companies across the country that joint operation was felt to be anti-competitive under the provisions of deregulation, irrespective of the wastefulness of overlapping services from an operational point of view, not to mention the standpoint of the poor passenger, forgotten amid all this. However, while Leaside was ready for the changes, the first portion of which involved withdrawing the 102 between Angel Corner and Chingford and rerouteing it to Edmonton Green, strike action at Forest postponed that district's participation, prompting the laying-on of an emergency 102A across the breach. This also helped the 34 to shed its Walthamstow Titans and roads south of Walthamstow Central Station. Forest eventually applied its changes between the 19th and 23rd of the month.

On 26 November the 50 was allotted a Croydon share, relegating Streatham to Saturdays only. In the Southall area, the 120 was withdrawn between Southall and Greenford and the 105 rerouted intermediately over that section; new minibus E5

covered the rest. Another lost route came 'home' in the shape of the 200, which from 3 December departed Cityrama at its own request. Norbiton (Kingston Bus) stepped up on a short-term contract pending re-tendering; the official LS allocation was bulked out by what Ms remained at the garage, albeit without blinds or at least making an attempt with paper labels. From approximately this time black skirts began to appear on Norbiton vehicles, such an application having otherwise ceased at Leaside since July. Black paint was also, unfortunately, applied to the side blind box glass at this unit as a crude way of overcoming union objection to the correct use of side blinds.

Finally, the increasing need for transport on New Year's Night came to fruition in a big way on the 1988/89 occasion when several night routes received one-night-only allocations over and above their official complement; those with Ms were the N13 (Potters Bar), N19 (Victoria), N79 (Willesden), N89 (Hounslow), N93 (Fulwell) and N97 (Shepherd's Bush), while the circular service used Chalk Farm Ts and Ms from Holloway and Victoria. Such off-the-cuff enhancements were perhaps emblematic of the increased flexibility to be encountered in the years ahead.

Below: Cityrama was another independent firm not to meet with much approval, but magnanimously it surrendered both its routes before they could be taken away. Coming onto the 200 on 3 December 1988 wasn't the previous incumbent Merton, but Norbiton, which introduced its Ms in Kingston Bus trim. Rounding Atkinson Morley Hospital's small layby as evening falls on 20 December 1989 is M75 (WYW 75T), with MCW badge bolted lower down than is conventional and with the quite unnecessary 'BUS' sticker attempting to reassure passengers that standard fares are still payable, something that ought to be pretty obvious on a 'London Transport' bus! *Colin Stannard*

FOUR

Subsidiary Adventures

As 1988 came to a close London Buses Ltd sprouted eleven operating Units, all differentiated by a new name, separate management structure and purchasing policy while retaining the standard tapegrey livery and common fleetnumbering system. These were formed from splitting the existing five districts in half; thus Leaside District gave way to London Northern and Leaside Buses, while Wandle District spawned South London and London General. Cardinal District begat London United and CentreWest and Metroline completed the circle anticlockwise around London. All were formalised on Monday 5 December, the logos soon following, and on 1 April 1989 were given their autonomy as wholly-owned LBL subsidiaries.

Accordingly, while this 'divide and rule' business was taking place, comparatively little happened to the routes operated by Ms during 1989; for the first couple of months just termini were tinkered with, while 4 February saw the 217 projected from Waltham Cross to Hammond Street, three Ms being added to Enfield's complement for this purpose. The scourge of parked cars at the 43's Friern Barnet terminus forced the route to terminate at Muswell Hill (Hampden Road) between 25 February and 2 September.

During January private-hire M1437 was converted to single-door (DPH43/24F), the front wheelarch seats additionally being removed to provide luggage space. A further enhancement in time for this year's Milton Keynes shopping trips (beginning on 1 April) was the fitment of a Gardner 6LCXT 240bhp turbocharged engine and its coach seats gained headrests. Less prosaically, Fulwell began a programme to fit anti-vandal seating at the rear of its Ms' upper decks.

Above: The devolution of 1988/89 saw Leaside District split into two, its western garages falling under the aegis of London Northern. In this shot at Waltham Cross, Potters Bar's ex-WYPTE M1451 (CUB 540Y) has now taken on LBL's new corporate livery, but the fleetnumber transfers are incorrect, more properly belonging on numberplates. *Tony Wilson*

Right: The trouble with individual liveries is that they reduce flexibility; it was inevitable that Leaside-liveried buses would be subject to the same transfer process as other LBL vehicles, thus not only has M10 (WYW 10T) got across the river to Streatham following its release from Muswell Hill, but standard grey paint has been applied over the black skirt, producing a weird 'half-and-half' effect! Streatham garage, which commenced new route 250 on 14 May 1988 to allow RM-operated 159 to fall back from Thornton Heath High Street to Streatham, was part of the new South London subsidiary - unfortunately, none of its routes went anywhere near Tower Bridge, the unit's logo! *Chris Evans*

Due to large numbers of failures suffered by its second-hand buses, Potters Bar began regaining standard Ms in February with the input of six spare from Holloway and Muswell Hill; it was intended for all Ms to be gone from the latter through this small-scale shuffle (which also involved LSs), but still the Metrobus clung on.

The ceremonial unveiling of London United on 1 April was the reason for the repaint of M1069 (its fire damage repaired) into a superb reincarnation of London United Tramways colours of red and cream. After operating briefly from Stamford Brook (usually on the 91), in May it was transferred to Fulwell in connection with an exhibition in Kingston, sticking predominantly to the 281 and 285. In July it spent three days at Norbiton before returning to Stamford Brook (where this time it mostly worked on the 27), and in November it moved to Fulwell, there to settle for the rest of its London career.

Above: If only devolution and privatisation had brought liveries like this. M1069 (B69 WUL) spent its first year in London United Tramways livery visiting each garage of this similarly-named new LBL subsidiary. Its first visit was to Stamford Brook's 91 in May 1989 and is caught at Hammersmith. Otherwise London United's logo was a simplified white version of the crest seen here. *Geoff Rixon*

Left: The nearside aspect, pictured working from Fulwell in the same month. M1069 retained this livery until July 1997 and donned another historically-inspired scheme in 2004 when it was sold to Sullivan Buses. *Geoff Rixon*

Left: CentreWest London Buses Ltd encompassed Westbourne Park, Alperton, Hanwell and Uxbridge garages, represented by an arrow pointing in the direction of the bus's travel (and thus not always 'west'!). Both directions are shown on Uxbridge's M976 (A976 SYF) at Ruislip on 19 July 1989 as it works new route 98A, created to retain a double-deck arm while the 98 was otherwise renumbered U1 and converted to Mercedes-Benz 811D minibuses. *Malc McDonald*

The 28 lost its Sunday Ms when MA-class Mercedes-Benz 811D minibuses replaced them (and the weekday RMs) on 4 March, while the 52A was cut between Notting Hill Gate and Victoria, prompting the introduction of a Victoria allocation on the 52, both changes on Mondays to Fridays only. More MAs hit the streets, but under the 'U-Line' banner when on 27 May Uxbridge downgraded some of its 'big-bus' routes; the 98 was withdrawn, only its peak-hour replacement 98A (Hayes-Ruislip) meriting double-deckers (Uxbridge Ms), while the 223 lost its Uxbridge-Ruislip section and its entire Sunday service. The 224, which like the 98 had seen the odd M over the years, disappeared altogether.

After the closure of so many garages during the mid-1980s, a new one opened on 3 June – Colliers Wood (AA). Although this was just a fenced lock-up across the road from Merton garage, the input of the 200 from Norbiton required extra space. Accordingly, it assumed full-time M operation, taking its vehicles from Putney, where they were replaced by slightly older (and Leaside-liveried) examples made spare from Finchley. As an adjunct to Sutton garage, Colliers Wood also gained part of the 152 on weekdays, introducing it to Ms, while the 200's return to a 'friendly' operator permitted the turning point at Brixton garage to be resumed.

17 June saw the reverse of a scheme of 1971 when the 49 was restored to its Crystal Palace terminus, replacing the 249. On 1 July Ensignbus gained in strength through the purchase of Frontrunner South

East and its contracts for routes 248, 252 and 550; now its Metrobuses of both types could spread their net. At London Northern's Potters Bar, a surprise delivery of Scanias took over the 263 on 29 July, minimising M appearances. The garage's ageing second-hand buses were felt inappropriate to continue on the 84 and 242, the new contracts on these Hertfordshire County Council services applying from 2 September, so in good time a shuffle of age blocks was undertaken. Over the first ten days of July Potters Bar discarded all its second-hand Ms to Holloway, which released B-registered examples to Wood Green, which in turn provided Potters Bar with the C-registered buses it needed. Tottenham and Finchley also participated in this exercise, which additionally concentrated air-brake-fitted buses within particular garages. Potters Bar's Ms also began to have their handrails clad in orange to aid the partially sighted, and to match standards now mandatory on all new buses, plus protruding bell pushes and high-visibility step edges. While officially allocated to the 17 at Holloway, the second-hand Ms soon racked up visits to all of the garage's routes, even crossing the river on the 14 and 19 on Sundays. As the summer developed, re-registrations to RM marks began to pick up speed. M1379, already the recipient of a Routemaster registration, was only two months into a repaint (to match M1437) when on 29 August it was deroofed in Southend while on an excursion.

The transfer in August of M226/97 from Colliers Wood to Merton was a portent of future DMS replacement; Colliers Wood's M1372 had already visited both Merton and Sutton as a driver trainer. The two Metrobuses were to remain the only representatives of their type at Merton for more than eighteen months, but soon became a familiar fixture on routes 44, 77, 155, 219 and 280, plus the 19 and 49 on Sundays. 'Official' DMS/M operation took until 3 March 1990 to formalise.

On 19 August the 90B (Fulwell) was lost to London Buslines as plain 90, but its Metrobuses were transferred to Norbiton in time for the takeup of the 57 from Merton's DMSs as a Kingston Bus contract, applying from 2 September for a three-year term. Ten Norbiton Ms received yellow handrails and a 'Bus Stopping' sign on each deck, while a nice idea that was not to catch on saw M1336 receive a gold 'Kingston Bus & Coach Company' logo and phone number.

Right: Norbiton's tenure of the 200 was only temporary, and the route passed to the London General subsidiary of LBL on 3 June 1989 with a new base, Colliers Wood. M811 (OJD 811Y) was one of several Ms transferred from Putney to operate the route, and is seen in Streatham High Road on 12 June, bearing London General's B-type bus logo. *Colin Stannard*

An unusual bifurcation for the new school year took one route 317 journey in each peak over the 217 to and from Turnpike Lane from 2 September, rather than the usual terminus of Enfield Town. After some time without additions to the night bus network, new route N73 was introduced from 22/23 September with Tottenham Ms, its central section following the 73 but with termini at Victoria and Walthamstow Central. After terrorist threats to the Cargo Tunnel at Heathrow, the 105, 140, 202, 285, A1 and A2 were all withdrawn from that thoroughfare (and Terminal 4) on 30 September, never to return.

September saw Wood Green's M1367 gain coach seats, an enhancement also applied to Fulwell's Ms 1003 and 1251. Broadening their options, Stamford Brook's Airbus Ms were treated to adverts offering the vehicles for contract hire. Otherwise, the era of unusual liveries was ending following a study by LRT that uncovered passenger misattribution of complaints to the wrong companies, leading to a renewed emphasis on the 'London Transport' identity. A now rare overseas trip saw M1044 visit The Hague between 31 August and 11 September to celebrate the Dutch undertaking's 125th birthday; for this purpose it was fitted with a transponder to change Dutch traffic lights to green. When not required after the summer season, M1379 spent

December in normal service at Stamford Hill on the 67, 149 and 253, though its time on the last mentioned was short due to its coach seats upstairs suffering vandalism; they were taken out and replaced by bus seats.

The loss of the 107 to newcomer Pan Atlas on 7 October forced a reshuffle of adjacent routes in order to maintain the balance of work at Potters Bar; thus, the 134 was withdrawn north of Friern Barnet in favour of a new local service numbered 234 (Archway-Barnet Church), using Potters Bar's entertaining muddle of types and permitting the odd garage projection north of the border. In town, the 135 was extended from Marble Arch to Victoria, supporting the 16. Overnight on 27/28 October expansion to the Night Bus network resumed; new M-operated routes were N1 and N5 (both Holloway-run and both marketed as 'Northern Line Night Buses' to accentuate their remit shadowing that Underground line's branches to Barnet and Edgware respectively). Revisions saw the N59 and N18 concentrated at Edgware and Westbourne Park respectively, both losing their Stanmore-Edgware overlap, while the N59 and N11 were both curtailed at Trafalgar Square. The N2 lost its Holloway and Victoria Ms for Muswell Hill Ts, but Ash Grove Ts on the N50 gave way to Shepherd's Bush Ms. Victoria

took up new route N19, broadly following the daytime 19, while Brixton added new route N69 to its inventory; this route backed up the N78 before following untapped roads to Norwood Junction.

The straitened times had by now thoroughly cancelled out any desire both to avoid mixed-type working and progressively replace older types with new. A rare tendering victory that brought 'home' the 197 group and 403 from London & Country on 28 October required the use of Ls, which could only be procured for Croydon by taking large numbers out of Streatham; in their place came all 22 of Brixton's Cummins-engined Metrobuses and mkII M1441/2. Streatham's increased M fleet added the 50 to their remit upon its transfer from Croydon so that the latter could man the 197 group and 403. Having taken on Merton's DMSs lost from the 57 plus ten released from Stockwell on 25 November after frequency reductions, Brixton ended 1989 with just 13 Ms, of which M205 lost its Deutz engine in January 1990.

On 30 October Hertfordshire evening contract 360 was lost by Potters Bar, school service 842 taking its place. Between 11 November and 2 December Ensignbus began the phased transfer of its routes to its new site at Dagenham (DM). It was Purfleet, however, that was in charge of Boxing Day-only route 86B, which was operated by Metrobuses 284-6 and three Olympians.

The new decade opened with the advent of another localised cheap operation, the RiversideBus network centred on Stamford Brook garage. The 237 was reallocated in from Hounslow as the main effort and lost its Ms for brand new, albeit provincial-specification Olympians. Hounslow took the 27, 91, E4 and two Park Royal Asda free routes in exchange, plus the 9 on Sundays (leading to a very long run-in from Mortlake; the others also received garage journeys to and from their distant new base via whichever termini or changeover points mid-route). Stamford Brook also lost its two night routes, the N93 passing to Shepherd's Bush and the N97 to Shepherd's Bush and Hounslow, which pair also commenced new route N67 (Trafalgar Square-Staines) at weekends. Shepherd's Bush thus lost its share of the 49, which by virtue of Streatham losing its last Ls became wholly M-operated (as did the 50, 118 and Sunday 159), while the 10 on Sundays lost M operation with the loss of the Holloway allocation to Chalk Farm under Ts. All of Stamford Brook's standard Ms were transferred to Norbiton to replace most of the garage's DMSs, none receiving Kingston Bus logos but keeping their London United crests now that non-standard identities were being officially downplayed (and in the case of Kingston Bus, officially cancelled in May). One transfer was former Airbus M1180; the other Airbus Ms began to receive unofficial and somewhat irreverent local nicknames before the practice was frowned upon and discontinued by spring, as was a similar local initiative to dub them with aircraft names.

South of the river Brixton lost the 133 on tender to Stockwell as a London General contract with brand new Volvo Citybuses (VCs), filling the gap by taking over the 250 from Streatham. M1448-51 returned to Potters Bar from Holloway during January, in which month five more of the rare Alexander-bodied Metrobus variant appeared on the fringes of town, BTS of Borehamwood acquiring ULS 614/6/7X and CKS 385/8X from Kelvin Scottish; while earmarked for Hertfordshire commercial service 355, they soon wandered to the 292. In February Ensignbus acquired four more Metrobuses, 275-8 (FUT 39/6-8V), dual-door DR102/14-specification examples new to Leicester Corporation Transport. Put into action at Purfleet during April and May, they (like all Ensign's aquisitions) received LT-style blind boxes at the front. Even so, the era of the second-hand bus was petering out. Harrow Weald began to regain standard Ms in February when M20/73/90 were transferred in from Edgware; unusually M73 alone carried white 'HARROW BUSES' logos over freshly-applied LBL tapegrey livery.

Technological advancements to keep pace with legislation included the introduction of electric wipers, beginning in January with Stamford Hill's M988; this bus also received an audible reversing alarm which also soon became standard, and in March trialled a new design of rear door opening device. Air-brake conversions were widespread by mid-1990, Dennis adorning recipients of the equipment with a little badge to carry on the engine cover. Also at the rear, a new design of light cluster was beginning to replace the previous chrome-mounted version which had become prone to water ingress as its rubber shrank; the new version retained the same wiring and configuration but was more flush-fitting, with a hint of smoking to the plastic. Wood Green's private-hire Ms 1379/1437 (soon

named *Senator* and *Ambassador*) became the first of the class to have their upper-deck opening windows replaced with flat panes, producing a sterner look; although the rationale was that the increased speeds attained by these buses made the opening units rattle against wind resistance, a large proportion of the class would be similarly treated over the next decade as the window rubber perished with age. Titans had been undergoing the process in some numbers for over a year. Inside the saloon, Leaside and Metroline carried out experiments with advert mountings that would reduce the need to paste vinyls to panels, and this was successful enough to be applied to the whole fleet.

New night route N9 bowed on 10 February at midnight; Palmers Green-operated, it followed the N29 to its home garage and then shadowed the 121 to Enfield Town. One early morning journey on the 29 was extended to Enfield Garage so as to complete an N29 driver's duty more efficiently.

On 24 January Putney lost its Sunday share of the 14, Holloway's allocation increasing by shedding some of its route 19 duties to Merton's DMSs. Putney's OPO drivers working on a Sunday thus concentrated on the 22, which lost its Sunday extension to Homerton to the now-daily 22B (taken over by Kentish Bus), not to mention the entire service beyond Piccadilly Circus, a gap which was not filled. After a surprisingly-long 5½-year innings, the 226 was split again, but this time into three. From the Burnt Oak end, new route 204 (M from Edgware) operated as far as Sudbury Town, overlapped by new route 224 (North Wembley-Willesden Junction), which took on the Alperton share of the 226; this route now fell back to Park Royal Asda.

March saw Ensignbus's 297 gain white and blue overall advertising livery for Castle Glass of Hornchurch; it was the first Metrobus to gain the ColorBus treatment and made its home on the 165

Left: Leaside Buses' private-hire Ms had gone from strength to strength since M1437 was pictured on the 253 on page 57. Since then, two more Metrobuses had been treated to four-speed gearboxes and coach seating, with a modified livery to boot. M1379 (VLT 88, ex-C379 BUV), with extra badges and ephemera added, has been put to use serving a stamp fair at Alexandra Palace in May 1990, and is seen transporting some of its attendees in that direction. *Tony Wilson*

Above: For an ostensibly standardised bus, the MCW Metrobus could feature some real oddities thanks to the manufacturer's early deal with Alexander to construct bodies. This brought solid orders from Scottish concerns happy that their local industry could continue in work, even if the results did look exactly like Volvo Ailsas, radiator grilles and all! Thus did Alexander Midland MRM2 drift into the clutches of Ensignbus in May 1990, becoming 571 (BLS 671V). The reason was that new commercial route 348 ran under a low bridge at Cranham and thus needed low-height double-deckers, which LT and its successors had not ordered since the days of the RLH forty years earlier. The unusual vehicle, seen on 16 September in Romford, was joined by an equally odd variant in the shape of Alexander Midland MRM1, which took the number 570 (see page 86). *Malc McDonald*

Right: All-over advertisements had fallen out of favour by the time the Metrobus, came along, but by the early 1990s just about anything was tolerated as long as it was out of central London. Ensignbus 299 (JWF 499W) became the second Metrobus in London to receive an all-over advertisement, by which Nelmes Garages of Gallows Corner offered passengers on the 165 and 365 the competing charms of brand new Mitsubishi cars until March 1992. *Malcolm K. Allan*

and 365. To cover for Volvo Ailsas away for conversion to semi-automatic transmission, Boro'Line Maidstone hired three mkII Metrobuses from Maidstone & District during late February and mid-March; 5204/7/10 brought NBC green livery to the Crayford-based 233, with possibilities on the 132, 228 and 328. April saw Merton's Metrobus holding increased from two to six examples and Putney's M1389 re-registered 89 CLT. At Metroline, Harrow Weald's M1456 was repainted and given special transfers to commemorate the garage's 60th anniversary.

A key feature of LBL's struggle to survive in the late 1980s and early 1990s was the mass introduction of minibuses. So far none had threatened Ms, but the CentreWest subsidiary favoured them more than most other LBL companies and took several large batches, first 811Ds (MAs) and then Renault 75s (RWs). The first RWs took over Hanwell's 282 on 3 March, releasing eight Ms. Schoolday workings on the 282's busiest section remained double-deck, a pattern that would continue as it was realised how imperfect minibuses were. The London United subsidiary, however, took off Fulwell's 270 on 7 April and replaced it with new DT-operated R70, the first of these new Dennis Darts also assuming control of the 285 on Sundays; the R70 also permitted the 33's Sunday extension to Hampton Nurserylands to be withdrawn. Fulwell's Ms reached Chessington Zoo on summer Sundays from this date with the extension of the 281 from Tolworth.

Not only in expansive mood in London, Ensignbus cast an eye to its east, setting going commercial route 348 (Romford-Purfleet via the recently-opened Lakeside shopping centre in Thurrock). As this had to pass beneath the low bridge at Cranham, the pair of Metrobuses acquired were particularly unusual; from Kelvin Scottish in May came 571 (BLS 671V) with the extremely rare low-height version of Alexander AD bodywork, followed in June by 750 (UMS 751T). Further unorthodoxy saw 299 adorned with a grey and red all-over advert for Nelmes Mitsubishi of Gallows Corner (until March 1992). On 13 May the Sunday services of routes 165 and 365, plus the 349, were transferred from Purfleet to Dagenham.

On 28 April the N11 received a Hounslow share. This was also the date more DTs entered service, this time at Hounslow. The 120's peripatetic extension round Beavers Farm Estate was switched to new routes H21 and H23, while new route H22 directly replaced the 202 (but only to Hounslow West, not Heathrow). M1069 was loaned from Fulwell to work the last day of the 202. Far to the north the 242 was rerouted in and out of the Rosedale Estate at Goffs Oak, a decision that soon came into question when the buses started coming under attack. A Sunday contract saw the 205 transferred to Westbourne Park (CentreWest) on 6 May, upon which it lost its Metrobus on that day of the week. Still favouring the MA class, London General's Putney garage introduced new examples of these minibuses to the 39 on the 12th, in the process withdrawing this once-lengthy route beyond Clapham Junction; Victoria's participation simultaneously became new MA-run route 239, but to keep the Ms in use the garage was given a weekday share of the 77A and on Sundays,

part of the 22. Five Putney Ms transferred in. On 19 May the last red buses abandoned Hammond Street when the 217 was pulled back to Waltham Cross without replacement. The RW class continued to spread; on 26 May the busy E3 succumbed to the unpopular Renaults, which took up work from a reopened Acton Tram Depot (AT). On Sundays Hanwell Ms remained on this route, but not for long; casualties from the conversion were transferred to Uxbridge (for new route 607 from 21 June), Edgware (in readiness for V replacement at Harrow Weald) and Holloway (to ease transfers for the 2 June programme below).

By 1990 the oldest members of the M class were now well into their second decade, and LBL had to think about shuffling them about to satisfy age requirements, a new proviso introduced to contracts as standards at last began to tighten up from the free-for-all early days of tendering. On 2 June routes 217 and 231 migrated from one LBL subsidiary (Leaside Buses) to another (London Northern) under a two-year contract term; Enfield lost eleven Metrobuses (of W- and X-registered stock) to Holloway, which released thirteen B-registered Ms to Potters Bar. Ex-Tyne & Wear M1481/3 also returned to Potters Bar. The 231 dumped its Sunday run to Waltham Cross, while Leaside's losses were made up by allocating Enfield part of the 144A at the expense of Wood Green. One Sunday M route was extended (the 73, to Stoke Newington all day), but on 23 June the 76's last projections beyond County Hall to Victoria were lost. 23 June also saw the 260 lost to newcomers Armchair. Willesden's share of the 266 grew to compensate, though it lost a handful of Metrobuses, two of which helped double the complement of standard Ms at Harrow Weald at the expense of some more of the wearied Volvo Ailsas.

LBL's organisational changes had given several threatened garages a breather, but in 1990 it still needed to make economies, and to do this cynically pitted subsidiaries against each other. Palmers Green saved its neck by proposing to outstation its Sunday roster (comprising routes 29, 34 and 102) at Wood Green (using the latter's buses) so it could close on Sundays, and so it was that Muswell Hill (the other

Above: The ever-worsening traffic conditions in the capital had compelled LT to cut back so many routes that through passengers were alienated, most disliking having to change buses. An interesting option was therefore explored with the creation from 21 June 1990 of new route 607, which served only fifteen stops of the 207's eleven miles between Shepherd's Bush and Uxbridge. The number recalled the trolleybus route replaced by the 207 in 1960, but Metrobuses had to do in the absence of Q1s! M61 (WYW 61T) loads up at Shepherd's Bush Green on 22 September; this route was initially shared with Hanwell, another CentreWest garage. *Malc McDonald*

Right: South London Transport, the offspring of part of Wandle District, could field all of Ms, Ls and DMSs and had to start shuffling them around to satisfy the age limits imposed on tenders. The year 1990 thus saw Streatham lose all its Ls for Ms, then many of its Ms for DMSs, regressing by two generations! At least it had M1441/2, the two AVE-trials mkIIs that had moved on from Brixton following the exit of that garage's last Ms in favour of a 100%-DMS OPO runout. The 109 was one of the mkIIs' haunts while at Streatham, and Cummins-engined M1442 (A442 UUV) shows off a recent repaint as it heads south towards Croydon during August. *Chris Evans*

Below right: It got frankly silly when Norwood had to regain a handful of Ms so that an equal number of Ls could furnish the age requirements on the batch of tendering gains allotted to Thornton Heath. In the three years since Ms' last tenure at Norwood part of the 2B had been one-manned by the back door through new route 2A, which stuck to the southernmost end of this trunk route by day but in the evenings and on Sundays swelled to cover the whole 2B through to the West End. On 25 July 1990 M940 (A940 SUL) is seen in Central Hill, approaching Crown Point in Norwood. Further convolutions at South London would see Norwood's Ms replaced by Titans the following year, then return again in 1993, disappear once more in 1996 and then come back one final time later that year for a Bakerloo Line rail job. *Colin Stannard*

choice for closure) ceased operations after 20 July its viability not helped by continued tendering losses from the London Northern subsidiary. Despite its conversion to T in October 1988, this garage had held on doggedly to its two much-prized four-speed Metrobuses, M1393/6, and these had kept the M class alive all the way to the end. They were transferred to Holloway, together with route 43 (which regained Ms). The Ts, however, passed with the 134, W7 and N2 to Finchley and soon appeared on the 13, 26, 82, N13 and N21 alongside its Ms. Proportions of M and T fluctuated for all three years of mixed operation. Finchley, meanwhile, abandoned its share of the 17 to Holloway, which made further space by reallocating the 4 to Chalk Farm, converting it to T operation. BL-operated route C11 had fielded considerable numbers of Holloway Metrobuses on its King's Cross-Archway leg for some years, but could do so no more after 21 July with its transfer to R&I Buses with new Darts.

Related transfers on 21 July saw the other three ex-Tyne & Wear Ms return to Potters Bar, which together with the input of more standard Ms reduced the Volvo Ailsa to penny numbers; similarly only a dozen Vs could still turn out at Harrow Weald after another nine Ms arrived, mostly ex-Cricklewood. In July Ensignbus acquired Derby City Transport's only Metrobus, GRA 102V, as no 112 (101 briefly being carried).

Down in south London, extraordinary things were happening at the LBL subsidiary of that name. Faced with another age limit on a tranche of tendered routes it had just won, South London had to shuffle its buses so that Ls could assume control of the routes allocated to Thornton Heath. Having lost its Ls for older Ms, Streatham now had to regress by yet another generation by taking on a dozen DMSs! These released an equivalent number of Ms to Norwood so that the same quantity of Ls could in turn free the Fleetlines from Thornton Heath. Eight of these DMSs ejected the last Ms from Brixton, which by the end comprised M51/66, 205/14/32/3, 312, 454, 503, 909 and semi-showbus M1440; Metrobuses were thus removed from the 95 and 189, plus the 250, N69 and N78 (which were transferred to Thornton Heath with Ls). There were now three out of five South London garages with mixed operation, bringing unnecessary complications in engineering and spares terms. Norwood's second spell of M operation reintroduced the class to the 2 and 68 but brought Ms to the 2A, 2B, 3A and X68 for the first time. Under these contracts, the 50 lost Streatham operation and Ms, the 159's Sunday service also abandoning Ms with the loss of that day's Streatham portion. Streatham, however, received all of the 137 on Sundays, part of the 59 on that day and half the 109 during the rest of the week.

The 98A was reduced from peak hours to schooldays only and the 222 demoted to MA on Sundays, but a new route to Uxbridge Ms was the 207A, which was introduced to give the Charville Lane Estate a service from the west, adding buses to some unserved roads there. Considerably more glamorous, and with a route number to match, was new limited-stop express route 607 – not with Q1 trolleybuses this time, but fulfilling the same end-to-end role between Uxbridge and Shepherd's Bush Green. Hanwell and Uxbridge shared the 607 much as they did the 207, the latter route tending to fall back to its constituent ends (Uxbridge operating no further east than Acton Town and Hanwell no further west than Southall Broadway). 21 July was also the date of yet another onslaught of rattling Renaults into CentreWest Metrobus territory; the 274 was withdrawn and apportioned to new RW-operated E7, while the E3 was minibussed on Sundays and the existing E2, still clinging onto Ms while the balance of the RWs was awaited, lost its Greenford-Ruislip roads to new RW-operated route E9.

A curious bifurcation was appended to the 242 on 21 July, taking its Potters Bar Ms over the 359 (and former 217) roads to Hammond Street during weekday evenings, as a Hertfordshire County Council contract rather than an LRT tender.

Two important changes accrued to the M class during the early summer of 1990; one aesthetic (this being the commencement, upon routine repaint, of the painting of the entrance doors red rather than yellow) and one practical (the introduction of disabled-friendly measures like 'Bus Stopping' signs and yellow-and-black step-edge inserts in a sawtooth pattern). Both latter features were adopted as standard under the *aegis* of DiPTAC (the Disabled Passengers' Transport Advisory Commission) and, together with the painting green of handrails and the installation of an emergency opening mechanism within the rubber buffer of buses' exit doors, with a beeping audio device to accompany the exit doors closing) were implemented over the next two years. Westbourne Park's M1382, deroofed in July, was repaired (by Kent Engineering) with the roof unit (featuring plain front windows) from South Yorkshire Metrobus 1886, while that garage introduced a new mesh grille design to M884.

Continuing the theme of sectionalising central London's through routes, the 88 was hacked in two on 22 September by the withdrawal of its former southern (Stockwell) section west of Marble Arch. Its Sunday OPO M operation from Shepherd's Bush was lost to a similar function on new route 94 (Acton Green-Oxford Circus/Trafalgar Square). At Willesden, the shortlived 172 was withdrawn, its roads (and more) coming under new DT-operated 206, while the 205 remained M-operated but also subordinate to this new route. To assuage closure-threatened Chalk Farm's fears after its loss of the 168 to Grey-Green, the 271 was reallocated in from Holloway (with the accompanying M to T conversion). Twelve Holloway Ms passed to Finchley, increasing the balance of the type there by displacing an equivalent number of Ts indirectly to furnish the 131 at Westlink.

A week later the Kingston Bus network was thrown in the air; Norbiton survived, now fully-M once again after ejecting the final DMSs, but its PVR was considerably reduced after it lost the 85 to London & Country and didn't win back the 131. It was additionally compelled to curtail the 71 at Kingston from the south and surrender the 213 to Sutton as a London General tender. Sutton, however,

Above: There was no sympathy for Harrow Buses as the operation was heavily reduced in its particular round of tender awards. The mkII Metrobuses were returned off lease, the Volvos sold and what routes remained reverted to standard Ms as if Harrow Buses had never existed. One unexpected upshot was the conversion of the 245 back to Metrobuses, which it had only had to cede to provide buses for the 207's one-manning in 1987. On 19 January 1991 the route was transferred from Cricklewood to Harrow Weald, filling some of the space vacated by the loss of routes 114 and 140. Conversion to Darts would follow within the year, but M937 (A937 SUL), seen at work on 12 May 1991 is a nice sight while it lasts.
Colin Stannard

received its first Metrobuses so as to keep the 213 M-operated (these being C-registered transfers from Putney released from there by older examples ex-Norbiton), while the route's new 413 offshoot (taking over the peak-hour bifurcation to Belmont) was also scheduled for Ms. The transfer of the 152 and 163 from Sutton to Colliers Wood, while accomplished with DMSs incoming from Sutton, introduced the possibility of Ms straying from the 200. Sutton's Ms began to wander, their first capture being the 93 during November, followed by the 163 and on Boxing Day, the 164. Norbiton's departing Ms were divided between two destinations: the oldest passed to Potters Bar, where they finally ousted the last of the Vs, and the middle order was allocated to Merton, where the conversion from DMS now got going in earnest.

Fulwell now introduced more DTs with the 29 September programme, the 285 succumbing daily and the 290 on Sundays. The A1 and A2 were re-routed to and from Heathrow Airport via the M4 spur on 27 October (also spawning a six-week shuttle between Terminals 1/2/3 and 4, while the 141's Wood Green-operated section was diverted on Sundays to terminate at Liverpool Street and Potters Bar's evening contract 360 was withdrawn. On 10 November the 17 gained a Sunday service as far as Kings Cross. Another loss to Ms transferred Alperton's 92 to London Buslines on this date, while the arrival of new DTs at Edgware encompassed the conversion from M of the 288 (and of the 240 on Sundays). The 204 received an all-day projection from Burnt Oak to Edgware. 10 November also saw the completion of the E-Line network, routes E1 and E2 succumbing to RW operation and the former being split in half. One surprise, taking place a week later, was the reversion of the 245 from LS to M operation.

Private-hire M1398 received LBL livery (albeit with gold fleetnumbers), while Stamford Hill counterpart M1437 augmented its summer work with occasional

visits to the 149 during October, fitted with a ticket machine for the purpose. The names on M1367/98 disappeared with their repaint, with all private-hire Ms treated by year's end. In October Ensignbus added 111 (ULS 621X), Alexander-bodied ex-Kelvin Scottish, to its fleet. Part of its remit was new commercial route 565, added on 23 October to link Barkingside and Lakeside rather than extending the 165/365.

The London United subsidiary of LBL recorded a major victory by winning the 140 upon the retendering of the Harrow Buses network on 1 December, putting it into Hounslow with Ms transferred from Norbiton, Fulwell and Alperton. Harrow Weald (as a Metroline garage) was awarded the 182 from Alperton (CentreWest), which converted the 187 from M to DT operation. Another loss to Darts was the 297, which passed on tender from Willesden (Metroline) to Alperton (CentreWest) with new Wright-bodied DWs. The leased mkII Ms 1452-80 began departing off lease from this date, and all the Vs were gone (bar one dogged straggler) by late November; the latter not particularly missed but the loss of the former an opportunity missed strategically. Cricklewood withdrew from the 266 to allow Willesden a full allocation after its loss of the 297. At Hounslow, the 98 was withdrawn and replaced by new DT-operated H98; the new Darts took over the 232's Sunday service. Presaging future developments, the 105 was split in two over its length and a new Alperton allocation introduced to cover the Southall-Shepherd's Bush end, the Hanwell contingent proceeding no further east than Greenford.

The 1 December changes released enough Ms from Hanwell and Alperton (which broadly swapped their eldest and newest Ms) to furnish Hounslow's needs for the 140, provide for Willesden's increased route 266 complement and to further grow Merton's fleet in replacement of more DMSs; the Fleetline was definitely at the end of its career. This was also the case at Ensignbus, where on 1 December the 62 (home of ex-SYPTE 295-8 alongside DMSs soon to be replaced by Dennis Dominators) was rerouted at its northern end to terminate at Collier Row. The sale of the stage operations to the CNT Group of Hong Kong on 29 December prompted a renaming to Ensign Citybus, the revised fleetname being surmounted by Chinese characters.

London Northern engaged MTL to carry out DiPTAC work (including floor repairs) on its Metrobuses, while other LBL units had DiPTAC work performed elsewhere or, in the case of Leaside, did it in-house. Some Ms got by with just the handrails treated to green covering pending fuller attention later. Floor replacement for CentreWest Ms was done at Acton Tram Depot, with various repaint, DiPTAC and accident repair work undertaken by, among other concerns, Eastbourne Buses, Reading Buses, Dennis of Guildford and Merseyside Transport. The contract for the fitment of door equipment incorporating sensitive edges was awarded to Wilfred Overton Ltd. Meanwhile, conversions to air braking continued apace. Leaside commenced the fitment of fans inside driver's cabs (another advancement that would become standard), while a ceramic-filtered exhaust system bowed on Stamford Hill's Ms 544 and 754 in December, the former fitted with a 'green' Gardner engine. From the first half of 1991 the introduction of stainless-steel exhausts and water tanks, a low oil-level engine cutout switch, hazard lights, assault alarms and Band 3 radios all formed part of the general advancement technologically, with Leaside at the forefront.

In spite of the falling out of favour of autonomous operations and liveries, four Sutton Ms received the mushroom skirt of Suttonbus at the tail end of 1990, M1180 combining this with Airbus vinyls! CentreWest, meanwhile, introduced a brighter and larger half-arrow logo in yellow (and still pointing forwards). In December Holloway's M124 became the first normal recipient of plain upper-deck front windows; by comparison, over a hundred Titans had been so treated by this time.

Boxing Day 1990 saw Ensign Citybus on the 22B, including Metrobus 291, and the one-off 86B (with three Metrobuses and three Olympians), while New Year's Eve saw mass night oddities like Norwood Ms on the N2, Victoria on the N12 and N87, Fulwell on the N93 and the connecting service operated by Putney.

The first change of 1991 was on 6 January and saw the transfer of Grey-Green's 313 from Barking to Stamford Hill. This allowed the 103 to come in from County Bus with its own Olympians, though very quickly Metrobuses began to appear. Ensign Citybus's 165 and 365 pair were re-routed to serve the new Tesco in Rainham from the 12th, while the start of the new achool term on the 14th saw London United gain a spur off the 281 known as 281s, and operated with an M from Fulwell. One minor but important change to the first Metrobus-operated night route, N94, gave it a new number (N16) from 19 January, to bring it into common purpose with the daytime 16. On that day Cricklewood was downgraded to the status of an outstation of Edgware within LBL's Metroline subsidiary, as a more preferable alternative to possibly closing Harrow Weald after the tendering débâcle; the only routes to remain operating from Cricklewood were the 16, 16A and 205, with the 32 adding a Metrobus complement to what was otherwise a minibus roster at Edgware and the 245 passing to Harrow Weald. This restructuring was forced by the winding-up of Harrow Buses after its first and only three-year term. Harrow Weald cast off its mkII Ms and worn-out Volvos (the former returned off lease and the latter sold) for a more conventional-looking fleet of standard Ms (mostly ex-Willesden, displaced thence by ex-Cricklewood Ms) for the 183 and 209, while the 186 was transferred in from Edgware and the 245 from Cricklewood. Losses were particularly heavy; the 114 was taken up by BTS with new Olympians, the 258 and 340 passed to Luton & District, the successor to London Country North West) and the remnant of the 136 was withdrawn altogether, while the 209 was reduced to just one morning and one afternoon journey as an adjunct to Dart-operated route H12. M150 was barely bedded in, however, before being taken under Headstone Lane railway bridge on 5 February, and it was another bus to gain the roof out of a South Yorkshire Metrobus, this time 1840. DiPTAC conversions commenced that month with M270, but the more modern alternative in the form of M1471, the last mkII M at Harrow Weald, was taken out of service on 3 April after a day on the 183 as HD166. Following in the path of the MD class, most of them went on to Reading Buses, there to spend a fruitful seventeen more years.

The combination of tendering reverses and conversions to minibus was gradually edging the M class off its traditional preserve in north-west London, and the years 1991/92 would see them deployed to another task – the final replacement of DMSs. The reprieved B20 variety of Fleetlines had been concentrated in south London – split since 1989 between two subsidiaries, London General and South London – but from 27 January Ms started arriving in force at the former's Stockwell garage. Here they took over the 37, 77A, 156 and 170, plus the 88 on Sundays and the N87 at night. VC-operated 133 and 196 soon began to see Ms.

Below: The end of the DMS was at hand as Ms poured into Stockwell and Merton garages in the first half of 1991. M506 (GYE 506W) was one of them, moving from Finchley to Stockwell in February, and in September is seen at Clapham Junction on the 37. This route lost all its operations west of Putney with the Wandsworth-area changes of 25 June 1991. *Haydn Davies*

Right: Another not particularly welcome split was that of the 17 from 2 February 1991, removing an important link across Archway. An attempt was made to remedy it with the introduction of three-bus route 17A, but it lasted only three months. On 30 March Holloway's M1119 (B119 WUL) is at the Nag's Head, where this short-lived route terminated. *Mike Harris*

A scheme in Barnet was implemented on 2 February; its major contribution to the M class's fortunes was in the withdrawal of the 26 in favour of a backstreet minibus known as 326, twelve Ms leaving Finchley for Stockwell. To replace the 26's Brent Cross end the 102 was extended from Golders Green, while at the Barnet end the 84A was projected over its roads to Chesterfield Road; the latter route lost Ms for DW-class Darts other than a single schoolday M that studiously avoided the route's new routeing in Alexandra Park. With the concurrent extension of the 125 from North Finchley to Finchley Central, there was thus no further need for the 82 to go any further north than Golders Green on Sundays. On the Holloway Road corridor the 17 was controversially cut north of Archway, removing an important cross-Archway link; while the 263 was augmented (with four Ms, owing to there being no new Ss available as yet), the planners hedged their bets by introducing a Monday to Friday-only 17A between Holloway, Nag's Head and East Finchley only. Introduced in part to test the effects of traffic flow on the recently introduced Red Route along this particular corridor, it was perhaps designed to fail, and lasted only three months. The Sunday-only 263A was withdrawn so that the 43 could be introduced on that day of the week, but unusually bifurcating at Old Street to serve the Sunday markets beyond Liverpool Street on its way to London Bridge, a variation unusually not differentiated by a suffix. At Edgware the 143 was demoted to DT and SR operation, many of the Ms being sent to Stockwell, but on schooldays new route 143A kept a single Edgware M occupied roving over the old routeing, the 143 otherwise having been rerouted down Long Lane near Finchley Central.

South of the river three major trunk routes were tinkered with to cut some costs. Brixton's RML-operated 137 lost its service south of Streatham Hill and altogether during evenings and Sundays, at which times new OPO route 137A took its place. Ms operated on Sundays when Streatham was in sole charge; otherwise it was with Brixton's DMSs and the two surviving Hs. With the withdrawal of the 95, the 109 was altered to render Streatham the main ingredient, Brixton coming off entirely, and Streatham's loss of its participation on the 159 rendered it a 100%-OPO garage.

The affiliation of Colliers Wood garage (with its routes 152, 163 and 200) with Sutton ended on 23 February when its runout and vehicles (including a dozen Ms) were incorporated within the allocation of Merton; further changes came on 2 March when new route 70 (with MAs) replaced M-operated 52A in its entirety; further Ms were dislodged to pass to Stockwell. Victoria took on some of the 52 on Saturdays. The transfer of route 393 from London & Country to London General on 6 April gave Sutton's small fleet of Ms the opportunity to turn out if the six new DW-class Darts could not present themselves in full. Also in south-west London, the N14 was projected from Kingston to Chessington (World of Adventures), allowing the N87 to be re-routed to Hampton Court, forsaking the A3 and Surbiton; both these changes commenced at midnight on 27 April. DTs overtook the 205 on that day with its transfer away from Cricklewood, while a significant change to the 253 on 11 May cut it between Mornington Crescent and Warren Street.

The two Leaside Ms with experimental exhausts were loaned to the Road Research Laboratory at Crowthorne during April and May; M544's seats were removed and test equipment fitted to evaluate varying loads of passengers (here represented by sandbags). Their next trial was in relation to fuelling, where special monitoring equipment was fitted to the fuel filler cap.

Mixed-type allocations, hitherto a strict no-no, developed another twist from 9 May when Norwood's small fleet of Ms performing a support role to the garage's majority Ls on the 2, 2A and 68 began to leave, to be replaced by an equivalent number of Titans taking the same role! The T class was unknown in this region but would soon make its presence felt in a big way.

1991's most important set of changes was known as the Wandsworth Area Network and was carried out on 25 May. It involved the splitting of established longer routes as well as the inevitable influx of minibuses and Darts. Ms were in full control of Stockwell by the changeover date, and they made their debut on new route 337 (Clapham Junction-Richmond), the middle section of the 37, which fell back to Putney. The Hounslow end of it fell to the new DR variety of Dart as H37, the DRs also assuming the 111 on Sundays. Stockwell Ms also took over the 49, which was not only reconfigured as a solely London General contract, but was cut down quite harshly, its roads south of Clapham Junction given over to new route 349; this Streatham-operated route ran from its home garage to South Kensington before taking a hard left to follow the 30 to West Brompton. Again the outermost end was devolved to Darts, this piece becoming new DR-operated route 249 – but on Sundays the 349 covered it all the way to Crystal Palace. Metrobus operation left the 59 with the loss of this route's latterly Sunday-only Streatham share, and Streatham's own peculiar flirtation with DMSs had now come to an end.

The 77 and 77A were hacked in central London, the former now taking a south-of-the-river path to Waterloo rather than Euston and the latter falling back from King's Cross to Aldwych. The last residue of its former peak-hour journeys west of Wandsworth became new schoolday route 77C.

Merton replaced two-thirds of its DMSs with Ms ex Hounslow and Norwood, and one of their tasks from 25 May was new route 270, fitting neatly between the 220's southern end (withdrawn south of Wandsworth) and the 280's northern end (withdrawn north of Tooting). Merton's Ms (and a fairly large number of DMSs still remaining by this date) also gained the 22 on Sundays from Victoria, allowing Stockwell to gain part of the 11 on that day of the week and letting Victoria concentrate its resources on the 19, which dropped its Holloway Ms and Merton DMSs as well as its entire service south of Battersea

Bridge (the 219 being augmented to cover and the 349 also taking part). Merton's newish 355 was re-routed at Tooting to Mitcham over the 44, which route was also severed, losing its roads beyond Vauxhall to the new 344, Victoria-operated (with Merton on Sundays) and commencing from Clapham Junction. The introduction of the 344 allowed the 170, once a route stretching all the way across town, to be cut down into nothing more than a minibus feeder into Clapham Junction only, its path into town duplicated by the 77A. Thus the 170 lost its Ms for DRs after only three months, as did the 156, which was transferred to Merton and rationalised to Wimbledon-Clapham Junction only; its Vauxhall leg was covered by the new 344 and its Morden extension on Sunday was provided for by the introduction of the 163 on that day (with Merton Ms). Collectively, the 156 and 170 joined the 'Streetline' network of London General minibus routes that had made their debut with the 39's conversion in 1990; these were also joined by the 265, which lost its two Ms for ten new MAs and gained an extension to Tolworth Broadway over the 72, which was curtailed at Roehampton.

North of the river, Holloway withdrew from the 74, which was rerouted to King's Cross rather than Camden, new Chalk Farm T-operated 274 taking its place. In exchange the 271 was reallocated from Chalk Farm back to Holloway, converting from Titan to Metrobus and easily making up for the 17A's withdrawal.

Time-honoured route 91 was partitioned into two Dart-operated routes; H91 (Hounslow West-Hammersmith) and 391 (Turnham Green-Fulham Broadway) and losing the cross-river link to Wandsworth. The former, however, was allocated one Hounslow M over part of the route during schoolday rush-hours, assisted by an ambitious morning garage journey of the E4 to and from Hounslow garage. Existing blinds were unaltered other than the pasting in of an 'H' over the 91 panel; similar treatment allowed the garage's Ms to start turning out on the H98 (ex-98).

Left: The Wandsworth-area programme of 25 May 1991 was the largest single set of route changes in many years, and split up several long-established routes into more easily-workable sections. The 49, having flourished briefly with its return to Crystal Palace in 1989 in place of the 249, was now cut back even further and split into three. The middle section was christened 349 and took on the Streatham buses (now once again all Ms). Its peculiar contortion against the grain to West Brompton was to allow the cutting back of another still-lengthy route, the 30, and this terminus is where we can compare the mkI and mkII Metrobus in the shape of M1099 (B99 WUL) and M1442 (A442 UUV) respectively; the date is 14 February 1992.
Malc McDonald

The partial OPO conversion of the 137 in February had had to be performed under a different number after union objections and the risk of confusing the public, but opinions had changed by 25 May when the evening services of the 10 and 13 were converted to OPO; after about 7 pm the RMLs on each route would head home, to be replaced on the former by Holloway Ms coming off the 17 and 134 and on the latter by Finchley's still-mixed M/T fleet not needed after the evening peak on the 82 and W7.

Post-Wandsworth tinkering snipped off two routes' potentially most useful bits, 8 June seeing the 18 lose its King's Cross-Farringdon roads and the 33 pulled back from Kensington to Hammersmith. Hanwell withdrew from the 607 so that Uxbridge could add a between-peaks service to the 207A and extend the 98A to Uxbridge Station from West Drayton, while London United curtailed the 267 south of Fulwell garage in favour of new DR-operated R68. The possibility of Metrobuses on the 145 departed on 22 June with its loss by Ensignbus to East London; the vehicles started turning out on the 347 instead, plus new Wennington-area local 323. During June and into July Merton continued to receive Ms, with ten further examples being collected spare from Fulwell and Westbourne Park indirectly to continue the removal of DMSs from Sutton. On 29 June the X71 was withdrawn, leaving Norbiton with just two routes.

The summer of 1991 saw London Forest staff at Walthamstow withdraw their labour in protest at newly-awarded contracts which reduced pay and increased hours; with no buses at all on the road from 10-28 July LT had to scramble replacements, Ensign Citybus using its Metrobuses on the D1. The companies that filled in thus placed themselves ideally to pick up the work when the dispute was solved at the end of July by taking the contracts away from Forest.

The need for Stamford Brook's three coach-seated Ls to be detached from the 237 to furnish what turned out to be a short-lived third Airbus route (A3) to Stansted prompted return M appearances on this route between 20 July and 13 September. On 6 July the 149's projection beyond Liverpool Street to Waterloo was cut to one morning peak journey only as far as Mansion House, but on the 29th the Waterloo portion was restored in full during peak hours. The 118's Sunday service lost Ms for DRs on 10 August, and on the 31st a small round of changes cost the 413 its Ms when MRLs took over an expanded service; simultaneously the 151 was restored to its original Worcester Park Station terminus rather than Lower Morden and the 213 gained a schoolday journey to Glenthorne School in St Helier, replacing the 213s. Another schoolday-only service, the 189, began the new academic year transferred to London General (Stockwell), reintroducing Ms (albeit on an officially-VC service); the previous South London operation had expired with the summer term after 19 July.

In August Stamford Brook borrowed Stamford Hill's turbocharged M1437 and tried it out on the M4 in the interests of converting the Airbus fleet to turbo power, but a more prosaic, and quite extraordinary event was on the 14th, when M1009 was loaned to London Forest and used on Mobility Bus route 925 to save the day after the failure of one of its wheelchair-accessible Mobility Bus Nationals! Further improvement was on the cards for the Airbus Ms when a refurbishment programme was implemented. Awarded to Hants & Dorset at Eastleigh, the work

involved floor renewal, new heating and new seat moquette in predominantly grey. Seating capacity was increased to H41/9D with the fitment of a row of rearward-facing seats over the rear wheelarches, while the entrance-door stanchion was removed so passengers could get their luggage off. The work (including repainting into a new livery) was completed by June 1992, a late change being the alteration of the blind box to a single aperture in which green blinds (A1) or blue (A2) were carried.

After a bitter and expensive recent history, Norbiton finally closed on 7 September; all that Fulwell had to do to incorporate the 57 and 71 (with 25 of Norbiton's 33 Ms) was to give half the 281 to Hounslow (which took the other eight). The other big industrial tug-of-war of recent years was settled just as ruthlessly with the commencement of London Forest's progressive disbanding. Capital Citybus, another new name for what had begun as Ensignbus, was far and away the victor here, and took the 97A and 215 as early as 14 September, shuffling existing vehicles while 14 more former Mainline Metrobuses were prepared by Northern Counties. After livery experiments which had seen 282 adorned in yellow and silver in May and 297 taking on an extraordinary livery of maroon and silver on the front and offside and green and silver on the nearside and rear, a further revised scheme was introduced, being bold yellow with two red stripes. Meanwhile this firm's original Metrobus routes, the 165 and 365, were repositioned so that the former worked south of Romford town centre and the latter to its north. The 252 was also cut between Hornchurch and Gidea Park and the 446 abandoned Corbets Tey for good.

Right: Stamford Brook did regain service Ms when the 27 was won as a London United contract and supplied with very early examples. The RiversideBus name used by this low-cost operation was continued, though the 27 was a more conventional contract than the 237 and 283 that had started it off. In June 1994 M28 (WYW 28T) is seen in Bishops Bridge Road. *Haydn Davies*

On 28 September the 224 at Alperton succumbed to minibuses (MAs), while after less than a year with Ms, the 245 was single-decked again on 12 November, now with North Wembley DTs in lieu of Harrow Weald Ms, which when displaced effectively completed Merton's conversion from DMSs, the last Fleetline straggler leaving in January. The daunting conversion of eighty-DMS Sutton could resume in earnest, the routes covered here being the 80, 93, 151, 154, 157, 164, N68 and N88.

Stamford Brook garage regained stage M operation on 9 November when the 27 was commenced as a London United contract, forcing the Holloway allocation to withdraw; the new stock was composed of very early Ms which soon wandered to the 237 with the latter's Ls appearing in exchange. The route was unfortunately cut at both ends, between Turnham Green and Richmond and between Camden Town and Archway. At Holloway, the 135 was retained on tender with London Northern (and daily, to boot) but its Marble Arch-Victoria section became peak hours only. Route E4 at Hounslow was transformed into new MRL-operated minibus route H40, its schoolday M migrating to the H91. Merton's 280 was rerouted to terminate at St George's Hospital

Above: The second batch of Airbus Metrobuses is immortalised in LBL livery one last time before going away for extensive refurbishment in 1992; the likes of M1008 (A708 THV), additionally sporting a white registration plate when caught at Marble Arch on 26 July 1991, had already been converted to wheelchair accessibility through a ramp fitted in the centre doorway. Behind the M is Olympian L312 on short-lived Stansted link route A3, which released three Ms to make return appearances on the otherwise L-restricted 237 at Stamford Brook. *Tony Wilson*

in Tooting, rather than Colliers Wood Station. A small but significant change cut the 29 between Trafalgar Square and Victoria from 16 November, putting more pressure on the 24; at Wood Green the 144A was introduced on Sundays and Tottenham's 171A was reconfigured to terminate daily at Northumberland Park Station. The 607 was upgraded, in a manner of speaking, with the replacement of its Uxbridge Ms by coach-seated LSs and LXs, the Ms going to Sutton to join former Holloway machines. Two Wood Green shopping services (known internally as V1 and V2) linked north London with Lakeside in the six weeks prior to Christmas.

The fallout from the London Forest tragedy affected the M class but minimally; the most significant convolution of the 106's recent history now turned the route back over to Ms when Clapton (reopened in 1989 as a London Forest garage, but today transferred to Leaside) supplanted Ash Grove. This controversially-closed ten-year-old garage also bequeathed its share of the 6 (on Sundays) and the N6 (by night) to Willesden, thus converting them from T to M. 34 Titans from both Ash Grove and Walthamstow were placed temporarily with Stamford Hill, bringing mixed M/T operation to the 67 and 149, plus 73 on Sundays and N83 at night. Stamford Hill otherwise gained the entire 253. Capital Citybus completed its sweep of Walthamstow's routes, taking on the 97, 158 and 212; Dagenham was the base until the former council premises at Marsh Lane, Northumberland Park (NP) could be reconfigured as an open-field bus garage, which was implemented on 30 November (routes 97, 97A, 158,

Above: A sea change from the established order of things was palpable in 1992 with Ts now part of historically Metrobus-operating Norwood's allocation while the DMSs so familiar to passengers of Sutton's routes had been replaced by Ms in the same year. This West Croydon shot of March 1992 captures M386 (GYE 386W), with 'PAY DRIVER' sticker rather than the flipover plate, alongside T638 (NUW 638Y). *Chris Evans*

Below: Even Ensignbus could lose routes; the 62, that it had operated since 17 January 1987 and latterly with Metrobuses like 277 (FUT 37V) new to Leicester Citybus, went back to East London's Barking on 23 November 1991. This bus is seen on the 62A, an offshoot created to link the 62 roads with King George Hospital at Goodmayes, but withdrawn with the transfer. *Tony Wilson*

212 and 215 transferring in on that date but the 123 remaining at Dagenham). For all its rapid expansion this autumn, Capital Citybus lost one of its earlier gains, the 62, back to East London; the 145 had gone the same way on 22 June. The 62A was withdrawn altogether.

On 30 November the 152, which had only recently begun to take on Ms, was minibussed (with MRLs) and curtailed at either end; custom still identified at school times became new Sutton M-operated route 452 over the extent of the old route to Hook. It took a while before Sutton drivers grew out of the habit of displaying 152 panels on their Ms! Another route to make a 'return' during November was the 209, which is all that Harrow Weald Ms subbing for defective DTs on the H12 could display until new blinds were delivered.

At the end of November Capital Citybus started receiving 14 ex-Mainline Metrobuses from the single-doored batch new in 1980; of H46/31F capacity, in full yellow livery and slotting in around existing fleetnumbers were 101-3/6/8/10/3-20 (JHE 171/2/96/57/78/0/69/2/82/46-50W). Although the 97A, 158 and 215 at Northumberland Park were the type's intended employment, the company's flexibility ensured appearances on any route based, with reciprocation by the new rolling stock (Olympians and Dominators).

The highest-numbered LBL M, former Tyne & Wear M1485, was lost in action on 12 November when it caught fire in Hammond Street on one of the 242's bifurcations to this point. Accident-damaged M81 benefited from its front the following March. It was extremely rare for the second-hand Ms to appear on contracted routes 217 and 231, but one MCW and one Alexander managed once each in 1991. Other unusual appearances over the year were Ms to the 10 (Holloway), 11 and 19 (Victoria), 88 (Stockwell), 156 (Merton), 224 and 297 (Alperton), with Willesden using them often on the 6 and, for the first time on the 8 on 31 December. Fulwell, whose Ms had started

receiving blinds with upper-case lettering by the end of the year, put theirs out on the 290 and R70 (a schoolday journey introduced on 23 November and also known as R70s). Finally, on New Year's Eve Victoria's Night Bus standby worked the N68.

Tendering struck the Wood Green area on 1 February 1992; to compound its curtailment from the north the previous November, the 29 was now withdrawn north of Palmers Green to cement its awarding solely to Leaside; this meant Chalk Farm had to withdraw its participation. The Palmers Green allocation was transferred to new route 329 (Turnpike Lane-Enfield) and absorbed the Enfield allocation on the 121. Palmers Green could reopen on Sundays now. Two lengthy former trolleybus routes were hacked quite severely, the 221 losing its entire southern section beyond Turnpike Lane and the 279 falling back from Smithfield to Holloway (and now appearing on Sundays with the simultaneous withdrawal of the 279A); the 141 (lost by Wood Green to Grey-Green and curtailed daily at Moorgate) was expected to cover for the 221 and only a diversion of the minibus 153 was deemed sufficient to see former 221 and 279 passengers into the Islington or Caledonian Road corridor. At least here the renewed 259, introduced at weekends and stabilised between Enfield Garage (or Edmonton) and King's Cross (or Holborn Circus) in replacement of Thamesway's 359, helped out a little, but established links were severed. The 242's bifurcation to Hammond Street was introduced on Sundays in memory of the 359. Tottenham's 41 lost its Tottenham-Ferry Lane end to an extension of recently-introduced minibus route W4. Grey-Green lost the 298 to Capital Citybus and the 125 lost its Sunday extension to Enfield Town, while Capital Citybus's 212 was minibussed on that day of the week.

At CentreWest, Westbourne Park's 7 was minibussed on Sundays in lieu of Ms, which concentrated on the 18 on that day allowing the Alperton allocation to be withdrawn for good.

Above: With its victories of autumn 1991 Ensign Citybus transformed itself into Capital Citybus, now exploiting to the full the 'Chinese' connection that had applied with the sale of the business to the owners of Citybus in Hong Kong late the previous year. The Walthamstow area was flooded with yellow buses old and new; the 'old' comprised 14 former South Yorkshire PTE Metrobuses like 119 (JHE 149W), seen on the 215 at Walthamstow Central on 12 March 1992 and by then based at Northumberland Park garage. *Malc McDonald*

Despite the year 1992 heralding an era of recession that made it impossible for already financially-stretched companies to maintain overheads to the extent of the past, the closure of Streatham garage on 14 March after just five years of operation was still an appalling example of waste and shortsightedness. Its fleet of 63 Ms (including the mkII pair) moved to Croydon garage, where they not only ousted all but seven DMSs, but the five dozen Titans that had come south from London Forest to replace the rest only in November. Thus did Metrobus operation return to the 50, 68, 109 and 130; routes 255 and X30 saw the type for the first time as did the 64 upon its transfer in from Thornton Heath. Routes 197, 403 and 407, contractually limited to Ls, had to make do with occasional appearances. Streatham's routes 118 and 349 lost Ms with their transfer to Brixton, the 137A also losing the type upon its move from Streatham to Norwood, while severe reductions to the 59 and 159 allowed the 109 to return on Sundays; the route was now shared out between Thornton Heath (with Ts), Croydon M/L/DMS (on Mon-Sat) and Brixton Ts on Sundays.

Above: The closure of Streatham garage on 14 March 1992 allowed its entire Metrobus fleet to decamp for Croydon, reintroducing the class there at the expense of DMSs. New routes for the M at Croydon included the 255, a one-bus wander round the growing light-commercial district of Beddington, and M1102 (B102 WUL) is that way bound on 22 July 1993. *Colin Stannard*

Lengthy route 105 was curtailed from the west at Greenford Station, new route 95 (with Alperton MAs but capable of occasional Ms) taking over between Shepherd's Bush and Southall; on Sundays the 105 remained through to Shepherd's Bush. Fulwell's 290 now succumbed to Darts, new DRs joining the established DTs there and also converting the 267 on Sundays. More Darts edged out Ms on 29 February with the conversion to DR of Edgware's 204, the 226 at Willesden converting to DT on Sundays using the 206's spares. Thamesway ceded its contracts on routes 20, 167, 235 and 275 to Grey-Green on 7 March, bringing to the 20 and particularly the 275 the possibility of Metrobus operation from the stocks at Barking.

Below: The five ex-GM Buses Metrobuses had spent most of their time at Potters Bar, two spells there bracketing a wholesale move to Wood Green, but the loan of M1443 (GBU 1V) to Westbourne Park in March 1992 was most unusual. The single door is noteworthy, as is the replacement of its radiator grille by a later-model version; correspondingly, the recognisable fronts of this bus and two fellows found their way to Leaside M567, 624 and 903. *Tony Wilson*

On Mondays to Saturdays the 4 and 135 exchanged bases and types, the 4 returning to Holloway with Ms and the 135 assuming T operation from Chalk Farm. On Sundays the 4 remained with Chalk Farm Titans; to retain the balance on this day of the week the 10 was also restored to Holloway, regaining M operation.

Only one of West Midlands PTE's 1,124 production Metrobuses had never actually entered service in its home region, having been bought for development work by Optare following its purchase of the rights to the Metrobus model; this mkII example was acquired by Capital Citybus in February as 107 (G107 FJW). Grey-Green lost 451 to an accident in January, replacing it in March with 472 (DTG 372V) formerly of Newport. BTS sold its five Metrobuses to Bullock's after the conversion of local route 355 to single-deck prior to its re-tender. Fulwell's London United Tramways-liveried M1069 retained its special colours upon repaint that month. Leaside commenced the conversion of its private-hire Ms to turbocharged operation, M1379 being treated at Enfield in January. An unusual swap during March and April saw Wood Green's M1443 loaned to Westbourne Park and used on the 18 to evaluate the effect of single-doored buses, M887 going out in return. This wouldn't be the last flirtation the second-hand buses had with CentreWest.

The 52 was split on 28 March, withdrawing between Willesden Garage and Mill Hill Broadway Station so that new route 302 (also Willesden M) could take over; its overlap continued to Ladbroke Grove. The 226, already DT on Sundays, assumed the type on weekdays also. On 25 April the 452 was

withdrawn, only the section to New Malden becoming part of the 152. New route X767, three journeys between Uxbridge and Heathrow, was the Uxbridge M-operated livening up of a staff bus.

For once the replacement of Ms by Darts was not due to fashion; in the case of the routes crossing Hammersmith Bridge, the council had identified continuing weakness with the structure that it considered could only be alleviated by the imposition of a reduced weight limit rather than spend money repairing it properly; thus the 72 at Shepherd's Bush received its DRs on 11 April and the 33 at Fulwell followed suit on 9 May, just one peak journey as far as Barnes, Red Lion (turning at Barnes Pond) seen fit to retain a Metrobus. Ms from both conversions finished off the DMS at Sutton, the last Fleetline operating from there on 19 June.

Also on 9 May the 73 regained a Tottenham share on Sundays, forcing the 67 out to Stamford Hill and its mixed contingent. Four of the Harrow Buses Ms made a triumphant return to London as Capital Citybus 170/1/8/9 (ex-M1470/1/8/2), in full yellow livery for the D6, which was gained from East London and strengthened to force the 106's evening and Sunday services to terminate at Mile End Gate, some distance short of Poplar. Liverpool Street bus station opened from this date, all locally terminating routes being rerouted in and the 271 additionally being extended there at weekends from Moorgate. On 4 July the 209 finally bit the dust, a schoolday-morning M being added instead to the H12.

With privatisation still on the cards (if not deregulation) following the Conservative election win of April, LBL's subsidiaries started preparing

Left: It seemed that the fading London Buses Ltd lived in denial of the worsening threat posed by cheaper operators, and therefore it was no surprise when four of the mkII Metrobuses returned off lease after the winding up of Harrow Buses would bounce straight back to undercut LBL once again. Capital Citybus was the new operator of route D6 from 9 May, and got eleven more years out of these vehicles. 179 (E472 SON) in dazzling yellow and now fitted with London-style blind boxes, is seen at Prestons Road in May.
Tony Wilson

their own private-hire arms, emboldened by Leaside's success in this field. In May Metroline's M1185 became the first to receive Metroline Travel fleetnames and was reupholstered with red moquette. Leaside itself had enough spare capital to purchase 40 Leyland Olympians, which between 9 April and 18 August replaced the Titans at Stamford Hill to produce an M/L mix on the 67, 149 and 253. Enfield fitted its Ms with wheel-hub odometers connected with trials of a fuel-monitoring system. Continuing strange appearances in the first half of 1992 saw Ms on the 11 and 19 at Victoria in lieu of RMs, while at Stockwell they began turning out on VC routes 133 and 196 and at Shepherd's Bush on the 94. At Merton they sometimes subbed for minibuses on the 156; at Uxbridge the big-bus journey (normally an LS) was performed by M304 on 1 May while Alperton's M434 was first to visit the recently-introduced 95 and Edgware Ms wandered to the 288 still (and just once, to minibus-restricted 303). At Croydon Ms could often be found on L routes 197, 403 and 407. Return visits to the 72 (Shepherd's Bush), however, did not include Hammersmith Bridge or roads south. An additional Leaside Metrobus to be treated to private-hire accoutrements was M641, chosen to honour a recently-deceased long-serving Wood Green driver whose favourite bus this was.

The five ex-GM Metrobuses, M1443-7, made another move in June, transferring to Enfield for the 317 with M633/92, 716/9/58 going to Wood Green in exchange. July saw the first conversion to single-door in the form of Holloway's M804, treated by Eastleigh, followed in August by Finchley's M1080; both moved to Potters Bar with the other oddments in October. The London Northern unit similarly detached five Ms for dual-purpose training use through the fitment of a removable handbrake for an instructor; it was no coincidence that four of the six were the swift four-speed examples. In the second half of the year five very early Ms (19/39/43/86/96) arrived at Stamford Brook for conversion to permanent Airbuses in place of the present part-time auxiliaries of B registration; although the new moquette was fitted, it was to the existing bus seats; nor were wheelchair lifts or PA systems fitted.

'Catch the Central Changes' was the battle cry for the year's biggest programme of route changes, implemented on 18 July. Its remit was to split up most of the remaining cross-London crew routes in a vain attempt to cope with the stifling volume of traffic, and in the case of the 6 and 8, allowed for half of each route to be converted to OPO as separate routes. New route 98 (Willesden Garage-Holborn) replaced the western end of the 8, and fielded Willesden Ms on Sundays, while the 6 gave its roads east of Aldwych to new route 26. The Westbourne Park end of the 15 became new route 23 (Ladbroke Grove-Liverpool Street), with OPO Ms on Sundays (and inevitably with the odd crew M on weekdays). This day of the week saw the 9 lose its Ms for Darts, with the whole route now curtailed at Hammersmith to complete the weight limit-related changes to Hammersmith Bridge's bus services begun by the 72 and 33. The 76, meanwhile, now crossed the river over Waterloo Bridge rather than Blackfriars Bridge. At night route N67 was extended from Staines to Egham, while an extension of the N92 southwest to Kingston replaced the N93 over those roads, taking on its Shepherd's Bush allocation to boot. New ground was opened up to Kingston via Richmond in the form of new Holloway and Shepherd's Bush-shared route N65. The N6 and N8 received curtailments commensurate with their daytime equivalents, but N99 was the number chosen for the new Trafalgar Square-Queensbury route operated by Willesden, N98 already being in use. The N21 was marketed under the 'Piccadilly Line' brand name to accompany its rerouteing to Cockfosters via the stations of that Underground line rather than by the direct route.

A new idea bowing on 3 August was the X43, a limited-stop express route over and beyond the 43. While scheduled for Ss from Holloway, its Ms also turned out in numbers; at night the Scanias took over the N92. On the 15th the 88 became the first direct OPO conversion in three years; having gradually lost its mixed bag of re-registered RMs and dwindling RMLs for crew M operation from May onwards, it was further cut between Oxford Circus and Marble Arch. This day also saw Finchley's W7 transferred to Holloway, standardising it as wholly-M under a new three-year contract with London Northern. Holloway's garage journeys to and from the Muswell Hill Broadway terminus, unlike those of its predecessor, ran dead.

Nearly fourteen years had now elapsed since the M type had entered service, so the downgrading of prototype-batch M1-5 in September 1992 to become the first Metrobus trainers hardly represented a waste.

newcomers to the 139 (evenings and Sundays) and 274. In any case the 274 saw them only until the 26th, when it was converted to DRL operation over the following two weeks; the 46 had been treated similarly a month before. All Ts had gone by 24 October.

Now that the DMSs had all but gone, the brunt of withdrawals fell on the Titan fleet; so far the only Metrobuses to be taken out of service at this stage were M1-5, which were shifted to training duties in September. Metroline's own private-hire fleet now constituted M1185/236/73/429, all four-speed examples, with 30 other examples tachograph-fitted. Capital Citybus, however, was encountering social difficulties plaguing its routes south of Romford, and attempted to address this problem by commencing the conversion of its fleet to single-door; Metrobus 296 was the first treated, in September, with the mk IIs following. The conversions accompanied repaint into yellow livery. The majority were done by the end

Left: Now that the DMSs were extinguished, attention turned to the Titan, and one by one the garages that had had to assume T operation between 1988 and 1991 were converted to M. Chalk Farm was the first, exemplified by M921 (A921 SUL) rounding Marble Arch on the 135 on 17 September. Red entrance doors were now part of the LBL livery in its final years, the yellow being painted over upon repaint, while green handrails denoted one of the DiPTAC-suggested accessibility improvements applied to the fleet over 1991/92. *Tony Wilson*

On 5 September a handful of changes along the Edgware Road cut the 32's peak-hour bifurcation back from Mill Hill Broadway to Grahame Park. Further north the main body of the 84 and 242 ceased to operate as Hertfordshire County Council contracts and became wholly commercial services, the former additionally converting on Sundays from M to SR and the latter losing its Sunday service to Thamesway minibuses (on which day HCC conditions still applied). The 73's Stamford Hill allocation was absorbed by Tottenham and the 253 was extended from Mornington Crescent again, but this time to Euston. In south-west London the 200 was minibussed on Sundays and the 152 lost its schoolday Metrobus, while the 57 at Fulwell was lost on tender to London & Country. This released enough Metrobuses to begin the conversion of Chalk Farm's OPO runout from T to M operation from the following day; the 135 was used to Ms but they were

of 1993, other than 275-8 which were left alone. Curiously, the twin-intake roof domes were replaced at the same time by the more common variety with the single central vent.

The 91 number vacated with the Wandsworth scheme was reactivated on 10 October as a renumbering of the 14A; the new Holloway route (its daily remit allowing the removal of the 14's remaining Holloway Ms and roads north of Tottenham Court Road) operating southwards to Trafalgar Square rather than paralleling the 14; as part of this process the 74 was withdrawn between Baker Street and King's Cross. At Capital Citybus the 97A was extended from Walthamstow Central to Whipps Cross and the 257 and 296 were taken on ex-East London, with Metrobuses among the stand-ins on both routes (the former from Northumberland Park and the latter from Dagenham) until the intended buses (ex-Southampton Dominators on the 257 and

Right: West Midlands PTE (later West Midlands Travel) amassed the second largest fleet of Metrobuses after London Transport, taking 1,131, of which 442 were mkls. It was therefore inevitable that they should become hired by one or more London-area concerns, and when Capital Citybus needed to use some of its existing buses to prop up a pair of new tenders at the end of 1992, it filled the gap with 2419 (LOA 419X) and eight compatriots. It is seen on the 248 at Hornchurch in October. *Tony Wilson*

new Olympians on the 296) were ready. The 296's temporary vehicles were displaced by the hiring-in of nine Metrobuses from West Midlands Travel between 5 October and 30 January 1993; they were 2014/39/46/53/9/62 (BOK-V), 2281/4 (KJW-W) and 2419 (LOA-X), which worked on the 248 with the off wanderings. Grey-Green acquired two more Newport Metrobuses in October, 470/1 (DTG 370/1V). Willesden's M50 was damaged by fire and withdrawn in November.

It was unusual by now for Sunday-only routes to be introduced, but on the 18th a second 359 was created by combining the 259 from King's Cross with the 191 service to Edmonton Green. Enfield was in charge. Two new weekend night routes debuted on 31 October; the N17 (Trafalgar Square-Harrow Weald with Harrow Weald Ms) and N66 (Cricklewood-Edgware, with Edgware Ms).

On 24 October the 94's Sunday service passed from Shepherd's Bush to Stamford Brook and gained L operation, though its Ms from the 27 made sure to wander. Shepherd's Bush lost the 295 to London General (Stockwell DRLs), the Ms freed going to Finchley to begin officially the removal of Titans at this other T-operating London Northern garage. 1992 in fact marked the beginning of the end for the Titan, the first examples being sold at the end of the year, and starting on 28 November Norwood's Ts too were ejected by Ms made spare by the uninspired conversion of Merton's 155 and 355 to 28-seat Dart (DR/DW) operation. Merton handed over the Sunday service on the 344 to Victoria's basement (GB), converting it to MRL/SR minibus. The overlap between 52 and 302 was extended with the projection of the latter to Notting Hill Gate on 14 November, while M operation returned to the schoolday-only 189

Right: From a Metrobus that looks like a Volvo Ailsa (see page 70) to a Metrobus that looks like an Olympian! 570 (UMS 751T), Capital Citybus's other ex-Alexander Midland oddity acquired via Kelvin Scottish, was fitted with a front more befitting a Roe-bodied Olympian and is seen at Romford Market in April 1993, yellow livery having been applied three months earlier. *Tony Wilson*

with the transfer of the Monday afternoon journey from Stockwell to Sutton; the other weekdays remained with VCs.

The mkII pair, M1441/2 were treated to a rear-end rebuild at Enfield at the end of the year in order to cure vibration problems, while LBL was so pleased with the success of the safety doors fitted by Leaside to ten Ms during 1992 that it took over the patent and commenced the fitment of the entire fleet with them; they were now opened with a pushbutton rather than the traditional tap device. Meanwhile, some old features were withering away; black-on-white reflective numberplates tended to be fitted more often than not, while to save that little bit extra, foglights began to be removed and flush wings fitted. The majority of the class was so treated beginning in 1993. Coach seating was fitted to Putney's M1432 in January 1993, to accompany its re-registration to WLT 432. Another Putney bus, M818, became one of the first Metrobuses to receive a 'super rear' advert, another feature that would spread rapidly as new ways of income generation were explored. M978 at Sutton was given a between-decks advert for the Wimbledon Theatre, which was served by the 93.

Three otherwise undistinguished transfers, that of M168/70 and 410 to Croydon in November, marked the official replacement of the last three DMSs in London service; the final straggler was withdrawn on 20 January 1993. Another departure was the red livery of pre-tapegrey days, very few examples indeed surviving to the end of 1993.

1993's first change assimilated school route 281s into the regular 281 from 2 January; on the 31st the X767 was withdrawn. As part of a two-phase programme that wound down Hanwell's operations before its closure, the 207 had its proportions adjusted from 6 February to put Uxbridge into the ascendancy, while the 105 and the schoolday M operations of the 282 and E1 were transferred to Alperton and the N89 passed to Uxbridge.

On 10 February Ms began returning to Brixton, regaining control of the 59, 118 and 137A but making their first appearance on route 319, introduced two days earlier as a replacement for the 349. This route was also a partial replacement for the section of the 219 north of Battersea, reflecting changing travel patterns forced by the closure of Battersea Bridge since a barge hit it on 21 April 1992. In the interim most services had been rerouted over Chelsea Bridge. The 21st saw the Sunday service of the 154 minibussed at Sutton.

M804, already single-doored, became the first open-top Metrobus, the work carried out by Kent Coachworks in February; Eastleigh converted M1393/6 to single-door in the same month, adding luggage pens on each deck briefly. All three were to become part of London Northern's answer to the private-hire industry, followed in April by M1067 (fitted with a four-speed gearbox for the purpose). Leaside, meanwhile, upped the ante by renaming its private-hire arm Leaside Travel; new gold fleetnames in an attractive typescript were applied to the Ms, Ts and Ls allocated to the unit. Although Ms were still being re-registered with ex-RM marks, particularly at London General, in February M845 was the first Metrobus to lose its Routemaster plate (545 CLT); since the original OJD 845Y had not been held on to, an unused mark, OGK 708Y, was booked from Wimbledon LVLO in which London General found itself; subsequent similar re-registrations in 1993/4 saw M198 gain SGK 374V, M853 SGC 671Y and M1315 C109 NGH.

Above: After a year and a half with Titans, Brixton garage began gaining back Ms from February 1993; M936 (A936 SUL) is pictured on new route 319, introduced on 8 February 1993 as a rerouteing of the 349's northern objective (to Sloane Square rather than West Brompton). *Colin Stannard*

Right: M804 (KYV 804X) became the first LBL Metrobus converted to open-top configuration, losing its roof in February 1993 so as to become a popular choice for route Z1, a seasonal service to and from London Zoo that had hitherto been operated as a summer-only extension of the 2 (or later 2B). This bus had already been converted to single-door and continued to operate like that at Holloway until this grander role was found for it. It is seen at Regents Park on 12 April 1993. *Tony Wilson*

Grey-Green took ex-Newport 466-9 (DTG 366-9V) in March to add to 470-2, allowing its last ex-SYPTE DMS-lookalike Fleetlines to reduce in number and render the whole 173 Metrobus-operated; an extension of this route from 5 June brought them to King George Hospital in Goodmayes.

On 6 March a switcharound within Metroline restored Cricklewood to full use at the expense of the costly modern Edgware. Of the M routes only the 240 remained at Edgware (the site now restricted to just the hardstanding outside), the 32, 113, 143A, N16, N59 and N66 going into (or back into) Cricklewood. The security issue of open garages or even parking spaces outside was underscored when Sutton's M599 was burnt out by an arsonist in March.

Kingston over the 111 to Hounslow. At South London, the 2 group was rejigged, trunk route 2B becoming plain 2 and regaining an evening and Sunday through service with Norwood Ls and Ms, thus reducing the 2A to weekdays, Brixton-Crystal Palace only. Vulcan Way in Addington lost its bus service with the removal of the 130 from that point and DT-operated 412 gained a double-deck spur to Wallington Station, away from its normal roads. The 220 was also converted to Dart on Sundays, Shepherd's Bush Ms giving way to Wood Lane DRs.

Open-top M804's summer employment in 1993 was on Zoo Bus Z1, operated by Chalk Farm from 9 April (weekends only from this date). On the 17th the 76 was extended experimentally to Northumberland

Below right: Still able to reach Uxbridge, though rather slower about it than the express 607, route 207 was subject to an alteration in 1993 with the closure of Hanwell garage and the opening of Acton Tram Depot to take over its allocation. This is where M274 (BYX 274V) would work from for most of the rest of its London life, and in this 22 January 1994 shot has geared up for privatisation by donning CentreWest's new garage-based logos, this one being EALING BUSES. The foglights have also been pulled out and the holes replaced by blank wings, a fairly needless modification that would spread to the vast majority of Ms starting from about now. *John Laker*

Above: On 27 March 1993 DT-operated route 412 sprouted a double-deck duty to cater for school traffic; Croydon's M1090 (B90 WUL) is doing the honours when espied at Wallington on 30 June 1994. *Mike Harris*

Hanwell closed finally on 27 March, the minibus routes going to the former council depot at Greenford (G) and the remaining double-deck operations on the 207 swallowed up by Acton Tram Depot (AT), a new base for 24 of the M class. At night Shepherd's Bush discarded all its night routes, the N92 being absorbed by Potters Bar (and losing Ms for Ss), while the N50/N56 went to Westbourne Park, the N67 and N97 to Stamford Brook (with Ls, only the Hounslow share of these two retaining Ms) and the N11 and N65 passing to Hounslow; to get its Ms home in the morning, the N65's last journey was projected from

Park Tesco, an experiment which was successful enough to last beyond the initial six months. That weekend saw the 221 succumb to Darts on Sundays, in this case Wood Green DRLs from the 84A, but in the other direction the 84 regained its Sunday Ms. The 24th saw the momentous transfer of RML route 19 to Kentish Bus; Ms thus left the Sunday OPO service as well; to keep the increasingly doomed-looking Victoria garage's crews operational, the 14 was transferred thence on Sundays from Holloway. This garage's own 74 was withdrawn between Baker Street and King's Cross, while at Hounslow the 232 was transformed into new DRL-operated H32; the Ms displaced were sent to Brixton. M1069 was loaned for the 232's last day and then visited the 140. In order to let the new H32 accustom itself to its smaller size (a withdrawal between Southall and Northolt accompanying the single-decking), the 120 was extended to Northolt and on Sundays converted back to M operation, if just to standardise the service due to its choice as a future low-floor LLW route. Willesden's 302 was converted from M to LN-class Dennis Lance operation, shedding some Ms to Brixton. All these Dart and large single-deck conversions failed to dislodge Ms entirely, the type continuing to turn out on the 95, 156, 170, 226, 297, 302, 607, H32, H91 and H98 during 1993 and now beginning to visit the H23 and R70 converted earlier in the decade; debut workings this year included the 190 at Stamford Brook. Subs for Routemasters, meanwhile, continued on the remaining core of two dozen routes.

Two more RML-operated routes were one-manned during weekday evenings from 22 May, the 23 (Westbourne Park) and 94 (Shepherd's Bush's union insisting this work remain with the garage rather than ship out to cheaper Stamford Brook, though the latter's Ls did gain two journeys at these hours). The 222 at Uxbridge was strengthened in frequency enough to replace the adjacent 223 (and, for the same reasons as the 120, returned to M operation on Sundays). Not long after its reallocation, the N50/N56 diagram was withdrawn and incorporated into new route N23, which followed the daytime 23 from Trafalgar Square and beyond to Ealing Broadway. The last two evening 23s were extended to continue past East Acton via the 70 to Ealing

Repair Centre attached to Enfield garage) was M1253, which stood out from the rest due to its treatment to illuminated panels either side of the blind box, proudly displaying the Leaside cygnet. On each deck was fitted a digital clock (soon upgraded in size to examples powered off the bus rather than using a battery each), while its sliding side windows had been replaced by hoppers and 1992-style 'Eyes Down' seat moquette was carried to accompany its Transmatic lighting and new flooring. It was handed over on 13 May. Routine advancements involved the use of Datatrak fuel-monitoring equipment on Stamford Brook Ms, while at Leaside two fuel additive systems (US-manufactured Ceramic Monolith and Silicon) were evaluated.

Somewhat less welcome modifications saw continuing conversions to fixed front upper-deck windows; M1426 of Willesden only had its offside pane done, and would not be the first to be going around 'half-and-half'. For no particular reason, Chalk Farm swapped its recently-acquired Metrobuses for Holloway's very oldest, mostly T-registered examples in a process taking a couple of months over the spring. Looking to the future and taking a cue from the recently-introduced Uxbridge Buses identity, CentreWest began applying GOLD ARROW fleetnames to all Westbourne Park's buses from June, M892 and 952 being the first Metrobuses treated. In some cases at Uxbridge, the offside LBL roundel found itself re-sited ignominiously to the emergency door.

Left: Victoria garage bit the dust in 1993, but its last hurrah was to provide the buses for an augmentation of the 11 during repairs to Charing Cross station's trackwork. This was known as 11A, and on 29 July 1993 was being held down by M849 (OJD 849Y) at Victoria Station, with refurbished RML2606 (NML 606E), now working from the Red Arrow base at Waterloo, for comparison. *Malc McDonald*

Broadway and only then would change their blinds to N23, an unusual variation which was tidied up in the N23's favour just two months later) while also at Ealing Broadway a bifurcation was introduced to the N89, taking a proportion of it to Ruislip over the former N50. This was operated by Alperton, and worked on and off the 105. Grey-Green's 125 was from 22 May customarily operated with single-deck Volvo B10Ms during evenings.

In the absence of Aldenham, local initiative was undertaken to refurbish Metrobuses here and there; Leaside did M425 for CentreWest by April (this bus gaining, as well as soft trim throughout, new UXBRIDGE BUSES logos designed after the yellow CentreWest half-arrow) and London United cut a deal with Hants & Dorset for similar work. Meanwhile M162 was added to the permanent Airbus fleet in May, standing in for accident-damaged Ms 1006/10. Airbus grew and grew with the addition of six more Ms (187, 221/3, 462, 506/26) to the roster, their conversions carried out by Eastleigh. Metroline Travel, the new private-hire arm of Metroline, detached a handful of Ms (403/29/49/60) for this role with an appropriate fleetname and new red moquette, while M1236 gained blue seating. Leaside's pilot refurbishment (performed by the unit's Accident

One route to lose Ms had only just received them; this was the 88, which received 13 new VN-class Volvo B10Bs from 15 May; the five Ms Stockwell sent away were selected for Airbus conversion as above. A spring of strike action as LBL's jittery subsidiaries geared up for privatisation was accompanied by the abolition of the block grant system from 1 April and the concurrent re-tendering of jointly-operated services. On 26 June the night routes emanating from Enfield were tidied up, the N9 coming off and the N29 strengthened and extended to cover it, together with a single journey of the 121 projected over the defunct N9's routeing.

Another closure followed, that of Victoria, which had become unviable since losing the 19. The main site was closed on 17 July, the M routes (52, 344, N11, N19 and the three 11s on Sundays) being transferred to Stockwell and the 14's Sunday workings passing to Putney, ejecting the 22 wholly into Merton. The 11 itself was withdrawn west of Fulham Broadway so new Dart-run 211 could partially one-man it, and the possibility of Ms ceased with the route's weekday transfer to the Red Arrow base at Waterloo. The Z1 was introduced on Mondays to Fridays from this date. Victoria, however had one last hurrah when a dozen Ms were kept back to run a temporary 11A

Right: Threatened ever since the 24 was lost to Grey-Green, Chalk Farm garage staved off closure by redeploying its assets to adjacent routes, but was finally finished off by the announcement that two Holloway routes, the 4 and 271, would be passing to an independent and that Holloway could fill their loss and more by swallowing up Chalk Farm's entire runout. This took place on 31 July and in September M118 (BYX 118V) is seen in Abbey Road working one of Chalk Farm's former routes, the 139. The 'PAY CONDUCTOR' plate shouldn't be taken as gospel by this time, as the scheduled M element on this route (evenings and weekends) was OPO, so this picture (whose date is not narrowed down to a particular day in September) is quite probably of a crew-operated interloper, something quite common for the 139. *Tony Wilson*

(Victoria-Cannon Street) between 26 July and 13 August as part of a rail-replacement scheme covering for the rail lines in and out of Waterloo East and Charing Cross. Extras were also added to part of the 38 for this period, M1437 being one of the crew-operated Leaside Travel vehicles assigned, while M1379 and standard M1000 were also sighted. M593 managed to get out on the normal 38 with a conductor on 13 August during this period, otherwise a very rare working indeed. The 11A's stragglers were dispersed during August, being shared out equally between Sutton, Merton and Stockwell.

London Northern's tough 1993 continued with the inevitable closure of Chalk Farm on 31 July; its four routes (including M-operated 135 and its evening and Sunday cross-link to the 139) were swallowed up seamlessly by Holloway, returning all 17 early Ms that had been transferred there during the spring! Also going over was the summers-only Z1, the province of open-top M804. The unit was further rocked on 10 August with the announcement of the award of the 13 to BTS.

Fulwell's Ms on the 71 were rerouted via Surbiton Station on 28 August, the Hounslow allocation on the 281 coming off on the same day, while the 285 was partially converted back to M operation, the DTs and DRs not being able to cope on this busy link. Schoolday route 98A, however, did not survive after the summer term (ending on 23 July), also the last day the 189 worked from London General.

As Titan withdrawals topped 200, nine Ms

(16/26/37, 106/8, 229, 312/77, 501) were withdrawn in August, becoming the first examples of the class to be sold by LBL during October; as with the majority of the Ts so far, they made Merseybus their new home – for now, at least. M312 was broken up to provide spares for them. These had been London General examples; the company otherwise had plans for the rest of its very large fleet that involved a frontal redesign that gave the radiator greater breathing room and incorporated a cutout designed to fit a stylised B-type bus vinyl; the numberplate (increasingly in white) was resited underneath. M218 and 975 were the first. The first all-over advert to grace the class was a white-fading-into-blue piece for the Royal Academy of Arts' 'American Art in the 20th Century' exhibition, carried by Stockwell's M435 between September and December. M1440 followed in October, this Sutton bus receiving a white base coat with orange graffiti-style wording so as to perform a tour of PC World outlets promoting Olivetti computers.

Right: As privatisation crept closer, strictures against all-over adverts were relaxed as long as they were not put into service; thus M435 (GYE 435W) out of Stockwell garage received an advert for an exhibition shared between the Royal Academy of Arts and the Saatchi gallery in Abbey Road, and was put to work on a free service linking the two venues. In September 1993 the bus is seen at the latter. *Tony Wilson*

On 4 September new night route N253 was introduced over the existing 253, the Mile End Gate shorts of which were extended to a new stand behind Whitechapel Station; this was also the new southern terminus for the 106. Two hard-pressed minibus routes gained official M augmentation in September, Edgware's 204 on the 6th and Hounslow's H22 from the 16th. London Northern was hit hard with the loss of routes 4 and 271 to new Liverpool-derived independent London Suburban Buses on 25 September, but enough Holloway Ms were freed to oust Finchley's last Titans, additional transfers allowing Potters Bar's four remaining Tyne & Wear imports M1481-4 to be stood down from this date while still others reduced Brixton's T holdings to single figures. As part of the concurrent Newham-area scheme, Grey-Green's 173 was converted to Dart operation (other than one schoolday double-decker) and cut back to East Beckton, new double-deck route 473 (Stratford-Beckton) permitting the continued use of the Metrobuses. On 9 October Croydon took on the 50 from Thornton Heath, reintroducing Ms alongside Ls. This date also saw the introduction of a most unusual peak-hour service; operated by Stamford Brook's Airbus Ms as a cross-link to and from the A2, the 609 was a with-the-flow express of six journeys from Mortlake to Barnes, then into town as far as Bank. It was nominally worked by the low-numbered recent conversions.

At Leaside, Wood Green's M650 was unveiled on the 29th as the first 'Talking Bus' – inside a voice synthesiser (partially funded by the Disabled Passengers Unit) had been fitted, activated by the driver to call out stops along the vehicle's assigned route 29 for a period of six months. Contemporaneous to the first withdrawals were the first conversions to dedicated trainers at London United, the buses receiving a table and cabinet downstairs plus an instructor's seat and brake to render capacity H0/20D.

After a dozen postponements, the second Metroline route to take on the LN class was converted on 2 October in the form of the 113; already sufficient doubts had been entertained about the Lances' length to effectively convert the 302 on Sundays back to M after only four months, Willesden's hand being tipped by the necessity to divert the route on Sundays away from the canal bridge in Ladbroke Grove during its repair. For this purpose Willesden had to borrow extensively from adjacent garages' Metrobus holdings. Cricklewood's refugees from the 113 finished off the Titan at Brixton by the first week of October and made a start on Thornton Heath, restoring the M class to the 109 and introducing them occasionally to the 60, 250, 264 and 312. At Potters Bar,

the N92 was effectively converted back to M from 5 October due to the taller Scanias' fouling trees along the route's leafier sections. New schoolday route 326s bowed on 1 November out of Potters Bar, shadowing the 326 between Totteridge and Dame Alice Owen school in Sawyers Lane.

The loss of the 13 to BTS forced the closure of Finchley on 4 December, reducing London Northern to just two garages. Of these, Potters Bar took on the 82, necessitating a dead run almost as long as the route itself (and only reduced slightly by the route's extension regularly to North Finchley in place of the 13), plus the N13 and N21 (both sprouting extensions to Potters Bar garage), totalling 13 Ms, and Holloway gained the 134 and N2 with 19 Ms. The X43 moved from Holloway to Potters Bar, its special-liveried Scanias edging the Saturday Ms off the 84 (in theory if not generally in practice) plus one for the afternoon journey on schoolday route 326s. London General lost the 52 to London Coaches, the first of the LBL operating arms to have been privatised but only now commencing stage operation (with second-hand Titans); the shortfall from Stockwell poured into Thornton Heath, ousting Ts. Two more evening OPO conversions were the 6 and 98 at Willesden, but not enough Ms were in stock to service them both, so LNs from the 302 had to feature prominently. M appearances were eliminated from the 204 with its move from Edgware to North Wembley, but the type continued to wander, occasionally to DR-operated routes 288 and 303. A single schoolday journey on the 50 to Old Coulsdon was combined with London & Country route 409 and adopted the latter number; while meant for Ls, Croydon's Ms could soon be seen, additional to their increasing wanderings to the 197, 403 and 407.

With few new double-deckers entering service in such an uncertain era, the next best course of action

Above: Grey-Green added to its Metrobus fleet in 1992/93, taking seven ex-Newport examples to replace its DMS clones that had held down the 173 since 1987. On 4 September 1993 this route was single-decked and cut back, the Stratford-Beckton end becoming new route 473, as 467 (DTG 367V) demonstrates at Stratford on 21 July 1995. *Malc McDonald*

Right: The need for flexibility ensured Ms would continue to turn out on routes that had otherwise been converted to minibus or Dennis Dart operation, and the appearance of Hounslow's M1212 (B212 WUL) on the H23 on 1 July 1994 was typical of several routes during this year. As well as its white numberplates, spreading fast, it is displaying a sticker for just the latest ticketing experiment which this time delved into the realm of smartcard technology for the first time. This particular version did not find favour, but the Oystercard would a decade later, by which time the M class was just finishing its career. *Mike Harris*

Left: Metrobuses and Olympians battled it out for supremacy at Croydon garage for a number of years following the Ms' return in 1992, and on 12 March 1994 the 312 was put in from Thornton Heath. Either class could be considered standard, with M1359 (C359 BUV) accompanied by L99 (C99 CHM) on 29 April. *Colin Stannard*

was refurbishment; in the case of the LSs this meant conversion to Greenway format, and when Uxbridge's started going away early in December what should replace them but M1448-51, the ex-Yorkshire Rider mkIIs in their dotage! They popped up on the 207 and 222 as well as the 607. Even more unusually, M1449 then turned up at Westbourne Park, running on the 23 throughout January, but this was their last hurrah; all four were withdrawn in February.

BTS, preparing for the loss of route 292 back to Edgware (from 4 December), took the incumbent Scanias off three weeks early, replacing them with four Metrobuses hired from West Midlands Travel – BOK 46V and GOG 110/3/99W. From the same week mkIIs POG 583Y and A698 UOE from the same source were loaned to County Bus for use on the 310 and 311; they lasted until May.

Perhaps the one bright spot in another difficult year for London's buses was the official discarding of deregulation as an option, as announced in the Queen's Speech of 8 November; still, the timetable for privatisation would now be stepped up to take place in 1994.

Left: A year later M1359 (C359 BUV) became one of South London's private-hire representatives, also appearing on service as needed. The 68A was created on 12 March 1994 out of Croydon's allocation on the 68 and worked no further north than the Elephant & Castle, from where this bus has travelled to Croydon town centre one day in May 1995. In 1998 the route would be renumbered 468. *Chris Evans*

Garage. At London United, an official M journey was added to Stamford Brook's 190 (after several rogue runnings and the otherwise simultaneous conversion to DT-class Dart operation) and to Hounslow's H22 and H32; a similar exercise at CentreWest from the 10th had introduced one Acton Tram Depot M to the E3. The 173, however, lost its schoolday double-decker to new route 673, exemplifying the renumbering of such services into the six hundreds. At Stamford Brook the 609 became scheduled for the coach-seated Airbus Ms.

On 26 February more night-bus alterations replaced routes N65 and N67 by a new N9 (operated by Stamford Brook) and a bifurcation to the N97 (Hounslow) respectively; the former alteration also allowed

OPO conversions, while very rare at this point given the resurgence in favour of the Routemaster family, could still be implemented from time to time, and on 29 January the recently-revived 2 fell; as well as gaining M/L operation (predominantly the former, examples coming south from Palmers Green) out of its native Norwood, it swallowed up the 2A, though the two-section format continued. At Brixton the 59 (reduced to peaks only since 2 February 1991) was withdrawn, the 118 being one of the routes strengthened to compensate and the 109 losing its weekend Brixton buses to Croydon and Thornton Heath. Also on this date the 41 was lost to London Suburban Bus, this company also commencing at night with the takeup of the N6; other revisions to night routes took off all of N17, N59 and N66, transferred the N99's contract from Metroline (Willesden) to CentreWest (Westbourne Park) and improved the N16 to run Edgware-Victoria throughout (transferring it simultaneously from Cricklewood to Edgware); and finally the 139 gained a night service numbered N139 (operated by Westbourne Park). From this date Edgware's M operations on the 240 switched allegiance within Metroline, becoming outstationed to Harrow Weald rather than Cricklewood. In spite of being garaged around the Metroline fleet, the Commercial Services fleet took to carrying 'CS' codes.

The first conversion from M to LLW was of the 120 on 29 January. In preparation for its own low-floor buses (to be the SLW-class Scania variant) the 144A was reallocated from Enfield to Wood Green, losing its projections beyond Edmonton Green to Enfield

the N92 to pull back into town. Stockwell lost its portion of the N11 with its award to London United alone, while it was the turn of the 91 and 134 to sprout N-numbered night variants both operated, like their daytime counterparts, by Holloway's Ms.

Still-lengthy trunk route 68 was divided on Saturday 12 March, the Norwood section falling back to its home garage forecourt and new 68A (Elephant-South Croydon Garage) assuming the Croydon buses with just peak-hour Norwood support; only the limited-stop peak-hour X68 continued the through service. Croydon pulled out of the 109 but took on the 312 from Thornton Heath. Additionally, night routes N69 and N78 were withdrawn, removing Thornton Heath from night work. This garage's last Titan, T373, was withdrawn on 9 March, completing the conversion of South London to M.

The 222 at Uxbridge was converted to LLW operation from 12 March, the Ms passing to Norwood, Croydon and Thornton Heath. A curious swap between Wood Green and Palmers Green this month equalised their respective ages of Metrobuses, Ms numbered between 353 and 627 moving to the former and those between 635 and 929 to the latter. Both garages' complements were fitted with pooled blinds and carried each other's garage codes for maximum interchangeability, making this rather moot. The 46 at Holloway gained a morning peak M from the 28th.

The 317 (minus its roads to Upshire) was awarded to London Northern on 26 March at the expense of Leaside, Potters Bar Ms now replacing Enfield's five GBU-V-registered Ms, which were placed in store

Left: Metroline Travel added another word to the existing cross-hatched Metroline fleetname and deleted the grey skirt; the company was already refurbishing the Ms it had detached for various contract and private-hire roles under this arm of the business prior to privatisation. M460 (GYE 460W) has been assigned to rail replacement when caught at Camden Town on 5 March 1995. *Malc McDonald*

As the very last non-tapegrey Ms squeaked into 1994, they would soon have to be reliveried again as privatisation loomed. The first LBL subsidiary to jump ship was Westlink to its management on 20 January (and sold on to West Midlands Travel only six weeks later at a profit). The only Metrobus to attend the pre-privatisation press call at Hyde Park Corner on 24 March, represented by each LBL subsidiary, was Metroline's M444.

London United started the ball rolling by applying Airbus fleetnames to the *roofs* of that fleet (bar the oldest ones). Leaside and Metroline Ms were already coming back from repaint minus their LBL roundels, while in February London United made permanent trainer M30 the first recipient of a most elegant red and cream livery; M13/22/31/6/46, 147, 206/64 would follow over 1994. In May London Northern painted Potters Bar's M563 into the 'X43' livery of red with white roof and grey skirt, while South London gave Croydon's M1359 coach seats and a beige midriff to accompany its transfer into that subsidiary's private-hire arm South London Travel. Metroline dawdled somewhat in applying the grey skirts and tape bands, M97 in April being the first to appear in all-red, but did its best by re-registering five private-hire Ms with Routemaster marks. Best of all, however, Sutton's M1440 was repainted for London

Below: M1055 (A755 THV) of London General was treated to an all-over advertisement for the Whitechapel Art Gallery, including the 'oranges and lemons' of the locally-inspired nursery rhyme. In June 1994, however, it is a long way from the East End as it helps out on the Wimbledon tennis service, always a seasonal diversion for Sutton crews. *Geoff Rixon*

pending a decision on what to do with them next. The school journeys became 617 and 629 and passed to Leaside Travel's Titans, only occasionally seeing visits from the four-speed Ms allocated. Leaside Travel's new image included elegant gold signwriting, and M1379 was the first allocated private-hire M to get the treatment; all four were concentrated at Stamford Hill in June. Cricklewood's four-speed Ms, meanwhile, were upgraded with coach seating for Metroline Travel early in 1994, while M460 joined that fleet in January and M444 was refurbished with new grey seating and saloon walls plus yellow handrails; it was also the first M to receive blinds with fluorescent yellow characters, a fad adopted quickly by its refurbished fellows.

General in full 1933 livery with 'GENERAL' fleetnames, as the replacement for similarly-liveried RM89, which was sold. Allocated, as before, to Sutton, from April, it made its home on the 80 when not in special use. Further special treatment saw it fitted with coach seating and given a name – *The General*.

In March County Bus replaced its two loaned West Midlands Metrobuses with two older examples new to Newport Transport, M75/80 (JBO 75/80W) acquired through Ensign and there painted into company cream and green. No 2698 did not depart until June, when it was replaced by 2781 (B781 AOC) pending M75's preparation. The Birmingham connection endured when Kentish Bus found itself unready to assume fully its large swathe of south-east London tendering gains from 12th March; to displace existing double-deckers from the 132, 228, 328 and 492 at Dartford to Lewisham-based route 161 came three mk Is (BOK 48V, GOG 110/99W, the second and third having already been used in London by BTS) and seven mark IIs (ROX 659Y, A676, 734/5 UOE, A739/60 WVP and B781 AOC). Four (2048/110/734/60) went home after two weeks, the other six working largely on the 132 until the last week of April, by which time the intended new Volvo Olympians had arrived. Nos 2199 and 2676, however, were kept on briefly for school use at Northfleet before returning in June; 2781 moved on to County Bus and 2199 did not finally depart until 8 July. In April the ex-GM Buses Ms returned to service, M1443/5/7 at Stamford Hill and the other two joining them there after working briefly from Wood Green. A union agreement saw them restricted to the 149.

Increasing co-operation between Norwood and Brixton garages saw the former loan Ms to the latter for occasional crew work on the 137 and 159 during the spring, with plenty of indigenous Brixton Ms at work too; this was partly to cover for the 159's dedicated RM batch going away for mini-refurbishment as per that route's contract terms.

A most unusual occurrence was the loan of Shepherd's Bush's M1073 to Wood Lane (B) minibus depot on 3 May to perform a short working on the 9A between Hammersmith and Queen's Gate – further such loans followed throughout the spring and were also used on the 72, reallocated to this base since its conversion to DR in 1992.

In order to allow London General's Red Arrow depot at Waterloo to close on Saturdays as well as Sundays, the 11 was reallocated to Stockwell on that day from 9 April and converted to OPO M. The 152's M duty migrated from Sutton to Merton on that day, freeing space for the latter's 156 to gain one similar double-deck working. London General's London By Night Tour became the province of Putney's M47, fitted with a PA system for the purpose, while M1055 continued this subsidiary's head start in all-over ads with a light blue scheme (plus 'oranges and lemons'

decals) for the Whitechapel Art Gallery. After use on the appropriate service, it joined M978 and M1440 on the 93.

At Holloway increased M appearances on the 274 were to train the C2's drivers on vehicles as long as the DNLs with which they were about to be supplied early in June. On 25 June the 234 at Potters Bar was demoted from M to SR minibus operation to permit a rerouteing via untapped backstreets, while the 263 was rerouted to terminate at Barnet Hospital, leaving the roads across the border to Potters Bar Garage roads to a combination of 84 and X43. The Airbus add-on route 609 also came off after this date. After a

month with a single Lance SLF on a supplementary duty, the 186 at Harrow Weald assumed full LLW operation, though retaining one M at schooltimes and seeing still more due to the new buses' teething troubles.

The treatment of several stops along the 18 to Countdown vehicle-location technology earlier in 1994 was now applied to five Westbourne Park Ms (505, 1245/67, 1380, 1415) from June, a digital indicator being fitted on each deck to display the next stop in red LEDs. Conversions to fixed windows at Leaside gathered pace in 1994, Tottenham and Wood Green Ms being first in line to lose their openers. A return of past practice from May or thereabouts saw rear ads once again pasted either side of Ms' rear blind boxes, the horizontal frame being removed. Ten South London Ms from the T- and V-registered holdings were reclassified as dual-purpose trainers/service buses, gaining an extra external mirror for the use of an instructor.

The last service changes of unified London Buses Ltd, other than the 255's introduction on Saturdays from 23 July, came on 6 August when the split of the 112 produced new double-deck route 232 over the eastern section, commencing from St Raphael's Estate and then joining the North Circular to continue to Wood Green. London Northern was the winner, with Potters Bar taking Ms from Holloway (which was originally slated to run this route).

Above: The North Circular Road is hard enough on cars, let alone buses! The 112 used to do a good quarter of it until split in two in the 1970s, before being reunited and now, from 6 August 1994, split again. This time the eastern section was numbered 232 (the previous incarnation had been 212) and was promoted to double-deck with Potters Bar Ms like M1355 (C355 BUV), captured leaving Brent Cross on 18 August. One foglight is missing and the 'M' 'C' 'W' letters it had when new are long gone, while the nearside roof corner has been patched, a very common amendment to the M class in later years. *Tony Wilson*

FIVE

Privatisation and Return

Sixty-one years of unified London bus operation drew to an ignominious end in the autumn of 1994. The application of LT roundels had dwindled over the summer and became history upon privatisation, with 'London Transport Buses' now a regulatory authority only. CentreWest was the first LBL subsidiary to jump ship on 2 September, via a management buyout. The company promptly dropped its trading name in favour of the local identities it had been phasing in based on each garage, the latest of which was CHALLENGER for Alperton's services.

Leaside became the next M operator to go over to the private sector, this time to the Cowie Group from 29 September, and Metroline passed to its management on 7 October. On the following day the company acquired (or, in the case of Edgware garage, regained) the 107 from Atlas Bus, but due to the late arrival of the intended EDR-class 9.8m Darts and European employment law, sub-contracted back to them with Metrobuses on loan (usually M62/87, 135, 367, 1342); this situation lasted until 5 November, when the route (and its staff) were formally adopted. Metroline's relationship with Atlas Bus, which was to become considerably closer, had been initiated on 26 September when M87, 1342/66, 1428 were loaned to the Harlesden depot to fill in for recalcitrant Titans on the 52; these Willesden Metrobuses still carried route 52 blinds used before 4 December 1993! Atlas Bus logos were added to the sides of participating buses. The Metroline Travel imprint expanded that autumn, assuming first an X2 shopper's express on 19 October and, three days later, a Terminal 4 shuttle using the coach-seated Ms.

On 3 September the Airbus operation opened a new outstation at Heathrow, West Ramp (WR); 16 Ms at any time were kept there overnight. After just a year in Airbus colours, M86, 221/3/506 were stood down at the end of October and prepared for return to service, retaining their new seating; meanwhile, *bona fide* Airbuses from the elder contingent had been turning out on the 237!

On 2 November London General was sold to its management; M1055 (ex-Whitechapel Art Gallery) was first into the new livery, which consisted of just an extra yellow line above the grey skirt; the fleetname, however, was altered to the style of the 'Clapham Omnibus' VNs, with an orange vertical stripe. The frontal treatment on this bus and subsequent conversions was also revised to omit the B-type-shaped indentation and allow the new fleetname to take its place; a horizontal aluminium strip now bisected the grille so as to let the yellow band continue all the way round. A third variety still was just a plate fastened over the nearside third of the grille on which to affix the logo. On the nearside, the new logo's orange bar obstructed the running number holders, so these were repositioned forward to the bay between the doors. M256 gained 'GENERAL' fleetnames all round.

London United, another management buyout from 5 November, truly excelled, however, with the repaint of Fulwell's M813/5, 1262 into red with a light grey roof and grey skirt (both surmounted by a white line), complete with adverts for the 285 on which they were based. London United's new logo was a reworked version of its tramways-style crest and was applied to the front, leading to the removal of the PAY DRIVER/PAY CONDUCTOR plates. The company was also first to evaluate dayglo blinds on its Ms; these would be adopted as standard over 1995 by all contractors, funds being released by LTB to pay for their manufacture.

The first day of the new school year saw the 84A's school journey renumbered 684 and a new 699, emanating from Southgate Station, appended to the 84 at Potters Bar. The 112 sprouted a schoolday duty allocated to CentreWest at Alperton and proceeding beyond its new terminus of Brent Cross to East Finchley Cemetery.

On 10 September the introduction of routes 191 and 259 on Sundays obviated the need for the 359; that day also saw all three of 217, 231 and 317 at Potters Bar demoted to MW minibus on Sundays. The first Scania low-floor single-deckers made their debut on 17 September, 15 of these SLWs going to Wood Green for new route 144 (ex-144A); 14 Ms were transferred to Palmers Green, which then ejected its eldest Ms to Clapton to become trainers in place of the company's Titans hitherto used. On the 25th the E3's double-decker was introduced between the peaks to run along the whole route. Between 26 September and 7 October Capital Citybus 112 was loaned to County Bus for use on its route 510; amid the privatisation of the LBL companies County Bus and its parent, the Lynton Travel group, passed to West Midlands Travel on 7 October. The first of October saw the U1's big bus withdrawn to accompany extensive reductions throughout.

London Northern left LBL ownership on 26 October for that of MTL Trust Holdings. Late in the following month experiments were undertaken with potential liveries; M576's treatment to two shades of red separated by a white band was trumped by M1287, which was repainted allover red with the fleetname *MTL LONDON NORTHERN* in beige Helvetica italics over the blind box. The main fleetname was rather more ornate, being surmounted by a diagonal flash, and just to make sure the new company ownership was imprinted on those boarding, 'MTL Trust Holdings Limited' logos were applied above the entrance doors. This livery was adopted and repaints commenced, carried out at a rapid pace by Greengates; an early 'hearts and minds' move to cement the new order in the eyes of the public was the priority deployment of repainted Ms on the 82, 91 and 135 working into central London until enough were available to work on any route.

29 October saw Metrobuses introduced to Westlink; the company's swift purchase by West Midlands only six weeks into management ownership was now bearing fruit in that schoolday route 661 required three more buses and in WMT country, these were Metrobuses. Thus to Kingston came POG 594Y and B878/9 DOM from the parent company's large fleet of mkIIs. From mid-December they spread their net to the 411, created on 29 October out of the western end of the 131. Traditionally Country-area routes 403 and 407 of South London were returned to London & Country from 29 October; although these had been L-dedicated routes, thirteen Croydon Ms were delicensed. On the 30th the need to use Ms on the 113 and 302 on Sundays prompted the conversion of the 32 to LN on that day of the week, portending further developments with this route. Metroline duly assumed the 107 contract on 5 November, EDR-class 9.8m Darts now taking over but with official M support continuing at peak times. An extension to the N253's Euston end from the 26th connected it to the rest of the Night Bus network at Trafalgar Square.

Metroline spent the autumn preparing ten Ms (M313/5/35/76/80, 424/37/8, 937/68) to upgrade the ambience on the 292, with assistance from Hertfordshire County Council, into whose territory the route ran. This involved refurbishment (with new floors and blue-based seating taken from the existing Metroline Travel Ms, some of which were further downseated to provide extra luggage space), new Transmatic fluorescent lighting and a coat of grey paint over the brown surfaces), and repaints into all-red. So far all-red was the colour scheme chosen generally, the grey skirts beginning to disappear from existing Metroline Ms by year's end. The company became the first to spread its wings, purchasing Atlas Bus on 28 November and formalising the continuing loans of Ms to its Harlesden base, now coded HR. Not quite a new livery, but rather charming nonetheless, was the spraying of 'snow' around the windows of M428 and 1202 for use on the 16 in the runup to Christmas!

Below: The onset of privatisation cut away company after company between 2 September and 10 December 1994 until LBL was no more. Metroline jumped ship on 7 October and settled with its management, and no time was wasted casting around for acquisitions from among the independents moored in its territory. The regaining of the 107 for operation from Edgware garage necessitated a period where the former staff of Atlas Bus were taken on and the Ms used had Atlas Bus fleetnames applied; M1342 (C342 BUV), transferred from Willesden, displays two sets of fleetnames when seen at Edgware bus station in October. *Tony Wilson*

Left: London General's first forays towards the post-LBL world involved creating a new grille for its Metrobuses which included a recess milled to fit an increased-size representation of its 'Ole Bill' B-type bus logo. The application is seen on Stockwell's M214 (BYX 214V) at the Elephant & Castle on 4 March 1995. The design was subsequently altered so that a redesigned company fleetname replaced the B-type bus logo and the gaping grille was bisected by a chrome strip so that the yellow band added to the grey skirt could continue all the way around the bus. *Malc McDonald*

All the LBL subsidiaries were now gone – except for South London. Dogged by high staff turnover and chastised by the Traffic Commissioner regarding unsatisfactory standards of maintenance over the previous three years, the company had its Operator's Licence curtailed to just six months, giving it a very short time in which to pick up its act sufficient to tempt a private-sector buyer. This turned out to be the Cowie group, which exchanged documents on 8 December to add the company and its 160 Ms to Leaside Buses. M384's treatment to a dark green skirt and similar cantrail band did not find favour, so for the moment, livery and fleetnames were left alone, save for a *'COWIE GROUP PLC'* vinyl transfer added just above the bonnet at rear.

The surprise sale of Capital Citybus 292 to Ensignbus (as 192, with yellow livery quickly applied) on 25 November left 294 the company's last dual-door Metrobus of those planned for single-door conversion and yellow repaint, and this was undertaken in January. 570, nominally a trainer, was still escaping onto service from time to time, while 6 January saw the entry into service at Northumberland Park of 104 (JHE 194W) following its September acquisition. Although national regulations had mandated the fitting of roof marker lights for all new vehicles over 2.1m in length since 1992, Leaside Travel's M1437, often the recipient of new technological innovations, was the first Metrobus to receive them in December, followed by M1379; fellow private-hire bus M1248 became a part-time trainer by virtue of its four-speed gearbox enabling prospective drivers to propel the vehicle to 50mph, as was mandatory in the testing process.

Middle: The experimental livery London United applied to three Ms for the partial double-decking of the 285 was arguably even better than that on M1069 – elegant, sensible and with a clear nod to heritage. Followers of the science of route branding were also placated with a discreet treatment that showed the main points of the route. M1262 (B262 WUL), now at Fulwell and looking a lot healthier than it did on page 59, is seen on 15 July 1995 in Kingston town centre. *Malc McDonald*

Left: MTL London Northern, on the other hand, plumped for all-over red, and a slightly darker shade than LBL's had been. Buses likely to serve routes going into town and out again were selected for repaint first, Potters Bar's M79 (WYW 79T) being an early recipient. The rather attractive fleetname was augmented by a device over the entrance doors that emphasised the company's ownership by MTL Trust Holdings. *Malc McDonald*

The Countdown experiment commenced over route 18 was deemed successful enough to begin exporting to other major transport nodes of London, beginning with the Nag's Head area of Holloway.

Metroline Travel mounted a Romford (or Lakeside) shopping service numbered X2, while closer to home Brent Cross was experimentally opened on Sundays between 30 October and 18 December. The Christmas period was considered a good time to shut down the DLR for maintenance; one of the five temporary routes commissioned to cover saw Metrobuses, the D8A from Capital Citybus.

The first change of 1995 saw the 412's double-deck school journeys become 612 on 3 January, the possibility of M wanderings remaining. The whole Airbus operation was reallocated to Heathrow West Ramp on the 7th, not just overnighters. New market-days route 511 (Grange Hill-Romford) from Capital Citybus's Dagenham from the 21st was another route capable of Metrobus workings, while on 4 February Metroline's Dennis Lance problems were addressed with the switch of the 302's LNs to Cricklewood for the 32, Willesden's 302 reverting to M operation using the transferred Cricklewood Ms and simultaneously easing the pressure on the OPO elements of the 6 and 98. Another M route fell to minibuses, however, on 4 March when the 105 received MAs, its Sunday through service cut back by introducing the 95 on that day of the week. Again, only early and late journeys retained double-decks. By this time CentreWest was still operating ten Ms that were the property of London General; released by existing spare vehicles, these were now returned. 6 March also saw single-doored M1443-7 transferred from Stamford Hill to Enfield for a Middlesex University contract, backed up by regular M336/53; painted into all-over white during April, they supplemented this Monday-Friday work with regular Saturdays concentrated on the 191.

Trainer M445, meanwhile, gained an all-over black advert for the London Symphony Orchestra, and in May M422 became purple for The London Dungeon. The first inter-Cowie M transfers saw M14, 282/90 come to Enfield in April for conversion to training work; many more would follow, beginning in May with ten (two trainers plus four each for Enfield and Tottenham). M282 crossed the river in the opposite direction in August.

Metroline now commenced livery experiments; three Ms were repainted in February into schemes which were all red plus a secondary colour, carried just over the height of the wheelarches. Willesden's M326 had a maroon skirt and white 1" tape divider, M1035 from Harrow Weald bore a green skirt and yellow band, while the combination on Cricklewood's M550 was blue skirt and white band. It was this latter that was chosen in May, repaints commencing in June with a new logo also introduced (another product of Best Impressions); having been evaluated in yellow and grey, it was chosen in white, the 't' being surmounted by an orange flash. Fleetnumbers were now placed above the entrance door (nearside) and above the driver's cab (offside), with another above the registration number box at rear, as had already been the case for some time. M326 was repainted in July and M1035 in August. Cosmetic alterations saw the company take to displaying the running number cards (colour-coded based on the garage) in the windscreen, removing the traditional side-mounted holders. Private-hire M449, meanwhile, had both rear windows panelled over to improve structural integrity (and permit the application of rear advertisements), its numberplate being bolted amidships. From time to time it and its fellows turned out on the Tesco Brent Cross route in place of the allocated blue SR.

Despite having, in this author's opinion, the runaway best post-privatisation livery in the route 285 scheme, London United was not yet convinced, and in February repainted recently accident-repaired M1238 of Hounslow with a yellow roof and three horizontal yellow stripes above the grey skirt; the effect proved to be a little *too* much, and following the official adoption of red and grey in July, repaints commenced. M1238 received it in August.

The closure of the East London Line for refurbishment from 25 March prompted three replacement bus services; that awarded to Capital Citybus, the double-deck semi-express ELX saw some Northumberland Park Metrobuses visiting alongside the orange-and-white Dominators otherwise acquired. No 111, meanwhile, was sold to Cardiff Bluebird in February.

Events surrounding the closure of London United's Wood Lane depot on 1 April saw the 94's Sunday rota moved back into Shepherd's Bush, ex-Stamford Brook, while it was now Shepherd's Bush's own Ms making forays to the 9A. Another closure, that of Leaside's Stamford Hill from 13 May, transferred the 253 and N253 to Clapton and the 67 to Wood Green, while the bulk of the 149 was absorbed by Enfield, only a limited Tottenham allocation springing up in the peaks for the run to Waterloo, now limited to start from Shoreditch Church only. Tottenham also took

(but retaining a single M at schooldays, while rogue visits continued, now encompassing the 201). The Ms regained from CentreWest were thus further cascaded indirectly, most passing to Metroline but then being leased by that company to London United. Their use at Stamford Brook allowed other Ms to pass to Fulwell to release DTs into Airbus Direct support vehicles in time for 15 July (on which date the A2 was extended to King's Cross and both services abandoned Terminal 4 at Heathrow); all the reserve Ms were returned to normal service by then, increasing the proportion of the type at Harlesden on the 52; on 1 April this route had abandoned its commercially-inspired projections beyond Willesden Garage.

With M804 (repainted in March into MTL SightseerS livery of white and dark red with turquoise separation) joining D2556 as the normal complement on what would turn out to be the final

Left: Were it not for a belated decree that 'London' buses should be predominantly red in accordance with the otherwise discarded traditions still needed to attract tourist business to the capital, this would have been closer to what MTL envisaged for a livery. The red of its MTL SightseerS commercial arm, which inherited the London Northern Travel Ms performing the same role, was more like maroon and there was a lot more white. M1067 (B67 WUL), fitted with a London General-style grille (without the chrome bisection) has been put to work as a trainer when sighted turning right out of Potters Bar station forecourt in April 1997. Tony Wilson

the N83, while the school routes 617 and 629 were moved to Wood Green, all with the appropriate transfers; the 106 already at Clapton was thus partially converted to L operation. The Leaside Travel Ms were divided between Enfield (M1248, 1367/98) and Clapton (M1379, 1437). In the interim the 107's schoolday M element was transferred from Metroline to BTS, commencing with the school term on 24 April; this did not prevent rogue M appearances from Edgware, especially of the refurbished examples straying from the 292 to this and other formerly-M routes.

From 29 April the 200 had one last fling before its split and conversion to Dart; as the new vehicles (DPL-class) were not ready the route was extended from Streatham Hill to Tulse Hill over the extremity intended for its new eastern end; on 17 June this was formalised as 201, the 200 falling back to Mitcham

incarnation of the Z1 from 14 April, a second open-top Metrobus debuted in March as General-liveried OM171, the opportunity created out of M171's deroofing at Battersea the previous August; from 7 May it worked on the 70D, allocated to Sutton, running on Sundays and Bank Holidays from Clapham Common to Dorking as part of the Surrey Sunday Rider network. M1440 was the standby bus. However, for the duration of Wimbledon it gained an all-over ad for Nike, with Pete Sampras on the nearside and Andre Agassi on the offside. Four-speed M1393/6 at MTL London Northern also gained SightseerS livery, the former also gaining a London General-style grille without the horizontal bar ('normal' Holloway M961 being the only other company M to receive this adornment at this time, the others receiving them by year's end). MTL Trust Holdings' purchase of London Suburban Buses on 12

Right: MTL London Northern was also the focus of a surprise increase in M numbers in 1995 when most of the Metrobuses sold to Merseybus in 1993 came back. M501 (GYE 501W), seen at St Albans in June 1995, had spent the latter part of its exile on the MTL Lancashire Travel operation in and around St Helens, and was put into service at Potters Bar still in that livery and retaining for the moment the traditional metal fleetnumber plates of Liverpool Corporation and its immediate successor, which identified it as 3501. For now the repatriated Ms filled a gap made by the need to help out MTL London Northern's newly-acquired sibling, London Suburban Buses. *Tony Wilson*

April was followed on 26 May by the bringing back of M229, 377 and 501 from MTL Lancashire Travel to cascade three Potters Bar Ms to Edmonton (ED), which was isolated from its three routes (4, 41 and 271) by rebuilding along the North Circular Road; the trio retained white and red with black window surrounds, but their rear doors had been disconnected and padlocked while at St Helens. They were assigned to work the 84, 310A and 310B safely out of sight; however M229 was moved to Edmonton within a fortnight, to be followed, bizarrely, by the two Vs! M139 arrived in August and was put to work on the 4.

The Night Bus network underwent some rejigging from 10 June to standardise day and night numbers; thus the N91 (Holloway) was introduced over the daytime 91; its projection to Cockfosters and Potters Bar allowed the N21's withdrawal as well as that of the N13 north of North Finchley; similarly new route N43 replaced the N92 and N93 and permitted the N2 to be rerouted over the 24 to Hampstead Heath rather than North Finchley. The N1 was renumbered N20, though the daytime 20 operated some distance to the east; apparently the number, the only one available this low in the sequence, matched the postcode through which it passed (N20)! The N13 passed from Potters Bar to Holloway, but both garages shared the N20. The only M route in the second phase from 1 July was the N38 from Leaside's Clapton, replacing the N96 to Chingford Mount plus a bifurcation over new roads to Chingford Hatch. Phase three involved no Ms, but phase four (19 August) took off routes N68 and N88; new route N77 (over the 77A and thence via Wimbledon and Kingston to Hook) also served to replace the N14 south of Kingston (but leaving its Roehampton-Kingston and Tolworth-Chessington sections fallow), while new route N44 followed the daytime 44 before replacing the N88 to Sutton; the N87 (renumbered N155 to match its closest daytime equivalent) was also pushed south to this point rather than Hampton Court (also abandoned) or Streatham. Stockwell had the N44 and N77, Sutton the N155.

One final bit of nocturnal tidying-up renumbered route N99 to N98.

Although the return of the sold Ms meant that numbers had actually increased, the movement of the type onto training work continued; from July and August London General began replacing its DMT-class Fleetline conversions by the conversion of private-hire examples to serve as trainers between their more glamorous duties, while Ms 144 and 271 were even sent to Plymouth to recruit drivers for the company! In July and August Capital Citybus's Dagenham depot standardised on mk IIs, transferring 295-99 to Northumberland Park. The last blue-and-silver-liveried bus was repainted yellow this year. Although West Midlands 2781 was now beginning its second year on loan to County Bus, a second example was taken on hire in the shape of coach-seated 2959 (D959 NDA) from the Timesavers fleet; it had a Sampson fleetname applied!

Midsummer changes are relatively few; 29 July saw the 221's Sunday service revert to M operation, while on 5 August the 27's northern end was projected from Camden Town to Chalk Farm Safeway and the 29 was split into two overlapping sections. Notting Hill Carnival extras on the 18, 28 and 31 on 27/28 August were performed by Alperton Ms, which also, most unusually, were allocated to part of the 12. One route returned 'home' on 2 September when the 293, since 1986 a Surrey County Council service, was awarded to London General on a commercial basis with Ms from Sutton; the following Monday (4 September) saw Capital Citybus's 345 school route take its place in the six hundreds as 645. MTL London Northern retained its 840 for Hertfordshire and added an 841, formerly with Sovereign. On 15 September National Express sold Westlink to London United; the 411 passed on tender in the same direction on the 23rd, gaining M operation from Fulwell and making Kingston's three Metrobuses redundant; they returned to West Midlands Travel, one of them (2879) on tow. The 411's new stock, as well as being drawn from solely repainted Ms, was fitted with reversing buzzers to warn errant pedestrians or staff that they were backing out of Cromwell Street bus station's pioneering nose-in stands. Finally the 18 lost its remaining service to King's Cross on 14 October, its terminus being standardised daily at Euston.

London General trainer M1432 received a black-based advert for the musical *Jolson*; it was one of a handful of guest buses to turn out on the 111 for Hounslow's open day on 16 September. Occasional M operation on the 11 was carried out by necessity with OPO buses from Stockwell in the absence of Waterloo crews and RMLs during September, the same having to happen to the 139 in October but with Holloway Ms. From 2 October the Airbus routes at London United began to receive their new Alexander Royale-bodied Volvo Olympians (subsequently to be coded A); the long-serving coach-seated Ms were stood down, to be divided among London United's garages, their wheelchair lifts removed but their four-leaf exit doors remaining in place. Despite an upsurge in vandalism, the majority of these buses retained their plush coach seating (capacity DPH41/28D, the deficit of two arising from the turning of the rearmost pair backward upon conversion). For their last few months, the existing Airbus Ms adopted the Toshiba V3 advertising now being applied to the 'As' and took it elsewhere when subsequently put into stage service.

MTL London now moved to take back all the Ms sold by LBL in 1993, barring M312 which had already been scrapped and M26, 1481-4 which were not acquired; M108 arrived in October, M16/37 in November and M106 in December; they could be identified by their 1970s-style embossed numberplates fitted while in Liverpool. Two (M16/37) went to Edmonton, which with the surrender of the London Suburban O-Licence from 11 November was now a *bona fide* MTL London garage) and the rest to Holloway. Meanwhile Grey-Green,

hit with the news of the impending loss of its 473, began disposing of its W-registered Metrobuses, 457 and 465 passing to Ensigns in September and going into that undertaking's London Pride sightseeing fleet. Upon the addition of Brents Coaches to Metroline's stable on 10 October, Metroline Commercial Services was renamed Metroline Contract Services, the strapline taking on a new form in yellow underneath the main fleetname. M1045 and 1067 donned SightseerS livery for MTL London, again working as trainers when not needed for private hire, while M961 made do with just red and smaller logos. A random acquisition in November was by Capital Citybus of JHE 138W, acquired from Stevenson's (although new to SYPTE) and numbered 105; it joined its fellows at Northumberland Park on 1 December.

After a year in which to take stock, the Cowie group began experimenting with a new look, the ground being laid by all-red repaints from August (although some Tottenham Ms had had their grey skirts overpainted red to accompany fitting with reflective registration plates). Enfield's M533 was treated early in October to two diagonal blue stripes at the rear of the saloon and extending over the rear roof dome, with an extra horizontal line at front. M1173 at Wood Green received a yellow variant, and it was this that was chosen, along with a new fleetname – COWIE LEASIDE. South London simultaneously metamorphosed into COWIE SOUTH LONDON. A similar exercise connected with MTL's purchase of R&I Buses on 24 October prompted the dropping of the Northern appellation from MTL London Northern, all subsequent repaints gaining just 'MTL LONDON' fleetnames. It was intended to replace all existing fleetnames, but this did not happen. On 11 November (first day 13th) the company ceded the 699 to Leaside Travel, first from Enfield and then from Wood Green (27 November, starting on the 29th).

Left: Although Cowie had picked up two former LBL companies in the shape of Leaside and South London, no attempt was made to update their LBL-derived livery until October 1995, when Enfield's M533 (GYE 533W) was repainted red and then had blue diagonal stripes added to match Cowie's car-dealership logo. In the last week of December the bus is captured in Tottenham High Road heading north towards Waltham Cross. *Author's collection*

Three days short of a year since purchasing Atlas Bus, Metroline now mothballed its Harlesden garage and transferred the 52/N52 into Willesden, the Titans going with it; Atlas Bus fleetnames endured, but the proportion of Ms increased still further. At Leaside, the N83 was renumbered N243. The most unusual change of the post-LBL era so far came on 1 December when CentreWest commenced a new operation far from its heartland through the award of the majority of the Orpington-area Roundabout contracts from Stagecoach Selkent. Only the 61 was a double-deck route (and on Mondays to Saturdays at that), but its 12 new Volvo Olympians had not arrived yet so M369, 421/51/99, 941, 1328 (Alperton) and M1378/82 (Westbourne Park) were sent south-east to fill in, Alperton covering for its contribution by taking six Ms (143, 245, 509/82, 781/8) on loan from Cowie Leaside; they were used mostly on the E1 and occasionally on the 83. After having trained from Ebdon's premises in Foots Cray (in M499), drivers from the new ORPINGTON BUSES operation

worked initially from the former London Country garage at Swanley until the new base at St Mary Cray (incorporating an office block where signing on and off took place from the start) was complete – both were assigned the code Y. All the Vs were in place by 23 December, M1378 remaining until February, just in case.

In November Cowie South London's Croydon-based M410 was unveiled after a comprehensive refurbishment, the most visible alterations being the respraying of the brown surfaces grey, the fitting of new Treadmaster flat flooring downstairs and new grey seating with yellow handrails and DiPTAC step edges. No more Ms were done, but it did get to be the first bus from its fleet into the new yellow-striped livery, volume repaints not getting underway until 1996 here or at Leaside. In the same month trainer M445 discarded its London Symphony Orchestra advert for one extolling Capital Radio, a scheme also applied to London General M1389. Tottenham's M317 was repainted green in December for the North

Left: The upheavals of privatisation released the Metrobus from its traditional dispersal areas towards points unthinkable; who could have imagined Ms working in Orpington, for example. This is what happened, however, when CentreWest bid on a clutch of tenders fifteen miles from its geographical heartland and won enough to set up a new operation known as Orpington Buses. Its only double-deck route was the 61 between Bromley North and Chislehurst, and until new Volvo Olympians were delivered spare Ms were gathered. M451 (GYE 451W), wearing the CHALLENGER fleetnames of its normal home at Alperton, is captured between Petts Wood and Orpington in the last week of December 1995, amid the snowfall of that year's unusually hard winter. *Haydn Davies*

London College, which used it on a student service, but before that the bus turned up at least once on each of Tottenham's OPO routes, including the 73 on Sunday 20 December! Otherwise two Ms were sold, becoming the first to leave the company altogether; Leaside's M24 and 123 passed to London Coaches which set them to perform closed-top Original London Sightseeing Tour work for the winter season, and in so doing dubbing them, quite unnecessarily, an MB class.

From November the former Airbus Ms were redeployed by London United; those allocated to Stamford Brook did not adopt the identity of RiversideBus, which quietly faded away. Their repaints also included another new feature – yellow fleetnumbers in reduced-size Gill Sans Bold, these also serving to identify the garage codes; Fulwell's recipients concentrated on the 411. MTL London acquired four DAF SB220s to help out on the 310A and 310B from 14 December. On 21 December Capital Citybus was sold to its management.

The run-up to Christmas saw extensive Shepherd's Bush crew M operation on the hard-pressed 94 (the two Sundays leading up to Christmas and the Sunday after, 31 December) plus the odd Metrobus on the 72; conversely DRs were stepping in on the 220 due to the Ms' lack of upstairs heating in what was turning out to be a cold and snowy December. 'Fake' snow, meanwhile, adorned the windows of Metroline M550 and 1031 (plus coloured interior-lighting inserts). For the first time in many years, Christmas Day itself saw isolated bus operations, performed on a commercial basis with locally-determined fares charged; Metroline Ms from Willesden ran a 716 and 732 centring on Cricklewood and sponsored by the TGWU. Boxing Day saw the usual running of curtailed routes over their former extent (29 over 329, 37 over 337, 68 over 68A) or further (149 over 279), plus Kempton Park race work with Sutton Ms. On 30 December the 293 was extended commercially to Leatherhead, while New Year's Eve saw Hounslow cover Stamford Brook's night routes. The rest of the

Left: The nearside treatment on Cowie Leaside and Cowie South London buses unusually had two fleetnames. M410 (GYE 410W) of the latter's Croydon garage and seen at East Croydon station in April 1996, was refurbished in 1995 to what was intended to be a new standard for the group's London Ms, but was to remain unique. The 64 had gained M operation on 14 March 1992 upon its move from Thornton Heath to Croydon, and Ms would leave when the route was transferred to Metrobus (the company) on 30 August 1997. *Chris Evans*

month had seen the first Ms on the 170 in five years, this time operated by Putney (which also unusually had one or two out on the 14 with conductors).

Having operated Surrey routes 555/6/7 and 575 with special-liveried DRLs since 1994, London United's Hounslow had put out large numbers of Ms, but from 2 January 1996 an official M journey was added to the former trio. Upon their return to Cowie Leaside from CentreWest, M143 and 245 were sold to London Coaches on 5 January 1996; these were the first into open-top configuration in February, albeit with the alteration of the front upper-deck windows to two widely-separated and not terribly attractive panes. On 3 February the 84A at Cowie Leaside became 184, the schoolday M complement responding likewise now that Ms had been cleared to serve Alexandra Park Road, though the early delivery of blinds for Wood Green had already led to Ms making appearances with not only this number, but the new 684, also a schoolday offshoot but which did not run via Alexandra Park Road. The award of the 263 to Cowie Leaside from this date immediately saw Wood Green Ms paying visits alongside the scheduled DBS-class DAFs. Two more all-over advertisements for this company affected trainers Ms 14 and 382, both reliveried in white during January for Carling lager; South London's corresponding pair were M149 (pink for Salon Selectives cosmetics) and M65 (white for Oscar de la Renta perfume).

At Metroline, the first few weeks of 1996 were spent exchanging Metrobuses and Titans so that the former could dominate the 52 and allow ten of the latter to pass to the Contract Services fleet; about half the 52 was M by mid-January. A similar exchange at Cowie South London towards the end of the month saw Norwood's Ms all pass to Croydon in exchange for Ls; this removed the type from the 2, 68, X68, 137A and also the 249, where they had been out in strength covering for failing Darts for much of the previous year. In March Thornton Heath also had its type standardised through the removal of its Ms; again Croydon was the beneficiary, though with such a large allocation this garage continued to field a mix of types, just seven Ls clinging on in support of Ms. Alone among South London garages, Thornton Heath had fitted its Ms with reflective registration plates late in 1995; Tottenham and Enfield were the only Leaside sheds to take a liking to the phenomenon (also during 1995) and the rest, wisely, left well enough alone, other than Wood Green which used its own transfer set with straight-backed 6s and 9s.

In the interests of reducing pollution, a quantity of Cowie South London Ms at Brixton were converted to run on Greenergy low-sulphur diesel, and six fitted with catalytic converters, in conjunction with a five-year experiment based on Brixton garage and including M-operated routes 118 and 319. Leaside adopted the Shell-manufactured fuel type as a whole.

After an extraordinary loan span of eighteen months, County Bus 2781 home to WM in January, but in February six more Metrobuses joined Capital Citybus's fleet. All ex-MTL, only three were new to SYPTE (100/9/11), the other three having started at Bristol (coach-seated 175-7). They were put into action, 109 still in MTL livery, on services covering for the IRA-bombed Docklands Light Railway after 9 February. Once things had calmed down, the sextet transferred to Northumberland Park, 175/7 joining the ELX fleet in orange and white and the others donning yellow for normal service. The ELX had been prolonged for at least another year, while a new Capital Citybus logo and 'here today... here tomorrow' slogan made their debut on 111. No 176's normal employ was on Dagenham's Lakeside-area commercial services.

Below: Yellow buses had ejected both red and blue from much of east London as Ensignbus/Capital Citybus advanced, but in 1996 it introduced orange buses when its East London Line rail-replacement service ELX was extended beyond its original year. No 177 (DAE 513W) was one of three acquired from Bristol, or Badgerline as it was now known, and when captured halfway round the Rotherhithe peninsula in November 1996 was working from Capital Citybus's new facility at Waterden Road, Hackney, having transferred from Northumberland Park on 19 October. *Haydn Davies*

Stamford Hill was brought back into use as a storage site and base for the trainers and Leaside Travel fleet between 26 February and 4 March. Cowie now bought County Bus from West Midlands Travel on 29 February and links sprouted immediately; in the last week of March Leaside Ms 790 and 996 were despatched to Grays to assist failing Atlanteans on routes 370/373 and 383, the former pair once LT routes; two weeks later they were exchanged for M474 and 782, plus M388 from Croydon, which in turn was replaced in May by M170/5 from the same source. At Ware, meanwhile, M509/746 arrived from Clapton in April; the semi-permanent nature of their work was underscored with new dayglo blinds for local route 395 and LeaValley fleetnames. Otherwise M75 received a revised livery of mostly cream with a green skirt. Grey-Green's loss of the 473 to Stagecoach East London on 3 March saw all but three of its Metrobuses sold to London Pride, and those three would appear at County Bus later in the year.

An unusual physical change to Sutton's M412 and 822 in April or thereabouts reflected the fact that the M class was ageing and structural strengthening was needed; their rear windows were replaced by glass panes of a third the height. Although half a dozen more London General Ms followed suit, the modification was not adopted universally; indeed, some of the Metroline Travel Ms had their rear windows removed entirely, on both decks! During May M808 was also refurbished with new seating and lighting.

On 27 April further renumbering of the Night Bus network saw Enfield's N90 become N279; one journey ran to Upshire, now otherwise far beyond the reach of daytime red buses thanks to the late-night journey of the 279 coming off. As day broke, Cowie Leaside found itself down by two routes; the 67 struck up with its new operator Capital Citybus and the 106 was demoted to Dart operation under Docklands Buses. Also on this day MTL London transferred the 4 and 271 back into Holloway garage, the former with twelve of the Ts and the latter with the Volvo Olympians but both capable of seeing Ms from Holloway's large fleet; Edmonton's Ms ceased their

assistance. The move of the 46 to North Acton (the former R&I garage) removed its single Holloway M.

A week later, on 4 May, Cowie Leaside lost its third M route this spring, Thamesway taking over the 191 with Darts. On the 5th the 70D appeared again for 1995 with OM171 (which broke its work of this nature with another Wimbledon-themed all-over ad). Another summer enhancement involved the 267's Sunday service, which was restored to M operation with the customary extension to Hampton Court; this year, so was the Sunday service on the R68. London General's second open-top General-liveried Metrobus was OM241, converted out of M241 and deployed on a Medway Towns-area service. In June M409 at Metroline received an all-over ad in white and black for AA Vodafone Roadwatch.

On 1 June MTL London closed its Edmonton base, transferring the N6 into Holloway but surrendering the 41 to Cowie Leaside where its allocation to Wood Green helped fill some of the losses of six weeks previous; the Ms lost from the 67 had stayed put and six had come in from Enfield. Wood Green also absorbed the Palmers Green share of the N29. A debut

Above: As well as MTL, the Cowie group was also expanding, buying County Bus from West Midlands on 29 February 1996 and sending Leaside Ms to help out at Ware. Loaned from Clapton, M746 (KYV 746X) displays LeaValley fleetnames when sighted at Hertford in June 1996 on local route 395. *Tony Wilson*

Left: MTL's acquisition of London Suburban Buses was not all roses, especially when comprehensive reconstruction of the North Circular Road separated the Edmonton garage from its routes operated; eventually the operation was absorbed into MTL London and one route surrendered. This was the 41, which returned to Wood Green but now under Cowie Leaside. Displaying two nearside fleetnames, M1070 (B70 WUL) is tailed by M548 (GYE 548W) westbound along West Green Road on 12 October 1996. *Malc McDonald*

garage to the M was London General's Battersea Bridge (BB) minibus depot, which from 8 June gained a rotating complement of six Metrobuses and part of the 49 on which to use them; both route and buses came from, and remained subordinate to, Stockwell.

On 23 May the Go-Ahead group purchased London General from its management, adding it to London Central. Orders had already been replaced for vehicles that would take over from the current Ms at Sutton. M1, however, evoked the past when Metroline repainted it into its original livery. Having already bought County Bus, the Cowie group now went for the brass ring and bought British Bus plc in its entirety on 18 June.

29 June saw an extensive programme based on south-west London; Westlink's 131 passed to London United, Fulwell receiving new Volvo Olympians but now able to put out its own Ms, released by the loss of the 285 to London Buslines. To cement the 155's welcome conversion to double-deck, the 131's Titans were loaned to Merton until it could gather enough Ms; the sacrifice here was the upper deck on the 219, which took the 155's DRs and DWs instead. Another double-decking was the R70 at Fulwell, already the beneficiary of the type at certain times of the week; this was accomplished by the last of the former Airbuses' replacement by further new As by August. The Bank branch of the Northern Line was closed

from 30 June, the replacement bus service unusually receiving a number; this Kennington-Moorgate appendage to the 133 (known internally as 133E) had a partial Cowie Leaside element (Clapton Ms doing the honours) and probed beyond the 133 in the late evenings and at weekends as far as Euston. Underground strikes on 3 and 8 July saw the appearance of Reading Buses Metrobuses (and Titans!) on the Airbus routes, while London United Ms turned out on the 9 as OPO and Metroline Ms helped out the 6, 98 and 113.

6 July saw Acton Tram Depot's holding on route 207 increase in size at the expense of Uxbridge (which needed the space for two new contracts). Cowie Leaside's white Metrobuses migrated from Enfield's Middlesex University contract to the 221 at Wood Green while the schools were out, green M317 staying behind at Tottenham to perplex local passengers by making appearances on regular routes. Two of the white Ms (M336/53) would not return to Middlesex University work when the rest did in October.

Above: The double-decking of Fulwell's route R70 by London United on 29 June 1996 brought Ms back to their spiritual starting point, as this route was once the 270. Passing St Stephen's Church in Twickenham on 6 September 1997, M1344 (C344 BUV) only has the middle letter of its original badging left, but that was more than most Ms that had them new could do by now. *Geoff Rixon*

Left: The five ex-GM Buses Metrobuses managed a decade in service in London, passing to Cowie Leaside upon privatisation. A departure from run-of-the-mill work came in 1995 when they were repainted white for a service operated for the University of Middlesex. This duty belonged to Enfield, but during the summer holidays of 1996 all five were seconded to Wood Green and assigned to ply the 221. M1443 (GBU 1V) arrives at Edgware station in July. *Tony Wilson*

The end of the school year fell on 19 July in Metroline territory, and saw the 143A and the Grahame Park bifurcation of the 32 withdrawn. At Grey-Green the 235, numbering a solitary double-deck working, finally bit the dust on the 27th, to be absorbed into the W13 once the schools came back on 2 September; similarly the 143 spawned a double-decker of its own, cleverly curtailed before having to tackle the narrow section of the route; this was covered by new route 643, also by Cricklewood Ms. The Grahame Park run formerly on the 32 became new route 632, operated unusually by the Contract Services department. Out in Surrey London United picked up the 681 from London & Country, using Fulwell Ms, while Croydon's 612 sprouted extensions at either end.

Summer-1996 miscellany included the appearance of Ms on the 31 for the Royal Tournament on 14 July (and again for Carnival on 25/26 August (together with the 28 and four Alperton extras on the 18). The last lowbridge Metrobus, Capital Citybus 570, was withdrawn in July. Space problems at Brixton forced the move of Cowie South London's M trainers to Croydon during August, while the 245 was partially M-operated on Sundays between 11 August and 8 September. The last Airbus M operated in August, the final examples (M1011/9/23) going away for conversion to bus spec that month and of these, only M1019 retained its coach seats upstairs. M500 was another Leaside M to head to Ware, albeit for only two weeks between 31 August and 14 September to cover an increase on the 395. Atlas Bus ceased to be from 13 August, the 52's operations now coming under an increased allocation of Metroline discs, with the appropriate fleetname changes.

With new-vehicle orders only manifesting themselves in sensible numbers as management-owned companies weighed up their financial options, sometimes vehicles of different ages had to be shuffled instead; thus from 31 August London United switched its Ls from Stamford Brook's 237 to Hounslow's 140, the 237 both regaining M operation and losing its roads beyond Hounslow Heath to a new route 235, also Hounslow-operated. These roads, however, lost their night service when the N97's bifurcation in this direction was pulled out. The loss of Ls from Hounslow also saw the N9 and N11 returned to Metrobuses. The 111 regained its Sunday Ms and the 116 returned from London & Country, immediately seeing volume M operation alongside its scheduled Lynxes; to furnish this, Hounslow surrendered its portion of the 281 to Fulwell and its M complement on the H91 to Stamford Brook.

Brixton's 319 was demoted from M to LDR-class Dart on 14 September. In partial compensation eight Monday to Friday workings on the 109 were transferred in from Thornton Heath, restoring M operation to the route. Plans to send ex-Brixton Ms to County Bus to replace the 370/373's ANs prior to Dart SLF conversion did not occur, and in the event only five were sent across the river to Leaside for storage, the other nine coming from Croydon. The 395 did, however, get its new buses, allowing M500 to return to Wood Green. Two weeks later the 255 at Croydon was reconfigured into new Dart-operated 455 and the 14's evening service at Putney (plus a couple of early-morning journeys working off the N14) was one-manned.

On 28 September Capital Citybus lost the 246 and 446 (both withdrawn) and the 652 (to Stagecoach East London) but gained new school routes 651 and 670, shadowing part of the 252 and 370. Some of Dagenham's Metrobuses (of both varieties) moved to Northumberland Park, converting the 257 at the expense of the ex-Southampton Dominators; appearances on the 97, 97A and 158 ensued. One of the two Brixton workings on school route 689 was transferred to Norwood on 7 October while on the 12th CentreWest's Uxbridge garage gained the 698 from London Buslines, this being the old 98A after a couple of number changes. Its Ms also assumed new night route N207 (renumbered from N89 and shorn of its Northolt-Ruislip leg in favour of an extension of the N23 in that direction, though the N89's Alperton share also migrated to the new N207) and continued to visit the 607 despite its conversion from LS/LX to Volvo Olympian (V) operation; these new buses then quickly made the N207 their own. The

Below: 31 August 1996 saw a reshuffle of Hounslow's M routes to introduce new route 235 over the western end of the 237. Displaying the yellow Gill Sans Bold fleetnumbers that had now become standard for London United and added to the front of buses for easier recognition, M1358 (C358 BUV) picks its way round the southern flank of Hounslow town centre, otherwise pedestrianised. *Malc McDonald*

N43 was extended from Archway to Muswell Hill Broadway on Friday and Saturday nights.

Even as their third decade approached, the Metrobus family was still subject to improvements; M1248 was the first Leaside Travel M to be treated to refurbishment, which gave it a slightly different look externally with rear lower-deck window removed, roof marker lights, square headlights (uniquely) and a 'London General'-style grille. Inside were new grey panels and carpeted seat backs and walls surmounting new flat flooring. Completed in October, the work was topped off by the application of a new livery of maroon and off-white, with the diagonal Cowie stripes in maroon and dark blue. M1367/79 quickly followed, the latter converted to single-door, and finally six Ms recently on loan were accepted into the Leaside Travel fleet to replace the unit's school-bus Titans and private-hire DMSs. At MTL London only eight Ms remained to be repainted after just two years since privatisation, and second repaints were now rocketing along. Strengthening work to London United Ms 15 and 17 involved reinforcement of the engine housing, while Cowie Leaside commenced a programme to treat corrosion issues on its fleet, always something of a problem for the mk I Metrobus, but generally cured following the experiments undertaken by Optare with what was now Capital Citybus 107. By October M14's Carling Black Label all-over ad was replaced by one for Calvin Klein, but at Sutton M1432 lost its Al Jolson ad for full General livery. Instead M202 donned a black-based ad for Police sunglasses and M978 one for the Harlequins rugby club. M209 was sent to Plymouth to trawl for staff once again, and M236 became the first sold outright, passing within the group to its Go-Ahead Northern operations as the vanguard for many more.

Four of the Ms stored at Stamford Hill came back to Cowie South London in October, and unusually returned the type to Norwood for a *fourth* tour of duty, albeit in this case to assist London Central on the Bakerloo Line replacement 'BL1/2' between 10 November and 14 July 1997; M64, 74, 205 and 220 were the buses in question. Clapton Ms also featured until 14 February 1997.

Capital Citybus had grown by now sufficient to require a new base, and this was opened on 19 October as Hackney (H) at Waterden Road. First in was the ELX, including its two Metrobuses (175/7), Olympians, Dominators and seven new Dennis Arrows in orange. The '133ᴇ' extras came off after 27 October, but the changes to the 155, 219 and 355 that had involved the former regaining its upper deck were not rescinded. Two routes to entertain the possibility of Metrobuses as they changed operator were the 179 (Grey-Green to Capital Citybus's Dagenham from 19 October) and 313 (Grey-Green to Cowie Leaside's Enfield on 2 November); the extra Ms for the 313 soon started wandering to the 307, which had gone a year since its acquisition without seeing any Ms.

Stamford Brook closed operationally on 9 November, but was held on to by London United in case an upturn in tendering fortunes manifested itself; routes 237, N9 and N11 passed to Hounslow (the night routes retaining M operation) and the 27, plus the evening- and/or schoolday M elements of the 94 and H91 went to Shepherd's Bush; the 94 was withdrawn between Piccadilly Circus and Trafalgar Square. The incomers for the 27 were kept separate in operation from those Countdown-equipped Ms used on the 220, these vehicles soon being identified by the painting yellow of their running number plate holders. The 190's temporary move to Shepherd's Bush (to clear out Stamford Brook garage prior to the route's transfer to Armchair on 7 December) cost it the chance of any more Ms appearing. Hounslow's M workings on the H22 remained in spite of the introduction of a Hounslow Heath allocation (this being the Westlink base) and the 391's move to Fulwell increased the likelihood of Ms. Stamford Brook now became London United's training base (for which all the Shepherd's Bush-based red-and-cream Ms moved in on 9 November), MOT centre and storehouse for withdrawn vehicles. Also on 9 November, Capital Citybus's 347 came off, leading to the sale of 570, while the Airbus routes once again were re-routed to serve Heathrow Terminal 4.

New buses were now creeping in, sometimes but not always helped by the backing of big-group

Right: While buses were not generally permitted to carry adverts into service, rears were fair game and the flat construction of the Metrobus made it a perfect canvas — or would, were it not for blind boxes and numberplate housings getting in the way. Thus Holloway's M1284 (B284 WUL) of MTL London had the offending obstructions resited as shown; the effect is most peculiar. It is caught at Golders Green on 22 March 1998, showing how the Sunday OPO service of the 139 at the time worked onward from West Hampstead to this rather more convenient place to terminate. *Author*

venture capital. Between 9 and 30 November the M/T mix on the 52/N52 at Metroline's Willesden gave way to new AV-class Volvo Olympians and by the third week of the month the M standbys (and the ANs they supported) on County Bus's 370 and 373 had been replaced by the intended Dart SLFs. M474 and 782 remained at Grays for schools work, the other loans going back to Leaside.

On 23 November Capital Citybus's Hackney received the D6 from Dagenham, taking with it Metrobuses 107/12/70/1/8/9, 279/82 from Dagenham plus 117 from Northumberland Park. They could also turn out on the D5, placed at Hackney (with its associated route 678 afternoon journey) since 4 November.

Perhaps the first major threats to Metrobus totals accompanied the Sutton-area tender awards commencing on 30 November, in which London General (and its M-dominated Sutton garage) was the major beneficiary. Forty-two Volvo Olympians had already been ordered, just before the company came under the aegis of Go-Ahead, but almost enough LDP-class Dart SLFs of two lengths were ready on time, and they replaced Ms from the 80 (extended in place of the 393), 151 and 164, the 163 following a little later (by 16 December) and a schoolday M continuing on the 164. Sutton's evening work on several Surrey contracts, which were rejigged from this date to become 420/422/440, also assumed LDP operation. At least the 154 reverted to double-deck on Sundays as some kind of compensation, though the 155 went back to Dart on that day. However, Stockwell rotated some of its oldest Ms into Sutton for withdrawal prior to sale within the Go-Ahead Group, taking the

Left: M37 (WYW 37T), another Holloway Metrobus, had its rear blind box resited to the other side of the rear window and the original housing was plated over. It was pictured on 18 December 1998, laying over at the Tottenham Court Road terminus of the 134. *Author*

garage's newer examples in exchange. Cowie Leaside also sold its first Ms, eight going to London Coaches in November from the batch that had been released from South London with the 319's conversion to LDR. London General loaned M1391 to Nostalgiabus during the month, but disposed of 13 more Ms; of these, three passed to CentreWest to serve as reinforcements as part-exchange for three Uxbridge LSs needed in Oxford.

Since 23 November CentreWest had been assigned a couple of school journeys on the 79; once or twice an Alperton M was used instead of the intended ex-London Buslines Olympian. These red-repainted Olympians (known as LNs) then took over the E1's schoolday element from Ms. The 184 lost its schoolday M after 21 December, and the Metrobus family was not rewarded for Christmas as both the Airbus routes and this year's Metroline commercials (716 and 752) were with their new Volvo Olympians; at least Ms 1031 and 1189 were selected for 'snow around the windows' treatment. On Boxing Day the 277 was with Dagenham Metrobuses from Capital Citybuses, while extensions to M routes for this day were the 29 over 329, 37 over 337 and 149 over 279.

1997 began with the D6 partially converted to Arrow operation at Capital Citybus's Hackney (on the 6th), this day also seeing Westlink's Surrey-commercial 402 gain a Hounslow M on schooldays to address high demand. On 11 January Hackney gained another route, the 257 (and its cross-worked 215 on Sundays) coming in from Northumberland Park and bringing to the garage further Metrobuses in the shape of 280/1/3-91/3/4/7/8; this vehicular shuffle, together with the departure of 112/7, rendered Hackney predominantly mkII Metrobus with just five of the type left at Dagenham (112, 275-8, all mark Is). At London General's Battersea Bridge, the 295, struggling with DRLs, took at least three Stockwell Ms on loan during January, while Putney continued to put Ms out on the 170. Capital Citybus 108 was damaged in an accident on 9 January and left that fleet.

Clapton came off the Bakerloo replacement on 15 February; the Ms spared formed a float for corrosion-treatment work on the class at Cowie's companies, which was expanded to also be carried out at Stamford Hill and began to encompass the Ms of other operators as the year progressed, first London United and then Metroline.

The first big event of the year was the award of the 91 and N91 from MTL London to Capital Citybus on 1 March; the loss of these Holloway routes allowed the displaced Ms to stay behind and replace the 4's Titans. The input of the 91 into Northumberland Park (initially with Titans) helped soothe the company's loss of the 298, which had seen continued Metrobus operation despite having been allocated Metrorider minibuses for five years – its new operator, Cowie Leaside, specified new LDRs to be based at Palmers Green, but sure enough, the large stock of Ms available to the garage through its twinned status with Wood Green soon added it to their list of routes to visit. Metrobus sightings on Holloway's 274 disappeared when the route was extended east of Camden Town on 1 March, via roads unwelcoming to buses wider and taller than its DRLs.

The basically flat rear of the Metrobus lent itself to the craze for rear adverts rather better than its contemporaries, and dozens of applications followed; fittings did not need to be repositioned, but in or around January 1997 Holloway's M1284 suffered the plating over of both its rear blind box and its numberplate housing; the plate was fastened over the rear bumper, right at the bottom, with the mandatory covering light affixed to its right; the blind box was placed inside the rear window. Other MTL Ms were to have their rear blind boxes resited in this manner, but only M1284 had its numberplate moved. Two Cowie all-over adverts metamorphosed again in March, South London's M149 donning a scheme for Vittel and Leaside's M282 gaining a scheme for Pringle sportswear and golfer Nick Faldo; in April M450 received an advert for Vittel, ex People to People. Repaints of Leaside Travel Metrobuses into

Left: London General's classic-liveried M1432 (WLT 432, ex-C432 BUV) makes a stunning sight as it shows off to passengers of the otherwise mundane Surrey County Council contract route 540 anchored on Redhill. It was repainted into this livery in October 1996 and is pictured 11 months later. *Chris Evans*

Right: On 29 September 1997 Leaside Travel was reallocated within Cowie to the responsibility of County Bus. Eleven days earlier M625 (KYO 625X), now sporting an athletic livery of white, maroon and blue, picks up pupils of St Ignatius College on the Great Cambridge Road due north of Ponders End. *Mike Harris*

the new maroon and white livery were complete by the spring, the new colours also appearing on new coaches and three Titans converted to open-top. One special-liveried trainer returned to service, however, this being London General-liveried M1432 deployed to Sutton in March. A more unusual advertising gimmick that spring involved the application of Baby Bel cheese logos to the nearside wheel hubs of South London and Leaside vehicles!

The long-term closure of Hammersmith Bridge to car traffic from 2 February necessitated changes to the routes in its remit; on 8 March the 9 regained some glory with the conversion of its Sunday service back to M (again working from Hounslow), though the whole Mortlake service now passed to a strengthened 9A (which was renumbered 209). The 33's lone M augmentation was withdrawn. On 10 March Grey-Green lost the 20's schoolday element to Capital Citybus (Dagenham), but as both companies could field Metrobuses, the type continued to turn out. The loss of the '20D' (as timetables dubbed this portion of the 20) prompted Grey-Green to sell Metrobuses 467/72, which passed to County Bus as M367/72, still in Grey-Green colours. They were despatched to Grays to assist Leaside-loaned M474/782 on school routes, being joined by M80 from Ware; M75 was sold in May. Grey-Green 466, the company's last Metrobus, held on until July as the W13's sole double-decker before also passing to County Bus (as M366).

From 3 March Sutton's remaining Ms on the 93, 154 and 157 began to depart as new NVs arrived; the order for these Volvo Olympians was increased to 58 to allow the 213 to be done too but still the company hadn't ordered quite enough and a hardcore of Metrobuses remained, assisting where they would. Such would be the case with the purchasing policies

of not only this company but others as stricter budgeting led to corner-cutting, and such a practice would enable the M to last into the 21st century. M209, meanwhile, was wrecked in Plymouth while on assignment there and was written off. However, the class remained in favour when on 29 March the 88 was converted back to M operation, the VN-class Volvo B10Bs having proven too long for the route's narrow streets around the Tate Gallery; the VNs were rushed off to City of Oxford. M293 replaced M209 in Plymouth.

From 5 April the 310A and 310B had a County Bus component added, sharing with MTL London; while the routes assumed single-deck operation (cascaded DAF SB220s from both companies), Ms continued to appear. A couple of changes to the night bus network on the 26th introduced new route N37 (Peckham-Putney via the daytime 37) with Stockwell Ms, and the withdrawal of the N29's Trafalgar Square-Victoria and Ponders End-Edmonton Green sections. The 70D appeared for a third summer on 4 May with OM171/241, and for this summer the 267's summer-Sunday extension to Hampton Court (plus the entire R68 on that day) was accomplished with Fulwell Ms. The 26th saw the 196 reapportioned within Go-Ahead from London General's Stockwell to London Central's Camberwell to address staff shortages, and obviating (for the moment) M appearances. The 213 lost its Glenthorne Road school projections in St Helier on 17 May, but up stepped a diversion of Nostalgiabus's 613 instead. To accompany changes to the E-routes on 24 May the E3 lost its Acton Tram Depot M component.

Miscellaneous happenings in the spring of 1997 saw the repaint cycle of Metroline Ms complete and examples going for second repaints, while that company's Contract Services Ms finally received their blue skirts. At Cowie Leaside, Palmers Green's M545 was burnt out by an arsonist in April and scrapped in May. London United's unrepainted versions started receiving yellow fleetnumbers standard to that company. Capital Citybus scrapped its No 103 and sold No 275/8 in March/April. At London United, Shepherd's Bush Ms were cleared anew for the 283 and began popping up during June; this garage's Ms formed part of a LT-funded project converting vehicles to Euro-2-equivalent low-sulphur fuel. At Metroline, M1035 had its rear blind box replaced with the three-track unit from a DT, fitted at the bottom of the rear window; M102/25, 1034/1174 followed, the last mentioned keeping its old assembly as well!

The long-term problem by which Sovereign (formerly known as BTS) had to juggle its buses to get enough double-deckers for the 13's evening and Sunday OPO element was solved on 31 May when this arm was transferred to MTL London with Holloway Ms. Capital Citybus found that extra contract work taken on by Fashion Logistics, who shared the Hackney depot site, required the effective emptying of the garage of buses for a period; its work on the 179 moved out to Dagenham on 31 May, the 257 (and 215 on Sundays) following on 7 June (with Nos 280-89) and the 678, D5 and D6 going into Dagenham on the 28th with the rest (107/70/1/8/9, 279/90/1/3/4). It was at about this time that Northumberland Park's Metrobuses started making forays to the 67, gained earlier in the year.

Saturday 28 June saw the latest incarnation of Kingston-area contracts; the most important of these brought red buses back to the 57 when London United won it back from Londonlinks and London &

Country. In the short term it was set going from Westlink, but local objection to a proposed site in Hampton Wick forced its operation from Fulwell; plans to hire London General Ms were superseded by the expedient of making temporary cuts to some peak-hour services, allowing enough existing Ms to deputise (five each from Shepherd's Bush and Hounslow and nine from Fulwell), though all were based in the yard at Fulwell and separated operationally from the main runout there (and thus carrying 'On Hire to Stanwell Buses' notices).

Just as M964 became the last Metrobus at MTL London to lose its LBL colours, the MTL SightseerS arm was wound up on 10 August; the five Ms in white and turquoise settled down as trainers, gradually gaining red livery. M126 had a rear blind box placed in the rear window.

The retention of the 38 by Cowie Leaside from 19 July also included the Sunday OPO service, which was put into Clapton ex-Stagecoach East London; while meant for Ls, Ms also figured strongly, as they did on night route N38 which was transferred in the same manner. On this day Capital Citybus's Dagenham picked up the 369 from Stagecoach East London, using new East Lancs-bodied Arrows but also allowing its Metrobuses to wander from time to time. Three Ms (64, 74, 205) were transferred from South London to Wood Green to furnish a frequency increase on the 144 pending the receipt of three DAF SB220s in 1998; further amendment would accrue to the 144 shortly. M205's experimental past a decade ago was remembered by its selection to trial 'Electric Paper' illuminated side advert panels.

Croydon's Ms abandoned the 64 on 30 August, the date of this five-year spell's Croydon-area tender renewals, in favour of new Volvo Olympians

Left: London United Ms had ceded the 57 to London & Country in 1992, but five years later they took it back. This time it was Kingston garage that was in command, officially under the banner of Westlink now that this company was owned by London United. Two waves of Ms preceded the Volvo Olympians on order, first in the form of spares from other London United garages (like M89 (WYW 89T) loaned from Hounslow and seen in Kingston in October 1997) and then with Ms hired from London General. *Geoff Rixon*

operated by Metrobus. However not all of the new buses were ready, so Metrobus acquired nine Ms (76, 216/28/35/52/9, 320, 447, 527) spare from London General's recent conversion of Sutton to NV operation and painted them into blue and yellow for use on the 261, releasing compatible Volvo Olympians for the 64. Once the new buses were all in stock, the Ms departed for Metrobus's East Surrey school routes. Brixton's 118 regained its Sunday allocation from Norwood's DRs, ceding the 137A on that day in exchange and converting the whole route to L, while the schoolday M part of the 249 lost its Ms by passing to Thornton Heath. The 57 moved out of Fulwell's yard and into Kingston now that that site had been reprieved for a little longer, and this time did take London General Ms on loan in the shape of M231/42/4/61/2/75, 321/5/34/86 (till November). Further north, the schoolday portion of the 112 was transferred from CentreWest to Metroline Contract Services, while a portfolio of schoolday augmentations taken up by Nostalgiabus for this year (127, 156) once needed the loan of Blue Triangle's ex-GM Buses GBU 3V.

CentreWest's partnership with London Buslines now allowed the former to enrich itself with the latter's newer buses; on 13 September the 83 was converted from M to LN/LA operation, these being Leyland Olympians formerly on the 92, which was simultaneously restored to Alperton with Ms. Six Ms (unusually from the newest in stock) were stood down to be turned into trainers, and two more, one of which served at St Mary Cray briefly in this role, were scrapped. The tie-up with FirstBus (since 19 February) was slow to manifest itself on vehicle sides, but slowly a window sticker with corporate '*f*' logo

gave way to new fleetnames in which the local identity (in yellow lower case) was followed by the same '*f*' device; the new yellow-band livery common on the company's new buses would not appear on the Ms until 1998. Meanwhile, a change of mind at Cowie saw its logos torn off during August and a new design tentatively introduced; M712/1253 at Enfield were the first to display Lea*side* (the 'Lea' in white Helvetica and the 'side' in yellow italic Times), with similar treatment afforded for South *London* (on two lines), pioneered by Croydon's M240 in September. Lea*Valley* and Thame*Side* were County Bus's variants for Ware and Grays respectively with the Helvetica portion in red and the rest in black to lie against the cream bus sides. M1443-7 were transferred to County Bus in August following the standing down of the Middlesex University contract after 20 June; of these, M1/4/5/8/9 (as M1443-7 became at Ware) received a cream livery with red skirt and Cowie stripes to replace elderly LR-class Olympians on the 310 from 1 September, M372 replacing M474 at Grays. However, Cowie management didn't take to the new logos and applied comparatively few to Leaside and only four to South London (M240, 680, 1085/100); grander plans were in hand, and to that end yellow-stripe applications were terminated abruptly, with the result that buses repainted after September would be going around all-red and carrying no identifying markings at all. Then, on 11 October, a new fleetname appeared overnight – ARRIVA. Indeed trainer M6 was repainted white with the logo in huge letters to serve at the launch of the new brand on the 14th. As the offside application was fouled by the running-number brackets, these were relocated into the pillar behind the driver on a large number of affected Ms,

one below the other; but subsequent finalisation of the red version of the corporate livery and subsidiary fleetnames in 1998 would render this meaningless. The first national-turquoise (officially 'shimmering aquamarine and Cotswold stone') Metrobuses were examples refurbished internally for sale to Colchester at the end of 1997.

A programme along the Edgware Road corridor was implemented on 11 October; first the 16 was shortened by removing it between Cricklewood Garage and Neasden, while the 16A was withdrawn altogether and its Brent Cross remit transferred to new route 189, which broadly followed the 139's roads. The Ms spared were retained to convert both the 32 and 113 back to double-deck operation, the LNs now being given up on entirely. Lastly, two of the three duties on the 632 moved over from Cricklewood to the Contract Services division, allowing it a better class of Ms; these also had a schoolday complement on the new 316 that replaced the 16's northernmost arm.

Co-operation between the growing big groups was almost unknown in the ultra-competitive arena that was London, so the voluntary swapping of some services in south London on 8 November was most remarkable. South London took on the 166 and 198 from Stagecoach Selkent, Croydon Ms furnishing the former. The Arriva routes to pass to Stagecoach Selkent in exchange were from Kentish Bus, allowing the closure of its impractically distant Dunton Green depot. To allow room for the 198 at Thornton Heath,

the 264 was reallocated into Croydon, converting it from L to majority-M.

The 34 was taken up by new Dart SLFs on 8 November, its contract reassigned within Arriva to County Bus (LeaValley) in order to make full use of Edmonton (EC), the former London Suburban depot acquired three months earlier. This also became the new home of the Leaside Travel fleet (the Ms of which added a new schoolday element on the otherwise single-decked 34); Stamford Hill was effectively mothballed again, with the corrosion treatment done at the accident repair centre at Enfield; this work proceeded to take on CentreWest Ms at this juncture. After its increases of July, the 144 now expanded further to absorb the W2 entirely and spawn a new schoolday 644 (Crouch End-Wood Green over the old W2). The 15th saw the 290's school projections beyond Richmond to Chiswick transferred to the R70.

The second period of M operation at Kingston ended in December with the arrival of all the VAs; the London General loans returned first, followed by the existing company buses, which went into store at Stamford Brook. CentreWest converted two more newer Ms to trainers and sold two more to fellow FirstGroup company Leicester Citybus. Miscellaneous changes over 1997's last quarter involved the treatment of M1389 (London General) to an ad for *Hello!* magazine and the re-registration of OM171 to VLT 71 (both September); Metroline's M367 donned an ad for Malaysia in October (gaining a blue front later) and in December South London's M14

Above: The ups and downs of tendering meant that a lot of routes once operated by Ms gained them back, sometimes by the previous LBL-derived garage. Such was the case with the 92, which spent seven years with London Buslines and was then won back from 13 September 1997 by Alperton garage of what was now CentreWest, trading locally as Challenger. M499 (GYE 499W) passes through Wembley that month; the use of Ms on the 92 allowed London Buslines' Olympians to gain red livery and assume the 83. *Tony Wilson*

Right: The Cowie group's board decided it wanted a new and more thrusting 'brand' to take it into the 21st century, and this was unveiled at the end of 1997 as Arriva, an artificial name that would mean the same in all the group's markets, including foreign concerns as and when they came under possession. For the moment the 'wheels within wheels' logo was added over Cowie yellow stripes, in the case of buses belonging to the erstwhile Leaside replacing a shortlived 'Leaside' name like that carried on Tottenham's M1213 (B213 WUL) when at Waterloo in May 1998. The 171A would lose Ms that November, becoming First Capital-operated 341. *Tony Wilson*

Below: South London's interim identity was applied to very few buses indeed; Croydon's M680 (KYV 680X) was one of them and in September 1998 is seen in Chipstead Valley Road during the short period in which Ms had control of the 166 again; this was due only to a unique swap of services between Stagecoach (whose route this had been) and Arriva. Darts took over on 26 September and not a double-decker has been seen since. *Chris Evans*

received two schemes in one; its offside was for Cheers Cafe and its nearside exhorted passers-by to eat Ben & Jerry's ice cream. At Arriva's pair of M operators, a new style of mesh grille was cut into the engine cover on several Ms, the lower-quadrant rear vent grille also being converted to mesh type.

Following Cowie's rebranding to Arriva, FirstBus became FirstGroup in November; fleetnames were revised again so that just First appeared on the front, with the company fleetname relegated to secondary status over the front wheelarches. CentreWest's livery was formalised as red with broad stripe, the 'Barbie' chosen elsewhere being off-limits in London; the logos appeared in January and repaints to Westbourne Park's Ms followed in February, although for many only the lower deck was done. A training livery was also adopted, of mostly yellow with red uppers. 'Electric Paper' side adverts were fitted to five Wood Green Ms, though the

announcement of the 76 and 259's upcoming loss caused Arriva's anti-corrosion programme to be cut from 300 to 240 Ms. In compensation, Arriva as a whole acquired London Coaches and its OLST operation on 4 December.

As the M approached its 20th anniversary, routes still continued to favour the type; on 10 January 1998 the 116 at London United's Hounslow was converted from LX to M operation, soothing the loss of the 235 to Tellings-Golden Miller's new Dart SLFs (other than two retained school augmentations). Starting on 12 January the 74 at London General's Putney was converted to new Volvo Olympians (NVs), though five Ms were kept behind and ended up staying there for four more years! The conversion from M to NV at Sutton was completed at around the same time, though again several Ms remained operational. A period of staff shortage at London General that had already led to the voluntary surrender of three minibus routes continued to bite; on 24 January half of Stockwell's route 37 was reallocated to New Cross at London Central, introducing T operation for the first time. This allowed the conversion of the 295 back to M operation after admitting that the DRLs couldn't cope; former Putney Ms flocked to Battersea Bridge for this purpose. One Putney holdout, M1433, worked the 39 on 23 February, the first double-decker on this route in nearly eight years. Of those re-registered Ms selected for sale at this time, London General kept their RM marks and in most cases still owned their former registrations to re-apply, unlike Ms earlier treated.

On 31 January the 43 was increased to absorb the withdrawal of the X43, whose Ss converted the 84 from M. Within Arriva, the 125 was reallocated from Grey-Green to Palmers Green, taking its Volvo Citybuses along but now becoming subject to M appearances; Palmers Green moved the 298 to Wood Green (but the pooled status ensured continued M visits). This latter change was part of a rationalisation scheme which restored the Kentish Bus contracts to 'red bus' operation and closed Ash Grove, which that company had been using. On 28 February, thus, the 22A and 22B were combined as 242 with Clapton operation (chiefly the ex-Kentish Bus Olympians, but with Ms added from the first day). To fill the 22A's path to London Bridge Station the 149 was extended from Liverpool Street, leaving its Tottenham-operated peak-hour run to Waterloo as a bifurcation. Portentous of things to come was the 141's move on Sundays back to Wood Green so that Grey-Green could man the 19 on that day of the week; although intended for DBSs (DAF DB250s from the 221), Ms appeared before long.

On 7 March Greenford (G) received its first Ms when the 282's schoolday workings transferred in from Alperton; M494/9, 861 were the trio in question alongside LA- and LN-class Olympians. Metroline fitted seatbelts to commercial M1425/8, the first and only examples to be so treated; sponge over the seat rails was an additional safety feature.

MTL London continued the fashion of resiting the rear blind box to permit better use of rear ads; M37/1120 were done, but M114's was on the offside, as was that of M739/964 when done a little later. In preparation for a clutch of schoolday tenders, London Traveller, a new company based in Harlesden, began acquiring Metrobuses, picking up Rolls-Royce-engined ex-West Midlands GOG 228/34/5/7W in red livery to join green GOG 230W already used on Hertfordshire County Council contracts; rail-replacement work was their lot until the routes were implemented. M203 restored the type to Kingston on 13 March and settled on the 468, being joined in April by M881.

Capital Citybus, meanwhile, was restoring Hackney to full use, beginning with the input of routes D5 and D6 on 14 February, followed on 21 March by the 257 (and 215 on Sundays and morning 678), though this time only three Metrobuses went along; the routes were intended for Dominators, allowing the 165/365 at Dagenham to resume Metrobus operation. This cleared space at Northumberland Park to take on the 76 and 259 from Leaside's Tottenham on the 28th, but M operation endured as the new contractor had to take several second-hand examples to fill in while its new Arrows were manufactured. All came from London General, donning the new 'central London' red and yellow livery and taking the numbers 301-7/9/15-9, while M240/6/74 were loaned for a month. The 76 handed its Northumberland Park Tesco segment to the 171A. Also on 28 March came the first OPO conversion for five years in the shape of the 139, a simultaneous move to North Acton costing the route its Holloway evening and Sunday Ms. The newly-acquired Ms at Northumberland Park soon ticked off routes 67, 91, 97, 97A, 158, 212, 215 and 257, while five of the mkIIs moved from Northumberland Park to Dagenham to man the 369 so that its yellow Arrows could fill in on the 259 temporarily. These Metrobuses stayed put to effect a type switch on the 296 so that its Olympians could assume the 158.

The East London Line finally reopened on 28 March, allowing the ELX to come off, but doubts over the rebuilt line prompted the commissioning of an extension for one week only, this being operated by Tottenham with Ms. Capital Citybus 175 had already been repainted yellow in December, and now No 177 followed. Tottenham sent eight Ms to Clapton to displace ex-Kentish Bus Ls to Norwood, while the first of ten Ms were sent away for open-topping for new Arriva partner London Coaches, which needed to replace its ageing DMSs. After that, the opportunity was taken to improve the age profile at Clapton, ten mostly B-registered Ms replacing examples two years their senior. They were fitted with AVL and dispersed.

Metrobuses were recertified, and M266, 491 and 544 joined the fleet in April. The Arriva firms were among the first to introduce bus-lane cameras, planted in the fuselage to the right of the blind box; the practice had spread widely by summer. At Metroline Contract Services, M1429 lost its rear window upon repanelling in May and M1428 became the first to receive a tree-deflector bar protecting the nearside front roof dome.

The 137/137A pair were altered on 25 April to a more conventional pattern, the latter now assuming the southernmost corridor and the 137 returning on Sundays with Brixton Ms, but its evening service now reverted to RML operation. 2 May saw the 110 at London United's Hounslow allocated a lone double-decker for schoolday work, formalising wanderings of the type since the route was allocated there in January, and on the 3rd the 70D returned for 1998, together with Ms on the Sunday 267 and R68; OMs 171 and 241 also worked a 'Millennium Special' 600 to Greenwich on Saturdays for this summer. Capital Citybus's Hackney consolidated all the local school routes on 30 May, namely the 20('20D') and morning arm of the 678. At Dagenham the 296 was now first choice for the mkII Ms, some also popping up on the King George Hospital link route 396 alongside just about any other type that could be mustered.

An old friend returned in May 1998 with Ensignbus deciding to reconvene as a bus operator and awarded 22 discs with which to do so: naturally Metrobuses formed the basis of the new runout.

A third Metrobus at London General was open-topped, M420 becoming OM420 in May, but this time the livery was that on London Central's T172/803 and the fleetname London Central. It was assigned to the Greenwich Clipper service running from Camberwell alongside OM171 and T803. M202, meanwhile, gained a black-based advert for 33 export beer and CentreWest trainer M1418 a silver livery with red skirt encouraging blood donation; at MTL London M1393 was covered in orange, which was considered to be a more prominent colour for the task of attracting more driving applicants to Potters Bar. London United began taking delivery of more Volvo Olympians for the 281 between May and 25 July. County Bus stood down M80 in May and returned M782 to Arriva London North; M372 was withdrawn in June but the company took on M208 (with yellow stripes) and red M232, plus M419/93 to restore partial double-deck operation to the 370 and 373 and displace Dart SLFs needed at Southend. The latter pair were refurbished and converted to single-door (but with the bulkheads replaced) and were loaned from Arriva Colchester.

Some wrangling within Arriva's subsidiaries on 20 June saw the 141 restored daily to Wood Green with Ms; so went the existing Sunday share (ex-DBS) for standardisation, while the 41 was transferred from

Above: One of the final alterations to the Metrobus as it approached its 20th anniversary was the strengthening of the body structure on several London General Ms through the fitting of a smaller rear window. M207 (BYX 207V), allocated to Merton, demonstrates as it rests at the back of Upper Ground in Waterloo on 15 August 1998. The flush-fitting smoked-glass-effect tail-light units that replaced their long-serving chrome-edged predecessors on the vast majority of Ms can also be seen. *Author*

Enfield's M780 was the first bus to carry the new 80%-red version of Arriva livery (with beige 'cow horn' and yellow piping), appearing to accompany the group's Annual Report on 24 February. On 2 April the group then unleashed its formal renaming exercise, by which Leaside became Arriva London North and South London Arriva London South (trading as Arriva serving London); of the other M-operating companies, County Bus became Arriva East Herts & Essex. Leaside Travel alone was untouched; during February and March M353/89 had been loaned to Edmonton to cover the 34 while its existing

Right: The only glass surfaces not covered by Contravision on Potters Bar's M1393 (C393 BUV) are the windscreen, doorway halves and two windows on the lower deck. This four-speed Metrobus had during its life ensured that the conversion of Muswell Hill from M to T would never be completed, and after that was converted to single-door and fitted with coach seats (just visible upstairs through all the orange vinyl); privatisation saw it adopt MTL SightseerS colours. In May 1998 this particular livery was applied as a recruitment device, though interestingly is coy about quite for whom. MTL London was bought by Metroline on 2 July and renamed Metroline London Northern, and it was under this legal lettering that M1393 was taken to Duxford for the 1999 edition of Showbus. *Author*

Wood Green to Tottenham; the Ms needed came from the batch pulled out of Clapton in February and since fitted with AVL equipment for the penetration into this sector of the Countdown network. Arriva London South, however, used this set of changes to send the Ls spare from the loss of the 188 to Croydon to allow six of the garage's oldest Ms to be withdrawn; even so five of them were still scooped up by Tottenham for the 41.

The programme of 27 June saw London General's Battersea Bridge garage closed and the 295 (and residual 49 workings) moved back into Stockwell with the 24 Ms that had gathered there. London

Traveller, meanwhile, stepped up for its first LTB contracts, comprising schoolday augmentations on the 143 and 302 and self-contained school route 643. After a period of wandering, a second site in Neasden was settled. London United lost the 237 to Armchair, which ceded its own 260 to Metroline; Willesden took on the 260 with Ms, as before the Armchair period, and reduced its share on the 266 by restoring a portion to Cricklewood. The Ms for the 260 otherwise came from the stock already held at Willesden for the 302, which was single-decked again, this time with Dart SLFs (DLDs). At London United the 391 changed its allegiance again, passing to Hounslow.

Above: The final Arriva identity made its bow on 24 February 1998, London by necessity specifying a cut-down version with a hollowed-out scoop of 'Cotswold stone' anchored by 2in-deep white tape but in actuality mostly obscured by the advertising panels. To some acrimony, all subsidiaries' names were homogenised, Leaside and South London becoming Arriva London North and South respectively. The former's M939 (A939 SUL), working from Palmers Green, is seen at Edmonton Green on 9 August 1998. By this time over 300 Ms had been fitted with non-opening front upper-deck windows. *Author*

Two major purchases took place in one week in July 1998 – on the 2nd Metroline bought MTL London, soon renaming it Metroline London Northern (trading as Metroline). This was just in time for the 217 and 231 to be set going with new DMLs two days later, both routes losing their Potters Bar Ms; ten of the oldest were withdrawn and put into store at Universitybus's Hatfield premises. In compensation schoolday Metrobuses were added to the 231 (Leaside Travel) and Capital Citybus (191). The latter was the subject of the second buyout on the 8th, passing to FirstGroup as First Capital. A sustained period of tendering victories for this company brought in the W8 on 25 July, and all the new Arrows were in place on the 76 and 259 by then so the Metrobuses were put to work here (and on the N20 at night), after a period

which had seen 316 loaned to Dagenham. Both W8 and N20 were taken at the expense of Metroline London Northern, which with the recent single-decking of the 217 and 231 now had a lot of Metrobuses spare; M1234 became the first to gain a blue skirt but six more found themselves dismantled for spare parts. Also on 25 July the 10 at Metroline London Northern's Holloway was extended full-time to Archway to replace the C12, additionally regaining crew operation during Monday to Friday evenings. The two Ms at London United's Kingston had to have their blinds amended locally to reflect the renumbering of their route 468 to 568 from 25 July.

Despite having retained the 127 for a further term, Arriva Croydon & North Surrey (its Volvo B6s still carrying Londonlinks livery and fleetnames) had the

Left: The creation of the GLC in 1965 had produced a geographic anomaly on its southern edge when Epsom & Ewell opted out, leaving a deep salient based on Chessington. Provision of bus services across this line has been complicated ever since, passenger demand being no respector of arbitrary borders. Just such a route was what was known variously as 468, 568 and 467, operating between Chessington and Epsom. For a time it was the sole reason for a Metrobus to remain at London United's Kingston garage in the form of M203 (BYX 203V), looking very smart for a bus approaching its 21st year of service when seen in Epsom on 19 October 1999. *Geoff Rixon*

route taken away by a dissatisfied LTB on 1 August; up stepped London General with Sutton Ms (five being transferred in), the rest being subcontracted to Stagecoach Selkent with Plumstead DALs.

Following the conversion to VA of the 281, Fulwell now received 10.7-metre Dart SLFs (DPs) for the R70 from 11 August; only now did sales begin from this company, M34 becoming White Rose's first. Between 20-27 August and again from 10-31 September a temporary route 509 was operated by London United M from Shepherd's Bush (Fulwell lending those ex-Airbus versions that had managed to retain their

coach seats) while repairs were undertaken to Hammersmith Bridge; the route linked the Bus Station with the north end of the bridge. Ms also turned out on the 283 during this period and even once on the R69.

First Capital continued to advance, grabbing Stagecoach East London's N50 on 22 August. On the 29th, however, one tender did not go to plan when Capital Logistics, winners of the 60 from Arriva London South, could not take over as planned due to the late delivery of its new DAF DB250RS(LF) low-floor double-deckers (only one of which was present

Left: The tendering arena had become more stable than might have been expected by the end of the 1990s, five-year contract terms producing changeover programmes at regular intervals. That in the Croydon region came around again on 29 August 1998 and one of its facets had actually threatened the 166's existence altogether until its regulars protested. Instead it was reduced to a single-deck route and its eastern leg hived off into new route 466, which then proceeded south to allow the withdrawal of London & Country's route 400. Only partially repainted, with grey LBL skirt turned red but tape band still *in situ*, Croydon's M555 (GYE 555W) heads south towards Caterham-on-the-Hill in September. *Chris Evans*

at all in London by this summer); instead Blue Triangle and Stagecoach Selkent (Bromley) swung into action, the former's initial contribution lasting only a few days. The 60 shifted southwards to become Streatham Garage-Old Coulsdon, taking the southern section of the 50. Also in this sector the 166 escaped a planned withdrawal by itself probing southwards, losing its roads east of West Croydon to new Croydon M/L-operated 466 but gaining an Epsom Buses-operated portion beyond Chipstead Valley to Epsom. This new 466 linked the old Shirley Inn target of the 166 with Caterham-on-the-Hill, terminus hitherto of London & Country-operated 400 (now withdrawn). Again the L proportion at Croydon increased so that Ms could be withdrawn. The new vehicles for Metrobus's conquest of the 119 and 320 from Stagecoach Selkent were not all available, however, and as in the previous year with the 64, two Metrobuses deputised on the 261. In the interim, fleetnumbers had appeared at this company and the two in question were 320/1 (ex-M320/1, as it happened). They stayed long enough to stray to the 161, both appearing on more than one occasion; after their work was done 320 remained behind as a trainer (and occasional service bus, visiting the 119 on 25 April and 18 May 1999).

Carnival for 1998 again saw CentreWest throwing its Ms into the fray from anywhere it could find them, with Alperton assisting on the 18, 28 and 31 and Acton Tram Depot joining in for the first time.

Meanwhile, Arriva London South trainer M282, now in a scheme for Dark & Lovely cosmetics (like M1260 at CentreWest), became the first Metrobus to be used as a float in the procession itself!

The hard core of 20 remaining Routemaster routes continued to see regular substitution by doored buses, but in September M1107 was despatched from Stockwell to Waterloo (RA) to join the 11's complement as a more permanent helping hand; as a former trainer at Stockwell it lacked the ticket machine and assault screen required of an OPO bus. It soon became the only M to don 'RED ARROW' logos when a repaint was effected in December!

The 313 gained a schoolday M on 1 September, operated, like the 231, by Leaside Travel, while London Traveller added new school route 626 (the renumbering of the 326s, which had come off after 25 July). Further Ms were stood down when Metroline converted the 16 at Cricklewood to AV operation on 19 September, six C-registered Ms going into Harrow Weald to dislodge the company's eldest examples for scrapping on site. Plans by the former MTL London to convert the 84 and 242 back to M operation and cascade the more valuable Scanias to Liverpool died with the takeover by Metroline, but the 84 was single-decked on Sundays from 19 September, with the new DML- and DMS-class Dart SLFs bought this year. The R70 at London United, so recently single-decked, now gained back a schoolday Metrobus, this time from Hounslow.

The receipt of new Dart SLFs at Arriva London South had by now released enough Darts to convert Croydon's 166 from M, and this was carried out on 26 September. Changes to Thamesway services on this date brought the 191 proper to Capital Citybus with its Darts, allowing Metrobus visits over and above the scheduled schoolday workings. Another vehicle shuffle returned the balance of mkII Metrobuses to Dagenham to accompany the move of the 158 from Northumberland Park back into Hackney (otherwise with Dominators) and the conversion of the 257 to Arrows; 112 was sold this month, while the first (so to speak) to receive the new 'ƒ' logos replacing the 'C' devices either side of the blind box was 306, returned after an accident earlier in the year.

On 3 October Leaside Travel, with its Edmonton garage, was taken back into the Arriva London North fold after less than a year with the former County Bus management; operated with the 14 Ms were various portions of the 34, 231 and 313 and stand-alone school routes 617, 629 and 699. The troubled 60 now gained a more permanent measure of Blue Triangle operation, its distant Ferry Lane base at Rainham able to field the occasional ex-PTE Metrobus alongside two Titans. Preparing for a tender win to be assumed in 1999, Blue Triangle then purchased eight ex-London United Ms (19/28, 112/46/79/95, 462, 1012) from dealer Mike Nash; all Metrobuses at this company were dubbed an MCW class whatever their

origin. Newly-convened White Rose commenced with ex-London United M34 and began to assist on the 60.

Arriva London North's Tottenham lost its third M route of 1998, on 17 October ceding the 171A to First Capital which relaunched it as 341 with new Volvo Olympians; of the Ms sold, several began the mission of stiffening other Arriva fleets by heading to Arriva Northumbria and Arriva Scotland West (formerly Clydeside). At least the 220 got its Sunday Ms back at London United, and Tottenham commenced a route numbered (or lettered) SWX in association with the revamped Sadlers Wells Theatre.

Even now the net withdrawals of Metrobuses from their seven operating fleets had numbered fewer than a hundred examples, but the conversion of the 242 (the Clapton impostor at Arriva London North) to DLA operation from 5 November could be said to sound the death-knell for the M. These low-floor double-deckers were DAF's answer to the new standard of low-floor technology and already companies retaining or winning tenders were placing orders for similar vehicles, which at this stage was the Dennis Trident and Volvo's as-yet-unveiled new chassis. Only the long delay expected between the placement and fulfilment of these orders, not to mention the sheer numbers to be replaced, was ensuring the M a longer stay of execution. The DLAs displaced the 242's ex-Kentish Bus Ls to the 253, allowing Clapton's Ms to depart – all except M1138,

Left: The floats wending their way through the circuitous backstreets of North Kensington and Ladbroke Grove for the Notting Hill Carnival every August Bank Holiday need to be big enough to blast music as loudly as is physically possible. Making music of its own on the afternoon of 30 August 1998 is M282 (BYX 282V), a Brixton-based Metrobus trainer sporting an all-over advertisement for Dark & Lovely cosmetics. *Author*

Right: Capital Logistics of West Drayton had been awarded the 60 for takeup on 29 August 1998, but appealed for a postponement due to having gambled wrongly on the availability by that time of the first low-floor double-deckers.
Instead Blue Triangle and Stagecoach Selkent were allocated as stop-gaps, the former able to use Ms from a small but growing number of acquisitions. Still in London United livery when espied in the Purley region in October, M195 (BYX 195V) would soon be renumbered MCW195 to bring it into common cause with Metrobuses that had not derived from LT successors. *Chris Evans*

Left: The Passright experiment of 1998/99 depended on passenger honesty, never the most reliable of variables, unfortunately! If they had a ticket, they could simply 'pass right' of the driver while farepayers paid as normal. To simplify this some of the Ms on Wood Green's W3 had their doorway handrail removed, while the Holloway aspect saw the 271 reverting to M operation so that the V-class Volvo Olympians inherited from London Suburban Buses could go onto the W7. At Holloway Road on 14 May 1999 is Holloway's M67 (WYW 67T), one fitted with a bus-lane camera. With new Dennis Tridents already on order prior to the takeover of MTL London by Metroline, no need was seen to repaint any more Ms, and it showed. *Author*

which clung on for dear life. M788 was the first 'M' at Arriva North-East (ex-Grey-Green) where it became trainer 788.

On 7 November the 634 became the first intra-Metroline transfer, leaving the Contract Services department for the more mundane Potters Bar. Completing a good year for Capital, the 1 was taken on from London Central on 14 November; as well as the existing New Cross Titans taken on hire, the route (operated for the moment from Dagenham) was stiffened with two mkII Metrobuses (279/89) still in yellow (the repaint programme into the now-standard 80%-red livery not having reached this type yet). The N1, however, was worked from Northumberland Park with the other First Capital night routes, and four of these N1 duties finished on the 1 in the mornings.

The introduction of the Passright ticketing experiment on routes 41, W3 and W7 from 18 November prompted both the removal of the doorway stanchions from Wood Green's Ms (so that passholders could board on the honour system

without impeding the flow of cash payers) and the swap of the 271's Vs to the W7, Holloway's Ms coming back to the 271 in return. A late innovation was the treatment of many Wood Green Ms (and some at London United) to illuminated side advert panels.

After the problems experienced with route 60 and 127 (with more to come!) a similar situation developed when Q-Drive went into receivership on 20 October and its bus operations (Limebourne) were sold to this company's management on 20 November; the existing buses were repossessed by their lessors and emergency replacements had to be scrambled. First out was London Traveller GOG 230W on the 42 until Independent Way (the new holding company of Limebourne) could buy some ex-Metroline DTs, but the 156 had to be run free of charge with the buses of four operators; using Metrobuses were Metroline Contract Services and Nostalgiabus (this last using M11 that it had had on hire from London General since October); by the beginning of December the situation had stabilised – for the moment. At that point the 60 was formally reassigned to Driver Express, a Horsham-based company intending to trade as Omnibus London, with an anticipated start date of 23 January 1999.

Seasonal route K50 linking Chessington with Kingston was this year operated by London United,

with Ms from Fulwell and Kingston. On 5 December a sheaf of contract awards affected Metroline and CentreWest; the former's Edgware lost the 292 to a second spell at Sovereign but picked up the 113 on transfer from Cricklewood instead; Willesden withdrew from the 266 to give Cricklewood free rein, thus forcing the OPO segments of the 6 and 98 to accept as many DLDs as AVs and Ms. Willesden's Ms now wandered to the 297, taken on tender from CentreWest otherwise with DLDs. The 92 at CentreWest was rather unwisely single-decked with new DMLs, just the one afternoon schoolday journey keeping an M. Out went ten of Alperton's last 14 Ms to First Capital as Nos 308/10-4/21-3/8 (Ms 498, 369, 311, 339, 343, 434, 451, 487, 843, 418). M393, 427 and 465 were kept behind at the last minute to join M421, so the numbers at Dagenham were made up with the most unusual return to London of former M330/2/413 from First Leicester, becoming 330/2/3; of those that were repainted in January 1999, 333 was immediately distinguishable by the yellow band being carried at a lower level than on the others, this due to its repaint by First Leeds staff (where the bus had been seconded as a trainer) unfamiliar with the template.

Finally for 1998, the arrival of LDPs for a second crack at single-decking the 155 caused a dozen Ms to depart Merton.

Above: Another victory for First Capital brought in the 1 and N1 on 14 November 1998; after a few weeks hiring the previous incumbent's Titans, the company made use of its new tie-up with CentreWest by acquiring several more Metrobuses like 322 (GYE 487W), formerly Alperton's M487. Based at distant Dagenham, this bus is seen at Waterloo on 16 March 1999; new Dennis Tridents (TNs) were on order and awaited. First Capital's buses were fitted with Wayfarer TG150 ticket machines during that month, as a programme thus to fit all contractors rolled on. *Geoff Rixon*

SIX

Declining Years

The year 1999 began in the worst possible way – with literally hours to spare Driver Express defaulted on its commitment to take over the 60 in full on 23 January. Theoretically restored to the contract, Capital Logistics still could field none of its expected DAF double-deckers and Stagecoach Selkent itself had to withdraw to furnish massive gains in the Woolwich tenders, so an unprecedented emergency timetable swung into action, operated with a fascinating collection of just about anything that could be snatched from its normal employ and stuck on the 60! Where Metrobuses were concerned, all Driver Express could muster before fading away ignominiously within ten days (prior to complete collapse on 23 February) was ex-Reading Buses CJH 166/70V, while Nostalgiabus could only contribute between its school bus commitments. Weekends (rail replacement obligations permitting) seemed more predictable, First Capital sending mostly F-NHJ mkII Metrobuses, while Blue Triangle's growing fleet (adding M270/1, 463 in January) was in any of three liveries and White Rose, adding to M34 with M73/88 and 276 ex-London United and M2 ex-Metroline, turned out on the 60 by basing themselves at Nostalgiabus's Mitcham depot overnight. Part of this company's holding group identified as Sidney Road Travel, which was the nominal purchaser of these four most recent Metrobus acquisitions, and repaints into 'retro' livery of red with black grille and white top (only 'authentic' on M2/34!) were fitted in somewhere amid the maelstrom. Both Capital Logistics and Driver Express took these Ms on hire for the 60 at times, using their own discs.

With attention focused on the 60, not far away the 127 quietly became a majority-Blue Triangle service, Stagecoach Selkent and Nostalgiabus coming off and London General's Sutton Ms continuing in support. A week later the 264 was transferred within Arriva London South from Croydon back to Thornton Heath, losing Ms for Ls.

First Capital added ex-London General 324/34/8 (ex-M348, 434, 488) in January, while CentreWest's M421 left Alperton after all – for scrap. The 1's hired Titans had to be returned to London Central while Dagenham's latest M intake was undergoing repaints, yellow 271/9/89 deputising in the interim until the Metrobuses entered service at the end of the month.

Arriva's accelerating cascade of Metrobuses, while adding M441 to Leaside Travel in December, included two more trainers for Arriva London North-East, M63 and 280 (renumbered plain 063 and 280). The withdrawal of Ms from Wood Green's 221 furnished buses for a new cause still – Arriva Croydon & North Surrey, the former London & Country and/or Londonlinks. Owing to the extreme difficulty turning a profit in this affluent region, it was decided to replace the company's newest buses with refurbished Metrobuses; the need was such that most were pressed into service at Croydon (CR), Crawley (CY), Horsham (HM) and Merstham (MM) in existing condition, starting on 8 February on Dorking-area locals but soon penetrating into Kingston on the 406, into Croydon on the 405 and 409 and into Sutton on the 420 and 440. Arriva Derby and Preston Street Coachworks of Faversham were sub-contracted to do this work alongside Enfield. A total of 43 was taken, three for training work in December 1998 and the rest following over 1999. While the Ms for service retained their existing fleetnumbers, the trainers formed variously a YDT (Kent Thameside) or ZDT (the ex-L&C-area companies) class, M388 (YDT388) pitching up at Arriva Kent Thameside's Northfleet and M776 (YDT776) following in May via Limebourne; M417 (ZDT417) was eventually readied for service and replaced by M168 (ZDT168). Blinds were vestigial, just a number and destination going in the ultimate box, but upon refurbishment (which involved conversion to single-door without an increase in capacity) three-track blind boxes were fitted and internally the treatment was to Arriva's recently-introduced turquoise moquette with wall paint of roughly the same base colour. This part of Arriva even got hold of the ten mkII Metrobuses new to Maidstone & District (and already used once in London when loaned to Boro'Line in 1990; once or twice they managed to slip beyond the bounds of their local routes and reach the London suburbs on Croydon's route 405! The presence of widespread training facilities within the group allowed the Ms to roam as far afield as Maidstone. The first refurbished example (M596) was completed in March and all were done by February 2000.

At the other end of London Arriva East Herts & Essex's Ware began receiving refurbished Ms from

Above: Perhaps the saga of the 60 wasn't just a mess that the media devoured gleefully, but the true spirit of what deregulation would have brought – somehow, a myriad of unlikely operators succeeded in pulling together an even more eclectic selection of vehicles and saving the day. First Capital's ex-South Yorkshire Metrobuses were in their last year of service in north-east London, and in Mitcham on 23 January 1999, the first day of what would turn out to be about three months of this situation, 116 (JHE 146W) pitches in, far from its usual Walthamstow-area turf. *Geoff Rixon*

Below: Blue Triangle was also at the forefront of the 60's emergency array of buses, simultaneously holding down the 127 nearby, which had also faltered under similar circumstances. Its attractive initial livery is displayed to full effect elsewhere in Mitcham on former GM Buses MCW503 (GBU 3V) on 31 March 1999. *Geoff Rixon*

Above: Few post-London Country bus operators have really prospered in car-dependent north Surrey, the experience in 1999 of its Arriva-renamed local descendants being no different. They did try to cut costs by removing all the newish buses taken recently and replacing them with refurbished Metrobuses displaced from London by the advent of new DLA-class DAF low-floor double-deckers, and the likes of M551 (GYE 551W) was the result. Points to note from the refurbishment are the panelling over of the exit door (but retaining the bulkheads, leaving room only for a thinner window), the unattractive tree deflector fastened to the roof dome and the national version of Arriva turquoise, never a particularly comfortable colour and not helped by the yellow tape looking odd at a lower elevation than on comparable buses. It is seen on the 406 at Surbiton Crescent on 29 September 1999, though without any destination blinds. *Geoff Rixon*

Below: The Ms refurbished for the 310 and 311 at Arriva East Herts & Essex's Ware garage received a red version of Arriva livery with a full cream front and were generally better presented than those to the south, allowing three years of operation. 5348 (KYV 786X) is pictured in Waltham Cross High Street on 14 May 2000. *Andrew Jeffreys*

the same programme, just in time for a renumbering scheme which saw them join existing stocks in the 5300s. The livery for the 310 was meant to be red with full cream scoop but M5 (ex-M1445 and, from New Year's Day 1999, plain 5355) received turquoise by accident. This company's intake were also converted to single-door but received 'graffiti' moquette in red with black scrawls.

On 7 February the reborn Ensignbus got into its stride by taking over First Capital's commercial 324 and 348 with its growing collection of blue and silver Metrobuses of various types, which were soon branded for the route. So much for being a trainer, CentreWest's M1422 was put back into service from Greenford on the E1 from 8 February, still in yellow and red.

The 60 was settling down, at last; First Capital reduced its participation to Saturdays after 7 February and came off after the 20th, having introduced another Metrobus variation with the loan of refurbished Arriva East Herts & Essex 5349 (ex-M419) on the 13th, while Blue Triangle dwindled to mornings and evenings only. Finally Capital Logistics started putting its DAFs into service from 9 March and by 16 April all the standby operators had stood down their heroic efforts, the only Metrobuses remaining on the 60 being those that Capital Logistics continued to hire from Blue Triangle, M271, 462/3; between 16 April and the end of the month these were kept at Capital Logistics' own depot rather than

coming all the way from Rainham. However, an old wound reopened when Limebourne had its hired ex-Grey-Green Volvo B10M single-deckers collected by their purchaser on 4 March; the company turned to Arriva London North, hiring six Metrobuses. Off to deputise on the 156 and 42 (the latter seeing its first double-deckers in over a decade, and certainly its first Metrobuses) went M549, 612/31/2, 776 and 1134 on 4 March, M531, 1152/5 following on the 27th (M531 replacing M612). London Traveller, meanwhile, changed its mind about using Ls, selling them in February and taking more ex-West Midlands Metrobuses instead in the shape of GOG 233/8/45W, which ran around in blue for some time.

A clutch of London United routes retained from 6 March included some of Westlink's, which identity was now phased out; the Hounslow-operated double-deck workings on the 235 and R70, worked by nine Metrobuses on a shared basis with seven Surrey contracts, were all transferred west into Hounslow Heath (from this date coded HH), bringing this base its first double-deckers and immediate visits by Ms to the 81 and 216. The M on the H22 was withdrawn, while at night the N11 moved to Shepherd's Bush and the N97 did the same at weekends.

Further DLAs into Arriva London North took over Palmers Green's 329 from 8 March, the rest going onto the 144 at Wood Green in replacement of the SLWs and occasional M augmentation.

Above: Ensignbus returned for a second stint on 7 February 1999, taking over First Capital's pair of Romford-Lakeside/Bluewater commercial routes with a host of Metrobuses from various sources. 100 (ORJ 100W) was new to Greater Manchester PTE and is captured in Romford on 24 June, in the elegant blue and silver save for the panel that has supplied the blind box conversion. Copious branding is evident, covering both 324 and 348. *Author*

On 27 March changes to the route 68 corridor renumbered Croydon's 68A to 468 and added Croydon new night route N68 over both 68/468 and thence to Purley, while at Metroline London Northern Potters Bar's 317 lost Ms for three new DMLs upon retention of its contract. Where did the Ms go but straight back to the 310A and 310B, allowing the non-standard DAF SB220s to leave. Still at Potters Bar, a single M returned to the 84 when the journeys avoiding Potters Bar town centre were reconfigured to operate 'with the flow' into St Albans and back again in the afternoons, but at Arriva London North Tottenham's 243 (and 73 on Sundays) was partially converted from M to L operation when ten of the Kentish Bus-specification Olympians were released by cuts to Norwood's services; B-registered Ms were selected for withdrawal.

Stability for the 127 came at the price of its peripatetic Blue Triangle Ms when the whole route was taken over by Mitcham Belle on 10 April, with new Darts, but Nostalgiabus was restored to its schoolday working now that the crisis on the 60 was all but over. It wished it hadn't resumed the corresponding route 156 journey from that day, however, when sustained violence by the local schoolchildren forced its withdrawal on the 27th; Limebourne bravely stepped in with a hired Metrobus – complete with on-board security guard! At London General, Stockwell took back the 196 from London Central, helping to soothe the loss of the 337 to London United; Ms remained, only now from Fulwell – and to clear space here Kingston was given the 411 with five Metrobuses.

The 'future' commenced for Metroline London Northern on 19 April, for that was what surmounted the logos on the first of 65 new Plaxton President-bodied Tridents of TP class; their first conquest from this date was the 43 (and N43), dislodging some of Holloway's oldest Ms. No repaints at all had accrued to Ms since their inheritance from MTL London, and their appearance was disheartening in the extreme! Thus the transfer of M37 to Harrow Weald let the side down somewhat; it would be the vanguard of several all-red Ms to cross the inter-Metroline divide when four were put into Willesden to augment the 52 for the duration of the Circle Line closure in June.

Limebourne returned Arriva London North's Ms between April and July and in May bought six of London General's, M120/88, 237/79, 476/7; still that wasn't enough and M673/719 were hired from Arriva London North in July. Ms leaving this firm started turning up at Arriva Scotland West (Clydeside).

Blue Triangle had been stockpiling ex-London United Ms for a greater purpose than rescuing the 60, and this came to be on 1 May when changes surrounding the opening of the first stage of the Jubilee Line Extension introduced new route 474 (Canning Town-East Beckton, taking over the southernmost section of the 69 and then assisting the 101 round the North Woolwich bottleneck). In May M27, 160, 616 and 1033 arrived from Metroline London Northern, joining March acquisition M932 from London United. A new livery made its debut on M981, consisting of more red with cream cantrail band and a thin cream band below each deck, plus black window surrounds.

This year's 70D (and new counterpart 70) were with London General OM171/241 as usual, but based at Merton with Sutton's contribution being the drivers themselves. May saw Ms restored to Alperton, three (including Greenford's sole M1422 in yellow and red training livery) coming back following the removal of the school augmentations' LA-class Leyland Olympians. Alperton's night routes had generally forsaken Ms for the newer types by this year.

Below: It seemed that small operators were collapsing one after the other, despite much faith being placed in them by LT perhaps at the expense of bigger concerns. Limebourne called in the receivers at the end of 1998, losing all the new buses it had obtained since its creation out of bits of Q-Drive; instead, in came trusty Metrobuses no longer wanted at Arriva London North and London General. Borrowed from the former, and showing both Arriva logos and the green bookmark device of Limebourne, is former Wood Green M631 (KYO 631X) at Wimbledon on 18 March 1999.
Geoff Rixon

First Capital's red repaint programme had now reached its mkII Metrobuses; in June 179 was renumbered 172 to match its registration, the number having been freed by the exit of a Leyland Olympian.

Failing to learn its lesson, London General single-decked the 155 again on 29 May, this time with LDP-class Dart SLFs. Only the transfer of its southern third to the 219 negated this somewhat. This was a rough day for Stockwell, which lost the 49 to Armchair and the 344 to a rejuvenated Limebourne, both routes being single-decked but for one Limebourne M on the 344 at school times (and even the minibus-restricted C3!). To compensate it absorbed the London Central contribution on the 37 and received the 155 (naturally prompting appearances of its own Ms). At night the N44 was transferred from Stockwell to Sutton, still capable of seeing Ms despite the NV takeover. Even so, all the Ms on the routes retained by Stockwell and Merton were on borrowed time, as the contracts stipulated new low-floor buses by the end of the second year. Limebourne's M situation was extremely fluid; having returned all but two Arriva Ms and loaning its own M237 to London Traveller (on 30 June), it now had to take M34/73 on loan from White Rose. The all-over ad craze seemed to be over for Arriva's London North, M14, 382 and 445 (whose most recent scheme had been for Yardley lipstick) all losing theirs during June for fleet livery, which M617 took to Leaside Travel in the same month. M282 at Arriva London South was repainted in July and M422 (ex-London Dungeon livery) in August; finally North East London College-dedicated M317 lost its green livery for a new coat of white. A new training livery bowed in July when London General M202 and 978 were painted diagonal blue over the front and tapering up towards the back, with red starting on the lower deck and swelling towards the back. M1389 followed in September, but no others were done.

Above: The M class, though divided into seven portions, was really only threatened for the first time by 1999 when the first low-floor double-deckers began arriving *en masse.* Holloway's route 43 was converted to the Plaxton President-bodied version of the Dennis Trident (known by Metroline as TPs) from 19 April 1999, and by then buses like M1083 (B83 WUL), seen at Highbury Corner a month before the conversion commenced, were looking extremely rough; the only repainted segment at all on this bus is a replacement offside front wing! *Author*

Above: Eventually Ms taken off service gravitated to training duties, where they have been among the easiest of buses for potential drivers to get to grips with. In July 1999 London General painted two of its Ms into a startling blue and red diagonal livery, demonstrated by M202 (BYX 202V) on its way past the Asda store at Kingston Vale in June 2000. *Geoff Rixon*

Between the two major tasks of First Capital's latest second-hand M intake, they would be turned to the unusual employment of assisting the 23 between 12 and 25 June during closure of the Circle Line. The next day Dagenham commenced working its greatest capture ever – thirty-bus route 25. The company's new Tridents (TNs) had arrived only in sufficient strength to furnish the 1, and this only because a handful of ex-Stagecoach Selkent Ls came in on hire, but for two months Ms reached eastern targets never imaginable after the established deployment of Ms and Ts and even after the TN conversion they continued to appear. The M-to-TN conversion of the W8 at Northumberland Park commenced from this time, but only in dribs and drabs.

The '133E' came back on 3 July, in even greater strength this time, to once again cover the Bank branch of the Northern Line during another period out of service. Four Go-Ahead garages participated, Sutton, Putney and mostly Stockwell all able to supply Metrobuses and this time authorised to take 'last tube' passengers all the way to Edgware or High Barnet! Night bus changes on 24 July took the N6 from Holloway to Willesden, costing it its Ms, and added new route N94 over the daytime 94 and run by the Ms of Shepherd's Bush (London United).

More Metroline London Northern Ms were made redundant on 3 July when the 232 at Potters Bar was converted to DLD-class Darts; the 112's schoolday element at the other end of the route was reconfigured as 611, still with Metroline Contract Services. Not so lucky was Wood Green's 644, however, which was withdrawn without replacement. All these schoolday changes applied from the new school year beginning on 1 September, on which date the 232 gained back a M component operated by Leaside Travel.

On 9 July TNs began replacing the Ms on the 18 at Westbourne Park, also taking over the N18, N23 and N139 by night, but three managed to hang on as spares cover. The expelled examples congregated at First Capital from the 24th, seeing off the hired Ls. They constituted Nos 325/7/9/31/5-7/9/50-4/7/61 (M465, 872, 898, 941, 884, 866, 887, 319, 340, 1051, 952, 892, 874, 857, 861), fitting around a block of Dominators. Despite a foretaste of their future beyond the 1 and 25 when three were deployed to Northumberland Park, none of this batch received a repaint and thus entered service on the 1 and 25 in a variety of schemes. Midland Bluebird was another extra-London recipient of redundant ex-CentreWest Ms.

Although Ms had now left the infamous 60, M216 (formerly of Metrobus) was acquired by Capital Logistics in July as a backup for its 16 DAFs; converted to single-door during its spell with

Metrobus, it was repainted red with a black skirt. Having had M11 on loan from London General for many months, Nostalgiabus purchased it in July. Similarly Limebourne acquired M73 from Sidney Road Travel early in July but later that month took its Metrobuses off the 42 due to clearance problems in East Street, thus spreading them to the 156 and 344. London Traveller, now based at the former Scancoaches depot in Harlesden (HN), undertook several hires in July, comprising London Pride 108 (EYE 325V), 110 (BOK 72V) and 112 (GOG 233W), then bought seven of Metrobus's nine remaining examples, M76, 235/59/62, 320, 447, 527. One last foray to London service by a 'Metrobus Metrobus' was by 320 (M320) to the 119 on 25 June, and after the sale just 321/52 remained as trainers, just in time to see the company sold to the Go-Ahead Group on 3 September.

HH rather than WK. M1008 breathed its last on 23 July at Clapham Junction when it accidentally ran over a prospective boarder while on route 337 and was then forced to crash into a shopfront by his aggrieved compatriots.

From 19 August a mix of DLAs and DLPs started taking over the 279 at Enfield from its Ms, in time for the contract start date on 16 September. The 25 at First Capital started to receive its intended TNs in earnest during August, the effect on the second-hand Metrobuses being their progressive move to Northumberland Park to replace the ex-South Yorkshire examples, which had put in eight solid years; 101/2/10/6/7/9, 277/97/8 were withdrawn during August and 106/13/4 sold. By September all of 1, 25 and W8 were TN-operated. Sold Ms from CentreWest started congregating at First Leeds and First Edinburgh.

Left: The delivery of a total of 87 Plaxton-bodied Dennis Tridents for the FirstGroup pair's routes 1, W8, 18 and 25 (in approximately that order) during the summer of 1999 allowed the stopgap second-hand Metrobuses to make their way from Dagenham to Northumberland Park to see off the yellow South Yorkshire imports. Again, to those familiar with the long reign of the Titan east of the Lea (or Lee) Valley, Metrobuses were a strange sight. M465 had become 325 (GYE 465W) without receiving a repaint, and by 22 November, when this bus was captured at Chingford Mount on the 97, no more were being done. *Author*

The Passright experiment ended on 1 August, the 271/W7 gaining back their proper buses, albeit with continuing wanderings of M and V classes. On the 9th a reversal of the London General/Central staff shortage theme introduced a London General element to the otherwise Peckham-operated P11, M1055 working from Stockwell on behalf of the Private Hire unit at London Central, which had been deputised to cover peak-hour needs on this route. If Stockwell couldn't manage it, Putney was known to send Ms too! Similar special duties saw open-top OM420 turning out on the 11 in August.

Preparing itself for the loss back to Metroline of Hounslow's route 140, London United sold ten Ls during August and the route's last month was spent with more Ms on it than hitherto. Similarly, the sale of Westlink's Deltas brought a surge of Ms onto the 81 from the end of July until DPs arrived to take over; from about this time the garage was officially coded

Metroline too was a recipient of new Tridents, the ALX400-bodied members of which it dubbed a TA class; examples took over the 16 in the first fortnight of August, enabling Cricklewood's AVs to transfer to Willesden for the 266; Ms released ejected Metroline's last Titans from the Contract Services department. Simultaneously at Holloway TPs were arriving for the 134 and N134; on 6 September the opportunity was taken to convert the 10 on Sundays from M to TP.

This year's Notting Hill Carnival augmentations saw Ms appearing on Westbourne Park's 328 introduced this year as well as the existing 31; loans came from Acton Tram Depot as well.

The 4 September scheme, as well as bringing TAs to Metroline's Harrow Weald for the 140, also introduced them to the 182 in place of Ms, though the conversion was fluid as the 140 took priority for the new Tridents and new school offshoot 640 also needed some; to this end nine red Ms ex-Potters Bar and seven ex-Willesden were transferred temporarily into Harrow Weald. Ms also abandoned the 183, which was single-decked by its new contractor Sovereign; thus also departed the M element on the H12 in favour of a similar operation by London Traveller. Despite an operator change for the 79, its schoolday element remained with a single M from CentreWest's Alperton garage. London Traveller's new contracts, routes 187 and 487, immediately saw appearance by its blue-and-yellow ex-Metrobus Ms due to the late delivery of the company's new Volvo B6BLEs. The company abandoned its Hertfordshire work to concentrate on its LTB contracts.

Underscoring another beating for Arriva Southern Counties, the 85's contract was transferred to London United outright, with the DAF double-deckers, but sure enough Fulwell's own Ms soon started to turn out in strength. To allow this, the 337 was reallocated from Fulwell to Hounslow. Arriva Croydon & North Surrey's Croydon garage ejected the 409 and its increasing number of refurbished Metrobuses to Merstham. All double-deckers at Merstham, Horsham and Cranleigh were Ms by August.

The 133 extras came off on 5 September, barring three days' respite when the reinstated Northern Line suffered teething troubles. Another Underground-related programme took place on 18 September to accompany the opening of another section of the Jubilee Line Extension. The once-mighty 109 was cut back to Brixton from the south, its roads into the West End (and Brixton allocation) passing to another incarnation of the number 59. Commencing from its home at Brixton garage, this route diverged from that of its predecessors, however, by going up Baylis Road once past the Elephant and then following the 188 to Euston. The 159, diverted from this date over Westminster Bridge to replace the 109, was reintroduced on Sundays with Brixton Ms and Thornton Heath Ls, while the 137 on Sundays was reallocated from Brixton to Norwood, losing Ms (though appearances by the type in crew mode

remained as frequent as ever). The Waterloo run of the 149 was withdrawn, along with the small Tottenham allocation that had operated it.

The rash decision to cut back the 199 and expect its passengers to switch to the JLE led to massive overcrowding on the 1 instead, which was projected from Surrey Quays to Canada Water to feed into the new line; as quickly as Thursday 23 September Blue Triangle was called on to provide extras in the peaks. MCW160/271 were the two Metrobuses deputised. At First Capital, the D5 was withdrawn and the D6 converted to Dart SLF (DMLs), costing four Metrobuses (100/4, 276/95). Fourteen were sold in October, including 296-9 inclusive and even two of those acquired less than a year ago (311/3); First's operations in Plymouth and Southampton were new beneficiaries.

M1138 continued to fight on alone at Clapton, two Ms (1309/401) coming on loan from Tottenham briefly to turn out alongside it on the 38 during September, while M645 was added to Leaside Travel to furnish a PVR increase of one bus on the 699. Similar assistance to RML routes came with the allocation of two more Ms to Waterloo for the 11 between October and December, M211 and 1225. The Metrobuses passed to Watford & District by London Traveller tended to come back on loan, including GOG 233W in green and cream; to alleviate the need for such loans the company bought M231 ex-London General. Another former London General bus, Limebourne's M237, having seen service at London Traveller, was now loaned to Nostalgiabus during October on its commercial route 306 (Kingston-Epsom) which was otherwise the bailiwick of Routemasters. Nostalgiabus's red and cream livery was applied to its first Metrobus that month, M11, and to M755 when taken in December, but not M502. At White Rose, M2, 276 and 563 were formally separated out to Sullivan Buses and M57 (the former, and to be future *Aldenham Aristocrat*) acquired. M29/44, broken up by Wigley, donated their parts.

Right: The number 59 seems to have a pathological attachment to the Brixton Road corridor, and on 18 September 1999 a third broadly identical incarnation was introduced to allow the trunk 109 to abandon its aspirations towards central London. Brixton's M173 (BYX 173V), in all-over red without fleetnames, emerges from its home garage on 24 September, on its way to the Euston terminus of this new route. DLAs were due by year's end. *Author*

Left: The opening of the Jubilee Line extension offered new opportunities for Tube travellers to skirt central London on their way to points east, and obviated the need for the 149's stubbornly clinging-on leg to Waterloo (and since the beginning of 1998 operated as a peak-hour-only bifurcation while the main route was redirected south to London Bridge). Latterly it was operated as a self-contained section from Tottenham garage, with the appropriate black-on-yellow blinds as displayed by M1297 (B297 WUL) at Liverpool Street on 24 August. The replacement final radiator grille panel on this bus is unpainted. *Author*

On 4 October London General's Putney regained a portion of the 170, theoretically with DRs but able to see Ms. After taking over the evening and Sunday OPO elements of the 13, Metroline London Northern's third wave of TPs converted the 17 between 5-9 October; 35 Ms were sold in September and 30 in October. Transfers of the remainder saw newer examples displace some of Cricklewood's oldest Ms, but in spite of the theoretical changeover to TAs, Harrow Weald retained examples. The MTL SightseerS livery vanished for good when trainers M1045/67 and 1396 were repainted into Metroline livery in November.

The final JLE-connected scheme was implemented on 9 October, on which date the P11's M-capable extras came off with the renumbering of the route to 381. The 16th saw the 279 and N279's contracts retained, with the N279 withdrawn between Waltham Cross and Upshire. The 191 gained an extra schoolday M from Northumberland Park. London United brought Stamford Brook back into use from the 30th, putting 19 Ms in for the 27 (ex-Shepherd's Bush) alongside the 94 on evenings and Sundays and the peak-hour H91 extras. The return of the 49 to Shepherd's Bush (albeit with DPs) prompted the return of Ms as visitors, while Hounslow began putting Ms out in strength on the 391.

Arriva East Herts & Essex continued to take small numbers of refurbished Ms, which between September and October had edged the former M1443-7 (5351/3/5/8/9) off the 310 at Ware, while the 370/373 at Grays lost their Metrobuses for second-hand Dart SLFs and finally, December saw the sale of all First Capital's original batches of second-hand Metrobuses, plus six of the 1998 acquisitions.

13 November saw Uxbridge's 207A withdrawn to become new Wing's Dart SLF-operated U7, four Ms departing for Acton Tram Depot and M1415 becoming the fourth M at Westbourne Park. Due to staff shortages at First CentreWest, London Traveller stepped in to provide buses for additional journeys on night routes N18 and N98 from 20 November until

year's end, but Ms returned to the N207 with the introduction of an Acton Tram Depot allocation replacing that of Alperton. On the 27th, Holloway's N2 was cut back so that new route N24 could take over the roads paralleling the daytime 24.

From 12 December Brixton's recently-introduced 59 began to receive DLAs at Arriva London South, along with Norwood's allocation on the 68, the latter route (and its X68 express partner) cascading Ls to Croydon for further replacement of Ms. However, after just ten months as a bus operator Ensignbus sold its operations on routes 324, 325 and 348 to Town & Country Buses on 11 December.

This Boxing Day Shepherd's Bush worked the 27 in lieu of Stamford Brook, which was not open on this day, a similar situation at Norwood obliging Brixton to cover the 137 with its own Ms. On New Year's Eve night, a particularly busy one due to the millennium, London Traveller pitched in on routes N13, N16, N23 and N94 as well as its own routes; this month saw M447 become the first into the intended (but in the event, abortive) livery of red with blue skirt and yellow band.

At the beginning of 2000, over 750 Metrobuses were still in London service, but the timetable of replacement by low-floor double-deckers was accelerating, many contracts already being specified for new vehicles and now just awaiting them. At Arriva London South, Croydon's M stock was hit again two weeks into the New Year when the 468 commenced conversion to DLA, the N68 also going over. Four of Brixton's recently-displaced Ms formed the first allocation at Beddington Farm (BF or CN), the garage acquired from Arriva Croydon & North Surrey with the previous August's restructuring. Here they were meant for contract work, but just once one of them was sneaked into service on the 403. Further south the blue Ms concentrated at Crawley, but service reductions associated with this switch-around caused the refurbishment programme which had brought them to this sector to be terminated; the final refurbishment on an M for Arriva East Herts &

Right: The 60 just wouldn't keep out of the headlines. After all the adventures it had been through, it was reassigned on 4 March 2000 back to the company which had lost it in the first place, Arriva London South. This time Beddington Farm garage, inherited from the former Londonlinks, was in charge with the existing DAFs, but as support two Ms were gathered. M809 (OJD 809Y) was one of them, and at Purley in September shows the 'lazy' blind for the 60. *Chris Evans*

Essex was simultaneously carried out during January. A most unusual M working between 17 January and 5 February was by Stockwell's M837, which alone was fitted with specially-made blinds to assist on the 345 during a period where the route was bouncing between four Go-Ahead garages; Stockwell came off on 5 February.

Route 293 rejoined the fold of 'red bus' routes (in practice if not logistically) when Surrey County Council awarded this formerly commercial route's Morden-Epsom core to London General; Sutton Ms took over on 22 January.

Connex Bus joined the ranks of ex-London M owners, adding M54, 140, 303, 565, 656 and 802 to a fleet of 29 Dennis Tridents ordered to take over the 3 and N3 from London Central on 5 February 2000; appearances in service proved very rare, but some received the company livery of red with shallow dark blue skirt surmounted by yellow tape.

On 17 February the first of 43 TNLs commenced the long process of converting route 207 to low-floor operation; Uxbridge's third went first (including the N207 at night), few Ms remaining at Uxbridge. London United was not far behind, but its choice was the Volvo B7TL of VA class; examples took over the 220 at Shepherd's Bush between 21 February and early March, also covering the N94 at night and 94 on Sundays. This released five Ms to Stamford Brook to cascade five ex-Airbuses to training duties. At Arriva London North, Wood Green got in the way of DLA allocations despite the 468 not being done, taking seven DLAs to commence the W3 from 26 February. Further London United VAs took over the 120 at Hounslow between 16-18 March.

On 26 February a scheme developed in Walthamstow; withdrawn was the 97A, replaced by new route 357 (also with First Capital Ms from Northumberland Park pending the transfer of TNs) but only as far as Chingford Hatch; new school route 657 was created to assist. Hackney's Sunday share of the 257 was swallowed up by Northumberland Park

and Dagenham's 511 into Romford was single-decked. Three ex-Uxbridge Ms came from CentreWest to Northumberland Park, released by new TNLs, but now that First Capital management had expanded to cover CentreWest, retained their M-prefixes. M1422 resumed its role as a trainer, being replaced at Alperton by M1377. At London Traveller, M199, 571, 693, 764 and 801 were acquired to replace two Manchesters, MRJ 54W and SND 145X.

Low-floor operation was by necessity rolled back when the 13's evening and Sunday OPO element was reallocated from Holloway to Edgware (which now faced the daytime Sovereign RMs across fencing at the same premises!) on 4 March and converted from TP back to M.

After all the hell experienced with the 60 in 1999, Capital Logistics now gave it up altogether and it passed straight back to Arriva London South. Joining Beddington Farm, however, to assist the transferred DAFs (now DLO/DLP class) were two Ms, 680 and 809, now specifically for service unlike the previous four, which moved out. Another kind of hell was what the denizens of Nostalgiabus's route 156 school journeys were wreaking on this small and vulnerable fleet; so much so that Connex Bus had to be engaged to step in on 15-17 March with five more ex-Travel West Midlands Metrobuses (GOG 259/62W, LOA 387/95/8X) still in their blue-based livery and otherwise used on rail replacements. They became an MW class with Connex.

The H91's accessory Metrobuses were withdrawn on 18 March. On the 25th Arriva London North-East moved out of Stamford Hill, where it had lodged since the closure of its traditional premises, and into an enlarged Tottenham; this brought the 24, 168 and 188 into the realms of possible M operation once again; the 68, while also making the move, did not see any due to its further transfer into Norwood later. The training Ms were scattered; while most went to Enfield, some passed to the remainder of Arriva London North-East at Barking, but this time did not

take up parallel fleetnumbers. At London General Putney added weekend operations to the 170, which was by now mostly M-operated, allowing Merton's sole scheduled schoolday M to come off. The N2's operation shifted south of the river, Norwood Ls (Arriva London South) replacing Holloway Ms (Metroline London Northern).

Routes 212 and 215 became less likely for M operation at First Capital's Northumberland Park, the former being single-decked with DMLs meant for Tramlink's feeder routes and its Olympians replacing Ms on the latter. The three loaned Ms went back to CentreWest alongside three of Capital's own (325/9/36), which had originated there in the first place and now once more became M465, 898 and 866. In a twist, this trio pitched up at St Mary Cray (Y)

which began operating the 1's augmentation duties in lieu of Blue Triangle between 27 March and 28 April. During March the 85 at London United's Fulwell saw the beginning of considerable M operation after a ten-year gap, this due to the route's DN-class DAFs needing repaints out of Arriva turquoise.

Conversions to low-floor double-deckers gained pace as the spring arrived; from 29 March further Volvo B7TLs into London United swept into Hounslow for the 111, 337 and H32, the Alexander-bodied VAs being followed in mid-April by Plaxton-bodied VPs; at night the N9, N11 and N97 also lost their Ms. Beginning on 27 April the Acton Tram Depot allocation on CentreWest's 207 was converted from M to TNL. The lack of enough new buses to

Above: First CentreWest and Capital had now graduated to bigger Tridents, its TPL and TAL classes biting further into M stocks as 2000 opened. The spring saw route 207 converted to TPLs, Uxbridge's allocation going over first from 17 February. M1244 (B244 WUL) thus has not long to go when sighted in West Ealing in March. *Geoff Rixon*

Left: First's training livery was mostly yellow with red lower panels sweeping up across the back. M1418 (C418 BUV), detached for this role earlier into its career than most other Metrobuses, is seen at Uxbridge in April 2000. *Geoff Rixon*

cover the entire requirement at most companies meant that some Ms had to stay as backup at all of Uxbridge, Acton Tram Depot, Shepherd's Bush and Hounslow. The arrival of TALs for the 25 at First Capital owing to a need for more capacity displaced TNs to Northumberland Park from 27 April; following the conversion to TN of the 357 with this move the garage's Ms were widely dispersed. Again, a few remained following the transfer south of the 212's DMLs pending the receipt of a dedicated batch still to come, and loans from CentreWest resumed, three coming from Acton Tram Depot (M442, 859 and 943). No 317 (ex-M457) became the first yellow-and-red training-liveried First Capital Metrobus, while sales at this stage included First Edinburgh, First Mainline, First Hampshire and the Rider York operations in Halifax and Huddersfield. London United's losses, meanwhile, were Thorpe's gain, M415 and 815 being the first here.

April saw London General's open-top OM241, not yet required for 2000's 70D diagram (starting late this year, on 28 May) painted purple to serve as a campaign bus for ultimately victorious Mayoral candidate Ken Livingstone; the election took place on 4 May.

The Sunday rota on the 19 wandered again from 29 April; too far away for Arriva London North-East's Tottenham, it wasn't that much more convenient to Brixton, whose Ms took it over on that day of the week. Due to clearance problems in Piccadilly, the low-floor DLAs otherwise based here could not yet be sanctioned for this route. The 118 was one route to pay the price, releasing the Ms needed by converting to DDL on Sunday (these being the 319's latest stock of overloaded Darts), while the 159's Brixton allocation on Sundays was absorbed by an increase at Thornton Heath, thus ejecting the 264 on Sundays back into Croydon (albeit theoretically with Ls). At night the N19 was gained on tender by Arriva London South; for the same reason as the 19, Brixton Ms again had to do the honours in lieu of the perhaps more politically-correct DLAs. The concentration of

the 68 at Norwood was intended to displace VA-class Volvo Citybuses to the 243, but the Volvos were sold instead and Tottenham's Ms stayed put.

Leaside Travel gained another schoolday Metrobus service, new route 675 which followed the length of the 275 to Barkingside and thence to Claybury. At night many of the N-routes, some of which were still operated by Ms, were altered to more closely match their daytime equivalents rather than all converging on Trafalgar Square. A new livery for Ms was that adopted for Arriva London's training fleet, now made up of Ms and growing in number. All-white was relieved by a medium-height grey skirt which was itself broken by a yellow tape band. M478 (a trainer at Enfield) was the first to receive it in March. With fewer than a dozen repaints performed since the Metroline takeover, Metroline London Northern's remaining Ms were beginning to look particularly weary, but one final advance was that of dayglo yellow blinds to Potters Bar, the last garage to receive them, in May.

Perhaps the most important change of 2000 was the opening of Tramlink; on Wednesday 10 May the Addington line ran free with proper services commencing on Thursday 11th; on that day the X30 was withdrawn outright. Nine days later, the 130 was severely reduced; at one point complete withdrawal had been envisaged, but passengers living further away from the tram's path through New Addington still wanted it and it was reduced to every 20 minutes on Mondays to Saturdays for a three-month period (which ended up enduring), aided by an extension to Addington Village of the 466. The coming of the trams (as well as the completion of the conversion of route 468 to DLA in May) doomed the Gardner-engined M at Croydon, only four (M629, 731, 895, 1036) remaining alongside the 22 Cummins-engined examples after 11 May. Of the mkIIs, M1442 was scrapped on site but M1441 managed to escape and returned to its second garage, Brixton, there to spend eight more months (though only at night on the N19 or as an interloper on the 19 and 159).

Below: Probably the best of all training liveries applied to Metrobuses was that of London United, an elegant red and cream. In use since 1994, M36 (WYW 36T) is pictured in North Hyde Road, Hayes on 6 April 2000. *Geoff Rixon*

On 13 May Kingston closed finally; London United reallocated the 411 to Fulwell and kept the 568 going for two more weeks at an outstation also lettered K, but on the 27th the 568 was withdrawn.

Having held out alone for over a year, Clapton's M1138 was withdrawn in May, finishing off the class there (for now...). Now that three of Tottenham's Ms (M1131, 1229/81) had been fitted with blinds including those routes taken on from Arriva London North-East, the type began turning out on the 24 from mid-May, having not been seen since Chalk Farm lost the type at the tail end of 1986. Like the 85 and 131, the movement of vehicles between companies ensured such routes Metrobus swansongs long after their heyday. The 289, however, had not only never seen Metrobuses until now but had only recently had

a restriction removed that had obliged the route to be single-deck all its life; thus Beddington Farm's operational pair began to wander from the 60. The following month saw Tottenham M appearances on the 168 and for the first time, the 188.

Having returned to the 1 extras on 2 May, Blue Triangle came off on the 29th, Limebourne filling in on 30/31 May and 1/2 June before First Capital incorporated them into Dagenham's own schedule on the 5th; any M workings thereafter were strictly interlopers. Limebourne's M477 received a shocking reversed livery where green was now the main colour relieved by a red skirt; no more were done and only three Ms of the company's half-dozen were operational by now and none of them received the later Limebourne livery with green skirt.

Below: The summer of 2000 was bleak for London General Ms, Stockwell and Merton sharing 99 Volvo B7TLs to replace most of them. On 22 July Merton's M946 (A946 SUL) is seen for posterity at Wandsworth on the 44; this garage had perhaps not been so bothered about replacing the traditional white-on-black numberplates from its Ms, though fixed windows and the London General front are both in evidence. *Author*

Above: In the same area, Mitcham Belle needed a double-decker to provide for schools traffic on its 200, otherwise won from London General on the basis of new Dart SLFs. It came in the form of M1106 (B106 WUL) from London United, and on 12 June 2000 is in Mitcham with livery unaltered. *Geoff Rixon*

IRA attention to Hammersmith Bridge on 1 June 2000 caused the return of the 509, though not in number this time; Armchair now joined Shepherd's Bush on this 200-yard service. The 19th saw this number used again for a longer service bridging the gap across Talgarth Road near Kensington Olympia; four Hounslow Ms were allocated (M1345/51/8/68)

As summer approached the advance of Volvo B7TLs spread to London General, which had placed a large order for Stockwell's 37, 77A and 88 (plus 11 at weekends and night N44 and N155) and Merton's 44, 77 and 270 (and 22 on Sundays). The former's allocation of PVLs commenced entry into service from 7 June, while Merton's started appearing on the 28th, also encompassing the 280, whose own batch of PVLs was due later in the year. On 17 June the 200 passed from London General to Mitcham Belle (which added bigger premises in Beddington), but the latter was also assigned the route's schoolday double-decker and bought M1106 from London United with which to work it; its former livery sufficed, nor were fleetnames ever applied, perhaps setting the tone for this company's long-term future. At Metroline London Northern's Potters Bar, repaints into blue-skirt livery were at last commencing for this garage's exhausted-looking Ms, owing to their retention in the short term.

On 24 June the R68 was transferred from London United to Tellings-Golden Miller with new Dart SLFs; Fulwell Ms had continued to turn out right up to the end. The move of the R70 to the same operator had to be postponed, but this date also saw the 81 reallocated within London United to Hounslow, the 555/6/7 group passing to Hounslow Heath in reverse; up until the changeover the 555 had regained an official double-deck working (working off the 235 or Surrey route 655) as long as the bus (an L or M) stopped north of Walton Bridge. Hounslow Heath continued to field Ms on the 555 where necessary.

Little noticed amid the great changes of the past few years was the final change of name of London Transport itself - from 3 July it became the convoluted Transport for London, its bus-procurement arm turning into LBSL but basically remaining a regulatory authority with no responsibility for operations (apart from East Thames Buses, of which more anon). The 22nd saw the 121 at Palmers Green projected to the new Island Village development beyond Enfield Lock.

Another route to gain Ms in their dotage after a period of many years was the 112, which was reallocated within Metroline from North Acton to Cricklewood on 12 August; this was temporary pending the preparation of Darts, but welcome nonetheless.

On 19 August the R70 finally passed to Tellings-Golden Miller, its hitherto peripatetic Fulwell Ms now being formalised as a schoolday London United offshoot, but now from Hounslow Heath. This date also featured an unusual change whereby a Red Arrow route was replaced by the extension of an existing all-stops service; the 505 gave way to an extension of the 243 all the way to Waterloo, which by being daily removed the need for the Sunday-only 243A on which VAs and Ls had never appeared due to lacking a fourth number track in their provincial-style blind boxes. The 243 now received new DLAs, Wood

Green's W3 on the same Lordship Lane corridor simultaneously completing its conversion from M to DLA. At night new route N149 was introduced (M from Enfield) to parallel the N243 and thence to Edmonton Green and Ponders End. Presaging future developments, DLAs began to wander from the 243 to the 41 and N73.

Limebourne's six remaining Metrobuses received fleetnumbers in Travel London's system upon the move of Travel London's fleet into Limebourne's Battersea (QB) base on 19 August; 471-3/6/7/9 identified M719, 237, 473, 476, 477 and 279. At London Traveller, which was formally renamed Metropolitan Omnibus during September to match its legal identity, M76 was repainted yellow with a purple skirt and flash but M320 did not last the year, an accident claiming it. All the ex-West Midlands Metrobuses had similarly gone by year's end.

This year's Notting Hill Carnival augmentations saw the small number at Uxbridge and Acton Tram Depot lent to the 31 and 328 roads in the absence of any from Westbourne Park (RMLs did the honours instead). Metroline Contract Services' M324 was one of the floats. No less colourful was Arriva East Herts & Essex 5230 (M263), in August treated to a blue and yellow all-over ad (minus the front) for Fishpools furniture stores of Waltham Cross.

Another extension came on 2 September when the 135, still M-operated, was withdrawn; Holloway transferred its resources (and Ms) to a strengthening of the 134, but from the south the 88 was extended up from Oxford Circus. This route's conversion from M to PVL at London General's Stockwell was well underway, but more new buses would be required and these would come in October as PDL-class Dennis Tridents. The schoolday working of the 275, which had come off with the end of the school year on 22 July, resumed with Leaside Travel, but this time as 675; Limebourne took its fate in its own hands by adding a second M to the 156 on schooldays. The 568 was reinstated on 2 September, but on the 16th was transformed into a TfL contract numbered 467 by adding the K3's school journeys. Although scheduled for Kingston DRs, overcrowding required support by an M by the end of the year. Also on the 16th the 222 moved from Uxbridge (First CentreWest) to Hounslow (London United) with DPs (and an M at schooltimes). The temporary 509 was transferred from Hounslow to Fulwell, an even longer garage journey away for this mile-long route! The transfer of the 411 from Fulwell to Kingston reintroduced the possibility of Ms alongside the scheduled DPs (placed on the route on 19 August and now transferring with it). By late September the three TAs had arrived to assist the mix of VA/VP on Hounslow's routes.

The closure of Metroline's North Acton garage on 23 September prompted the reopening of Harlesden (HR), which had been kept hold of since the absorption of Atlas Bus; this time the 266 moved in with 27 Ms, only journeys working off the 32

Above: Finally Metroline London Northern started painting its wearied Metrobuses; in October 2000 M1403 (C403 BUV) of Potters Bar still has a year to go before its route 82 was scheduled to receive new vehicles and the existing Ms' condition was deteriorating rapidly. It is seen in Park Lane. *Geoff Rixon*

Right: One way to remove ageing Ms was to withdraw their routes; on 2 September 2000 it was decided to take off the 135 and split its resources between the largely parallel 134 at the northern end, while adding some purpose to the 88 at the southern end through an extension northwards from Oxford Circus. Holloway's M1065 (B65 WUL) is captured arriving at Archway on 21 March 2000; this bus would be sold in January 2001 and make its way to Glasgow with Coakley Buses of Motherwell. *Author*

remaining Cricklewood-operated. This time Harlesden was operated under Metroline London Northern's O-Licence, while the Contract Services wing was formalised as a Cricklewood responsibility.

M629 became the third M at Beddington Farm on 30 September, and was not the only M to leave Croydon this autumn as the Cummins contingent was now targeted, examples leaving so that nine new DLAs could finish off the 468 in mid-October. M1295 reintroduced the Metrobus to Clapton, like its predecessor M1138 working alone. On 5 October both the 324 and 348 were transferred to Arriva East Herts & Essex, Town & Country not having been able to make them a success. Three Ms were despatched from Arriva London North, M756/82 and 1404 (taking numbers 5256/62, 5254), the first mentioned being familiar at Grays. M1316 was also sent out but failed *en route* and was brought back on tow. Two days later the 257 was unwisely single-decked with DMLs from First Capital's Hackney and the 296 was cut in half, its remit beyond Romford passing to new Stagecoach East London-operated 496. After 14 years an M complement was returned to the 283 with the introduction of two morning-peak double-deck journeys provided by London United's Stamford Brook to support the normal Shepherd's Bush DRs. From 23 October Cricklewood's 16 at Metroline was the lucky recipient once again of new buses; these TAL-class Tridents displaced the year-old TAs to the 32 to replace Ms, another pair going to Harrow Weald to modernise the 186's double-deck complement; still, some of the 32's displaced Ms into Edgware allowed older examples to be withdrawn.

An interesting autumn beckoned for the Ms bouncing between First CentreWest and Capital; on 28 October the 295 was awarded to the former (ex-London General) and Stockwell Ms gave way to Westbourne Park's, which were composed of reactivated spares and transfers from Dagenham, backed up by four Volvo B6 single-deckers displaced by DMLs; new examples of these Dart SLFs were all in place by late November. Acton Tram Depot's protracted conversion was effectively completed through the transfer to this work of its last three Ms. Then on 11 November Westbourne Park gained a second route in the form of the 27 (ex-London United at Stamford Brook) which ensured another deployment for this miscellany of Ms, this time supporting LLWs displaced from the 222 in September, and again filling in until new buses were delivered; these were TN-class Tridents and all had arrived by the end of February. London United filled the gap at Stamford Brook by bringing in the 391 in its entirety; Ms were intended for this route but only ended up appearing as strange visitors, thus the Ms left at Stamford Brook after the 27's loss only worked on Sundays on the 94! One of these, M369 (sometimes known as First Capital 310, sometimes not) was repainted red but with just the upper thin yellow band. Finally, Fulwell's 267 regained its Sunday Ms for the winter season and permanently thereafter.

Stockwell's M complement was reduced but not eliminated by the loss of the 295, while the PVLs for Merton's 280 were all in place by mid-November; nor did Ms depart entirely here either. In November two holdouts, M1055 and 1306, became the first to receive the new, darker shade of grey chosen for the skirt colour at London General. On Monday 6 November the 324 and 348 dwindled further, being pulled back from Romford to Hornchurch. The Olympia bridge reopened again on 24 November, the 509 coming off. On the 25th Putney's small rearguard of Ms extended their capability to new night route N22.

The 188, which had burned through an extraordinary number of operators since first being tendered, was transferred once again with its takeover by London General (Stockwell) with PVLs on 2 December; Tottenham's Ms had worked very rarely but M1298 joined a planned appearance by all five types based on the final day. The DLAs displaced

were put into Enfield, where in concert with penny numbers allocated earlier in the year, they took over the 149. The Ms replaced were converted into dedicated trainers, replacing the earlier examples on a one-for-one basis and taking their adapted brakes and mirrors, while M1253 and 1320, with their tachographs, joined the Leaside Travel fleet. M1170 gained 'Rat on a Rat' branding on a white background for the Metropolitan Police's Crimestoppers initiative. M operation on night routes N29, N73 and N253, meanwhile, had yielded to DLAs during November, but new Tottenham-operated N41 (from 2 December) was a new venture for them.

Christmas Day services for the Metrobus were just in the form of Nostalgiabus's commercial route 755 (using three), but New Year's night saw Blue Triangle control a trio of services with Thorpe's and Sullivan Buses support.

On 4 January staffing problems reared their head again at Stockwell, the solution chosen this time being to outstation two duties of the 37 at Putney, initially with two Ms but very quickly with PVLs. The 307 gained a second First Capital double-decker for school hours. At Metroline London Northern, the VPL-class Volvo B7TLs ordered for the 271 and W7 were switched to the 43 instead, that route's TPs taking over the W7, the 271's Vs staying put and the Ms being ousted anyway; only ten remained at Holloway by the end of January, largely on the 4 but in support of all routes there.

Durham Travel Services, trading as London Easylink, had been awarded the 185 from Stagecoach Selkent for take-up on 20 January 2001, but an eleventh-hour bureaucratic hitch meant the company could not commence as scheduled; thus for two weeks Blue Triangle stepped in, with two Metrobuses (MCW27/8, ex-M27/8) and a Trident blinded for its two-bus allocation, while similar sub-contracts were issued to Stagecoach Selkent (ten existing Catford Titans) and London General; the latter provided six Ms otherwise on their way out (M845/67, 905/9/95, 1005) and all were based at the newcomers' Old Kent Road premises, coded DR by TfL. For its own driver training, M478 (in Arriva's white training livery) was acquired. London Easylink's O-Licence and VP-class Volvo B7TLs were all in place for the official re-start on 13 February, but this would not be the last time that either Blue Triangle, or Metrobuses, ran on the 185!

In this month East Thames Buses, the LBSL-owned company formerly known as Harris Bus, acquired ex-London United M831/2 for driver training; they took the numbers (317/8) of their DAF predecessors and donned white livery.

On 27 January the first wave of yet another progressive reduction to Arriva Southern Counties' services was the award of the 406's core Kingston-Epsom section to London United with operation by Hounslow; to provide the DPs for it, Kingston's 411 was converted back to M operation, additionally furnishing the 467 with an M. The odd M turned out on the 406 at schooltimes. Also in the Kingston area, White Rose struck up a new contract on route 461 with its mix of Ms and Ts. M819/42 came in January for these routes.

Arriva London South lost the 118 to London General on 3 February with new Merton-based PVLs, theoretically finishing off the M at Brixton; two, however, stayed behind to support a new intake of Ls for the 250 (on transfer from Thornton Heath for six months), Sunday 19 and night N19, with guest trips on the 59 (OPO) and crew routes 137 and 159. M984 was joined on 7 February by M1084, the only Cummins-engined M to survive the purge of the type at Croydon (routes 197, 312 and what remained of the class on the 130 and 466) taking place simultaneously; Croydon offered a measure of support to a series of cascades of Darts necessary to furnish Arriva London North's just-gained minibus route W4 by taking on two of Brixton's Ms (M517, 731) to use on the 166 until its imminent conversion to LDR operation. M1441 was withdrawn from Brixton at this date, effectively being replaced by M1084; it was the last AVE-trials bus in service, just pipping the three Ls. At Beddington Farm, just M809 remained in service, the other two departing. Croydon's last Ms (1036/1105) ran in April, the majority of the Cummins-engined examples becoming the next generation of trainers at Arriva London South. The addition of five ex-Brixton and Croydon Ms to Wood Green's still-sizeable M fleet in advance of a four-bus increase to the 29's PVR applying on 28 April represented one last throw of the dice for the class here, as new buses were already on order for autumn delivery for this route and other local contracts.

After finishing off Croydon's Ms, the final members of the latest Arriva order for DLAs completed Enfield's 149 in late March, with a further order imminent for the 41 at Tottenham.

School route 616 passed from First Capital to Leaside Travel on 3 February, converting to M operation, and Leaside Travel gained two journeys on the 121 alongside Palmers Green's own Ms, also extending the 629 to Wood Green. Continuing staffing difficulties at Stockwell caused the farming out of the 196 to London General's Commercial Services unit; not only did Ms come from all over London General to support Stockwell's VCs, but drivers too, and even Nostalgiabus pitched in at times, taking M904 on loan. At night from this date part of the N16 moved from Edgware to Cricklewood, this and Willesden's N6 retaining a modicum of M operation in the expectation of new vehicles; the N98 on its transfer from CentreWest (Alperton) to Metroline (Edgware) was returned to Ms entirely. New route N27 (First CentreWest from Westbourne Park) was by necessity M-operated for its first month, new TNs soon taking over this route in concert with the daytime 27.

Having stayed till 16 February to help London Easylink bed in on the 185, Blue Triangle rode to the rescue again on the 27th, helping out London Central's 492 in the Sidcup area; while the existing Bexleyheath NVs remained in use, MCW27 did make one solitary foray. Limebourne, still able to field three Ms, repainted 476 (M476) dark blue for the Westminster-Chelsea Hospital staff link (H1) starting on 5 February, on behalf of its associated company Excalibur Travel.

On 19 March the Metrobus era finished at Grays, three ex-Southend Olympians replacing the last survivors on the 324 and the 348 being converted to Dart operation. From 19 March Nostalgiabus's assistance on the 196 was replaced by that of Metrobus, which took on M904 (as 254) from that company, plus M953 (as 253); the indigenous support by now also included M1357/87 from Waterloo,

Above: Arriva London South was the first post-LBL inheritor of the M class to lose the type entirely. Its last was M984 (A984 SYF), which alongside M1084 held out at Brixton until the end of 2001, both able to turn out only as crew buses on the 137 and 159. It is seen heading down Whitehall on the latter service on a sunny autumn day. *Author's collection*

loaned there for the purpose and their role cemented by a repaint with new charcoal skirt, a livery now spreading to additional surviving London General Ms.

Metroline's latest order for VPLs (33 strong) dislodged six more Holloway Ms in mid-March and then started taking over Willesden's 52, allowing its AVs to transfer into Harlesden for M replacement on the 266. Still Ms clung on at both Harlesden and Holloway and would hold out for nearly three more years, and Willesden also still had four to use when needed.

Arriva Southern Counties solved its ongoing staffing problems in its Crawley core by pulling out of the operation altogether on 31 March. Metrobus took the bulk of its routes and the Crawley garage; Merstham closed, leaving just Warnham (WS – the new name and code for Horsham since February) operating a small remnant of buses further to the south. Metrobus indeed took on loan some of the refurbished Ms (M454, 522/34/6/47, 614/60, 717, 1210, to which were applied temporary fleetnumbers 224, 232, 234/6/47, 214, 260, 217 and 210) and returning the type to the company after a spell, albeit only for three weeks on the 409 with a couple sent to Godstone (GD).

Also on 31 March the double-deck complement on the 81 (nominally L, but capable of M appearances too) was removed; to engender a service increase on this route, the DPs from the 406 were transferred in, allowing Hounslow to convert the 406 to M operation. The unsatisfactory situation with the 94 on Sundays, where Ms lay idle at Stamford Brook six days of the week, was solved by converting it back to RML on Sundays, in anticipation of a few crew routes regaining Routemasters on that day of the week. Three Ms remained at Stamford Brook for the 283 school journeys and to cover the 391 (which lost its temporary Hounslow allocation on this day). London United's trainers began to have their classic livery revised to fleet red and grey but with a huge orange scoop over the front and appropriate lettering; M157 was the first, but the ostentation on subsequent repaints and new conversions (M46, 204, 1006/14/9/22/6/8/9 up to early 2002) was in yellow.

Arriva's downfall was completed on 21 April with the transfer of Surrey routes 405 to Connex Bus and 420 to Metrobus as partial TfL/Surrey contracts (the London General commercial aspects simultaneously coming off); further hires to Metrobus were M503 (233) and from 21 April, M521/59, 776 (221/59/76). All twelve lasted until 1 June, while Horsham-based Ms 717 and 996, Arriva Southern Counties' last, were stood down on 8 June, and that was the end of the Arriva-refurbished Metrobus in this part of the world. Most were sold to Arriva Merseyside. At Arriva London North, repaints to Ms had ceased, but M651 was done by mistake in the spring of 2000 and proved to be the last, at least for the moment.

Nostalgiabus pulled out of LBSL operation on 23 April, reconfiguring as Surrey-oriented Northdown, thus the 127 lost its double-deck assistance; in order to retain the upper deck on the 613, Mitcham Belle transferred the M hitherto allocated to the 200. Other school routes shifting for the summer term were First Capital's, the '20D' moving from Hackney

Below: London United developed a new training livery; not as ornate as its predecessor, it nonetheless allowed more identification with the existing company identity by plastering a huge orange blob over the front and nearside of the standard livery. M157 (BYX 157V) is seen at Hampton Court in June 2001 before a change of mind saw the secondary colour changed from orange to yellow on subsequent training-bus conversions from newer Ms. *Geoff Rixon*

to Northumberland Park in exchange for the morning 678 and the morning 645 passing from Northumberland Park to Dagenham.

Disaster struck at Armchair on 15 April when the entire double-deck runout at Brentford had its fuel tanks sabotaged; during a protracted repair process Metrobuses were hired from various nearby undertakings. From 19-21 April Limebourne supplied M279, 476 and 477 and CentreWest M1235/59, 1382, all working on the 65. When these had to go back, Ensign stepped in, loaning Ms from its sales stock comprising ex-Arriva M517, 630, 731/74 and ex-Metroline M461, 829. These shored up the 65 until 4 May.

On 28 April First Capital (known collectively with CentreWest as First London since 25 March) lost the 67 to Stagecoach East London; that was one option gone for Northumberland Park's 12 remaining Metrobuses, but another opened up when the 263 was assumed from Arriva London North on this day; indeed the M complement was official (alongside Olympians of various makes and vintages) on what was otherwise a short-term stand-in to ease the pressure on Wood Green. The type was also wandering to the 341 with some regularity, and at Hackney a double-deck arm was restored to the 257 during the peaks, five Ms coming in from CentreWest; these, M882-4 and 979, were joined by M369 (a.k.a. 310) in its odd half-livery.

One way to ease staff pressure on some routes was not to try too hard retaining them, and thus fell London General's 196 to Connex Bus on 5 May. The 191 did, however, continue with First Capital's

Northumberland Park, but its vehicle allocation became distinctly wild over the next few months while a strategy to cascade TNs was developed; naturally Metrobuses had a large part to play. The 369 at Dagenham had a frequency increase on the 19th and took 331/52 from Northumberland Park. Ponders End's closure brought the four training Ms to Northumberland Park on 20 June.

During May the three Metroline Contract Services Ms with Routemaster plates gained back their original marks, while Metroline's own M455 was fitted out with tables to serve as a rest room for Potters Bar drivers at Tally Ho Corner in North Finchley, the terminus of the 82. Arriva London North's white trainer M6 was sold for preservation. With the closure of Wembley Stadium for rebuilding, the Alperton-allocated seasonal 618 ceased to operate.

Another RML route to revert to crew on Sundays was the 38 from 3 June, relegating Clapton's M1295 to visits to the 253 only. Also at Arriva London North, Tottenham's 41 was converted from M to DLA during June, reducing the garage's number of available Metrobuses to just three, but a happy consequence was the transfer of the displaced Ms to Enfield to convert the 307 to double-deck in advance of a new contract retained by Arriva London North. Four West Midlands Metrobuses, GOG 208W, POG 524Y, A700 UOE and B875 DOM joined Thorpe's in June, M985 providing spares for them.

One last throw of the dice for the London United site using the name Kingston prior to the intended move of its runout was the reallocation in of the 406 from Hounslow on 30 June, allowing the Ms to stay

Above: Quite what possessed the Tendered Bus Division to accept a bid for the 257 based on single-deck operation is unknown, as the route, important to the passengers as the only route on the busy corridor north of Stratford, struggled immediately after new DML-class Dart SLFs replaced 80-seat Arrows at Hackney early in 2001. Creditably, however, dispensation was received by First Capital to add three Ms to the 257 and here at Walthamstow Central on 14 November, shortly before the route was converted to full-time double-deck operation with TNLs, is M882 (OJD 882Y). By this time Capital had stopped adding to its own numbering system for acquisitions, and M882 would remain so numbered until final withdrawal in March 2002. *Author*

Right: Very late in the day for the Metrobus, Armchair acquired two to bolster its route 65. MkII E748 SKR and F772 EKM derived from East Kent, and looked a treat in Armchair's orange and white livery. By the time this picture of the former was taken in Kingston in April 2002, Armchair had introduced class codes, rendering this bus M748. *Geoff Rixon*

put when the 411 was moved out to Fulwell. The latter was furnished with five ex-Hounslow Ms instead, leaving just two at Hounslow, of which M1194 was transferred to Kingston in July leaving just M1368 (though joined in August by M1352). The use of Ms on the 116 thus ceased in practice even before its official single-decking on 8 December. Meanwhile Stamford Brook, having taken on the H91 from Hounslow Heath on 30 June, put its own Ms out occasionally as had its predecessor.

Connex bought Limebourne's holding company Independent Way on 7 July together with its Travel London unit; as far as Metrobuses were concerned, the school buses stayed with Excalibur Travel but on hire to Connex; operating on the 156 only until the

end of the school year at the end of July, they were replaced by Connex's own Ls and sold. Connex's last members of its earlier intake, LOA 387X and M802, were sold in July and August, the latter joining Imperial.

The end of July saw the 82 at Potters Bar commence its conversion from M to VPL, which drew out until September due to gearbox problems on the new Volvo B7TLs. One new operator, however, was Armchair, which in August acquired two ex-East Kent mkIIs, E748 SKR and F772 EKM, from Ensign to furnish a PVR increase on the 65 applying from the autumn term. Carnival for 2001 saw Ms out for the last time, helping out the hopelessly-overloaded 22-seat Darts on the 31 and 328.

Right: An old friend of the author's from its days at Putney on the 265 when new, M1036 (A736 THV) caught him up at Wood Green in 2001, being added to that Arriva London North garage for just the latest service increase to the 29, a very busy trunk route that absorbed every extra bus thrown at it and still needed more. On 23 June 2001 it is pulling out of its new home into the High Road to begin another journey to Trafalgar Square. DLPs would replace Ms on this route during August and September. *Author*

Left: The Metroline duo's latest deliveries of VPL-class Volvo B7TLs were meant for the 113 at Edgware and the 82 at Potters Bar, and the first mentioned was converted from M during September 2001, seeing off buses like M1174 (B174 WUL) pictured at the Oxford Circus stand on 5 June. This was another Metrobus with the conventional rear blind box taken out of use, but on this bus (and M1035) the replacement was a three-track unit from a DT-class Dart. *Author*

Even now the twin-garage set-up of Wood Green and Palmers Green could still muster over 90 Metrobuses, but on 31 August their replacement began, DLPs entering service on the 29 and the 102, 121 and 141 awaiting examples of the new VLW class of Wright-bodied Volvo B7TLs. The fourteen Ms in the 1300s block of fleetnumbers were earmarked for cascade to Leaside Travel in replacement of the earlier school-bus stock, M1326 going first. Aside from school work on the 34, some of Edmonton's maroon-and-white Ms had been straying to the normal 34 outside school hours recently. September also saw Metroline's VPL intake take over the 113 at Edgware (plus the N16 and N98 at night) starting on the 17th, and by October leaving just the 240 M-operated at that garage. Three Potters Bar Ms (1141/7 and 1325), struck up a staff bus taking route 82's drivers from North Finchley to their base, and were given all-blue lower decks for the role.

Brixton garage's entire Sunday OPO complement on routes 19, 137 and 159 was removed on 1 September, and all that M984 and 1084 could do now was to wait out their days with conductors on the latter pair; simultaneously the 250 returned to Thornton Heath. With the loss of the 60 to Connex Bus, M809 departed Beddington Farm. To the north of the river the 13 was formalised with Sovereign alone, Metroline's OPO-M element from Edgware (plus the N13 at Holloway) coming off. In advance of new Tridents on order, First Capital's 165 (still mkII Metrobus from Dagenham) was rerouted away from Roneo Corner east of Romford. First Capital's school route 645 was renumbered 679 and awarded to Leaside Travel, and a little further to the east Stagecoach East London sub-contracted its own school routes 649 and 652 to Blue Triangle in advance of the official contract changeover on the 29th. The 656 also went in for a month before its move to First Capital. Saturday 29 September was when the 248 moved from First Capital to Blue Triangle, using Ms and Ts until the new Dennis Tridents (TLs) were all delivered, and in unofficial capacity thereafter

(helped by M475, 953 and 1357 on loan from London General); a more unusual emergency deployment was on Dart-operated route 368. Blue Triangle also took the 651 from First Capital, which, although losing the 670 to Arriva East Herts & Essex, commenced a new 686 as well as taking the 656 from Blue Triangle's temporary stewardship. Both Blue Triangle and First Capital were expecting new buses for all their contracts with the 29 September scheme, but two school routes to retain Ms officially were the 697 and 698, using the quintet left at First CentreWest's Uxbridge.

The small number of Ms left at Putney lost the 14's Sunday service to RMLs on 29 September but managed to hold on to the evening service, while forays to the N22's next extension took them to Richmond. A second Metrobus joined Waterloo's M1107 when M1301 was put in to help furnish three duties on the 77A transferred from Stockwell; the others were PVLs on rotation. Metropolitan Omnibus sold M199, M477 and GOG 245W in September, replacing them with M468, 708, 809 and 1206 from three sources via Ensign.

VLWs started easing Ms off Palmers Green's 102 and 121 from 20 and 25 September respectively; the 141 was last on the list pending the arrival of more VLWs in 2002, and continued to mix just about anything Wood Green could put on the road. Of the Leaside Travel fleet, M1437's coaching days were at an end once a yellow advertising livery for the company's training school was applied. M929, 1124/36, 1231/53/4 and 1303/14/32 went into maroon and white across the turn of 2001/2, M1126/30, 1130 and 1312 remaining in the 80%-red of 1998 and M1313 alone having its front repainted maroon. Another era ended when Brixton's (and Arriva London South's) final two Ms departed, M1084 (the last Cummins-engined example) joining the training fleet in October and M984 being withdrawn in November - both, ironically, replaced by RMLs. Luckless both at the beginning and end of its life, M1102 was damaged sufficient to warrant its

Above: From 1998, London Traveller, a peripatetic component of the Yorkshire Traction group, operated a handful of Metrobuses as schooltime help for Volvo B6BLE single-deckers; some were ex-West Midlands but subsequent acquisitions were Ms. In mid-2000 the company was renamed Metropolitan Omnibus, and although a red livery prevailed, M76 (WYW 76T) was acquired in this most unusual livery and is seen in Oldfield Road North during June 2001, showing off the company logo based on the shape of the GLC area. Metropolitan Omnibus was wound up at the end of 2002 and many of the Ms passed to Thorpe's for rail-replacement work. *Haydn Davies*

Right: Despite wholesale replacement of its Metrobuses by NV-class Volvo Olympians in 1997, London General's Sutton garage had retained a number, which continued to turn out where needed. M1315 (C109 NGH, ex-VLT 15, ex-C315 BUV), was a twice-re-registered example and is seen at West Croydon bus station on 1 September 2001, three months before the 157 was lost to Connex Bus. The nearside wing is in London General's new darker grey skirt colour, though few Ms would survive long enough to receive the full application (see page 157). After leaving London M1315 would migrate to Liverpool to spend a couple of years with GTL, which christened it *Pamela. Author*

sale, only just having become a trainer, while corrosion issues took M1093 out of the programme and M1099 was also written off in a collision with UKA 23V, the only Original London Sightseeing Tour Metrobus to receive training livery. Training-bus conversions continued into 2002 at Arriva due to plenty of Ms becoming available; in January M1084 was converted into a mobile recruitment bus to attract prospective drivers for them.

London United's new Tolworth (TV) garage opened on 3 November, its M routes numbering the 406 and 467 with wanderings still possible to the 57. Seven Ms transferred in from Kingston, soon to be joined by two from Fulwell.

The conversion of two routes to new Tridents at either end of First London's empire (which from 6 November was referred to on bus sides as plain First) negated the need for supplementary Ms, Hackney's 257 being treated to TNLs on 10 November and Alperton's route-79 workings subsumed into a new contract wholly with CentreWest (ex-Metroline) from

A full contract term had now come around again for London General's Sutton routes and still its Ms held on, but with the contract-change date on 1 December the 157 was removed from their remit with its move to Connex Bus. An increase to the PVR on the 61 saw M1376 deployed into St Mary Cray, working intermittently between 21 December and April 2002, when three more Vs were sourced. On the 8th the 307 was formally double-decked, First Capital's two schoolday workings coming off but with new DLPs expected for the main route.

No Ms were in service on Christmas Day 2001 save for a large batch of Ensignbus vehicles on London Pride tour work, for which some demand materialised on the day; so much so that Metrobuses recently shipped out to City Sightseeing Cambridge were roped in to help.

2002 began with the conversion from M to VA of the 406 at London United's Tolworth on 5 January, while the 19th saw the pulling back of Arriva East Herts & Essex's 324 and 348, the former losing its

Left: First Capital's mkII Metrobuses had now come to the end of their lives, being replaced at Dagenham in December 2001 by brand-new Tridents, but three were kept on to support the new TNLs. Looking very tired but still able to do the job on 29 March 2002 is 178 (E478 SON), once known as Harrow Buses M1478 but now concentrated on the 123 with two others. The new Turnpike Lane bus station was now in business and provided rather better photographic opportunities than had its dank, covered predecessor. *Author*

the 24th; still declining to depart, Alperton's six Ms had spread their net to the 258, taken back from London Buslines comparatively recently. Enough Ms remained at Hackney to visit the 1 when it was transferred in from Dagenham on 1 December, but the flood of new Tridents into First Capital during the month portended a bleak future for Dagenham's and Northumberland Park's Metrobuses. Similar M withdrawals accrued to London United when TAs began taking over Fulwell's 131 and 267, the latter finally losing Ms after 23 years. Two sales, M960 and 1039, became the second and third Metrobuses at Mitcham Belle, and some of the VAs from the 131 were readied for Tolworth's 406.

recently-gained Romford-Upminster section and the 348 abandoning Greater London altogether. That date saw Metrobuses leave the 42 with the route's sub-contracting to London Easylink with a mix of hired Darts.

Ejected from the 165 and 365 by new buses (Darts on the former, TNs on the latter) during January, Dagenham's Metrobuses, half of which were still in yellow, began to depart, mostly to First's operations in Manchester and Leeds via the group disposal pool. Three, however, were kept behind; 171/2/8 from the old ex-Harrow Buses batch made their home on the 123. The conversion of Northumberland Park's 91 to TN in February left just four Ms in service there.

Right: After 23 years, the tenure of Metrobuses on the 267 came to a close in 2002 with the arrival of TA-class Dennis Tridents. So much for continuity; the successors would last only three years. On 22 April 2002 Fulwell's M1439 (C439 BUV) leaves the garage by the western (and now only) entrance/exit, the gate through which M51 is seen emerging on page 8 now the territory of Tellings-Golden Miller. *Geoff Rixon*

Below: London United replaced Kingston garage, which was built over with a cinema complex, with new premises at Tolworth. On 2 February 2002 in came route 418 from Arriva, and until new Dart SLFs (DPSs) arrived Ms filled in. M203 (BYX 203V), at 22 years of age now the oldest Metrobus still in service, was among the Ms transferred to Tolworth and is seen in Penrhyn Road on 1 June. *Geoff Rixon*

In keeping with the greater integration with CentreWest, Capital's indigenous Metrobuses were all reclassified M on top of their existing numeric fleetnumbers; thankfully none clashed with existing Ms in the company.

On 2 February the 184 was renewed with Arriva London North, with the promise of a new VLW replacing the M on its Leaside Travel-run schoolday augmentation (personified by M1327 transferred from Wood Green specially). The 263 left First Capital for Metroline London Northern, losing one possibility of Ms but gaining another, with Potters Bar still holding several and many still blinded for the route from when the garage previously ran it; otherwise this tine it was TA operated. Tolworth scooped up another route (418) from the pitiful remnants of Arriva in this sector, and some of the Ms transferred out upon the 406's New Year single-decking came back! On the 22nd Enfield's 307 started converting to DLP operation, and Nostalgiabus gained a single journey on the otherwise London United-run 468 on the 25th.

Splurging as extravagantly on new low-floor double-deckers as any other London company at the beginning of 2002, London General could now finally move against its last Ms, but not before rallying them one last time on the 133 from late January, since its VC-class Volvo Citybuses had a decade's more book value left in them so were sold first. As well as collecting Ms for the 133, Stockwell also picked up NVs displaced from Sutton by the arrival of new EVL-class Volvo B7TLs.

Left: In later years the operation of Metroline's school routes was the responsibility of its Commercial Services division, whose coach-seated Metrobuses were spread around Metroline garages closest to where the routes ran. M1236, once more carrying B236 WUL after seven years under WLT 646, is found at Brent Cross on 28 October 2002 on the 611, the double-deck assistance for route 112. *Geoff Rixon*

White Rose encountered financial difficulties as 2002 opened and after a period of help that included M276 coming on loan from Sullivan Buses, folded on 27 February, the Ms and Ts worked on the 461 departing. M57 was kept by White Rose's owner. From February Armchair allotted class codes to its buses, the two Metrobuses becoming M748/72, while Mitcham Belle similarly renumbered but in the reverse direction, 047-9 now denoting M1106, 960 and 1039. Former London United M1010, still with coach seats upstairs, was sold to East Thames Buses for service as a spare for its Volvo Olympians, gaining all-over red livery. It was used on the 132 and 180 until 22 September.

The M-working school duties on the 283 came off on 23 February, while Metroline Contract Services' school responsibilities were separated out to garages; this brought the 611, 632 and the appropriate workings on the 316 to Cricklewood. Ms were apt to turn out on this Dart route outside school hours as well. Leaside Travel picked up two more school routes in March, the 667 (an adjunct to Docklands Buses' 167) on the 9th and the sole double-deck journey on the W13 on the 30th. On the 23rd the 678 was taken over from First Capital, which had already lost the '20D' to Arriva London North-East on the 9th; that was the end of Metrobus operation at Hackney (M369 and 884 being the last). Dagenham's Metrobuses had visited the 396 with regularity for some time, but not after the route was lost to Stagecoach East London on 23 March; on school routes 656, 674 and 686 Arrows were now specified.

Left: London General became the second post-LBL company to lose the M, all remaining examples coming off service in 2002. Like Sutton, Putney's conversion to Volvo Olympian had not included enough new buses to see off all Ms, and the Metrobus stragglers actually outlived many of the 1998-delivered NVs at Putney. One route to have seen M incursions for some years was the 170, in contravention of its official status as a Dart-operated shuttle route anchored on Clapham Junction since 1991, and on 15 January 2002 M818 (OJD 818Y), which had worked all 19 years of its life at Putney, is caught at Clapham Junction. It would pass to Stockwell, but for only two more months, after which it enjoyed a new lease of life at GTL, becoming its last Metrobus. *Author*

Dagenham itself closed for a long-term period, its services moving to the former London Pride site at Rainham, which was coded R for the occasion.

Despite 2002 being the Queen's Golden Jubilee year, not a single M was among the fifty buses chosen to receive gold livery, in something of a snub to this most faithful of modern types. Two Original London Sightseeing Tours examples, the latterly-named MB555/633 and until now in Harrods green colours, did receive a light blue version of Arriva's touring livery with limited Jubilee signwriting, working like this between May 2002 and May 2003. In March 2002 Metroline's M151 was converted to a mobile classroom, losing its front door for plain panelling and being wired for computers. In December it received the 33 LUG cherished plate inherited with an R&I Dart.

The end of the VC class at London General was followed in April by the move of Sutton's displaced NVs; firstly to top up Putney, where they had reduced the small M complement to just M1370 by April, and then into Stockwell (replacing the stopgap Ms) and Merton for the first time.

On 25 May Waterloo was stripped of its non-Red Arrow roster to prepare for the reconfiguration of the garage to accept articulated buses. This occasioned the transfer of M1107 and 1301 to Stockwell with the 11 and 77A, but they were soon withdrawn. Putney's M1370 did not last May out, striking one more garage off the list, and Merton was left with just two (M1177 and 1126). By the end of May total Metrobus numbers between their six operators had dipped below 150 with just one LBSL route officially allocated the type; this was the 240 at Metroline's Edgware, which

sidestepped its intended conversion to VPL when it was realised that the new Volvos would be better served reinforcing similarly-operated routes in the face of big expansion to come in 2003. Frequent exchanges of Volvo and Dennis chassis between Metroline garages barely dented that pair of companies' M stock, numbering fifty vehicles.

At London United Stamford Brook lost its final pair (M1050 and 1400) on 25 May when the H91 was reallocated into Hounslow Heath; the latter also gained the 411 from Hounslow, taking Tolworth's VAs to result in a reversion to M of the 406. During the last two weeks of May Fulwell's last M route, the 71, received new TAs from a big batch ordered for this route and the upcoming takeover of the 65 from Armchair, leaving few left but which still managed to make it into 2003.

1 June saw the 125 transferred from Palmers Green to Edmonton within Arriva London North, bringing the latter its first stage Ms; they could also soon be found on the 34 on or off school duties and, for the first time, the 444. This was so that part of the 141 could transfer into Palmers Green with VAs to accompany a service increase; still Wood Green's remaining Ms, now down to seven in number, held on. Some Leaside Travel Ms turned out on the 125 when defects were discovered in the intake.

On 29 June three changes in south-west London removed M possibilities - Armchair's 65 was lost to London United, which lost the 85 to London General. Tolworth's 418 was also converted to DPS operation. On 1 July a new Blue Triangle operation was added, unusually, to support Stagecoach Selkent's major trunk route 53 while it was rerouted cumbersomely

Below: The Edmonton garage of Arriva London North (not to be confused with the LT premises of the same name closed in 1986, and even more confusingly, once belonging to London Suburban Buses under another code again, ED) received its first normal-service Ms on 1 June 2002 with the transfer of the 125 from Palmers Green; on 5 April 2003, as they were on the point of being replaced by DLP-class DAFs, Ms 772 (KYV 772X) and 651 (KYV 651X) pass in Southgate's semi-circular station forecourt. *Author*

away from a hole that had opened up along its line of route in Blackheath. These peak augmentations were predominantly Titan-operated (though Metrobuses did turn out occasionally) and ran between New Cross Gate and the Elephant only.

Metroline London Northern's Potters Bar staff bus was single-decked in June, while at Metroline proper Willesden's three Ms (391, 432, 595) departed for Harlesden and First Capital disposed of Northumberland Park's final pair in July. Arriva London North kept chopping and changing, Enfield losing its pair in July and Tottenham adding three for RML support. Clapton's M1295 remained in service after FFD work. Quite ludicrously, Westbourne Park's M859 had two enormous fluorescent spots applied to its bumpers (where the foglights used to be) in the interests of increasing visibility - after realising how

stupid these looked on all buses so marked, the company restricted this application to wing mirrors only.

At London General, Sutton's last two Ms (472 and 975) were withdrawn in July after one final fling on the Wimbledon Tennis services. M1435 (also recently ex-Sutton) was repainted all-over white with black Friesian cow markings to accompany an art exhibition of sorts in which various cow statues were positioned around London – not long after this work was done, it was re-registered from 435 CLT to C637 VMX, in a block including M1434 (C629 VMX, ex-WLT 434). At the end of July the arrival of TAs at London United for Tolworth's 57 released enough VAs to oust the recently-returned Ms from the 406; only two were retained for the 467. Fulwell's 23-year association with the Metrobus was now down to just

Below: Carousel of High Wycombe was another firm mobilised by Blue Triangle to save the 185, and its M598 (GYE 598W), acquired after a life spent at south-western (and later London United) garages Fulwell and Hounslow, is pictured at Victoria on 30 August 1992. The numberplate characters are of the rather mean variety mandated in 2001 with the onset of the new registration system and which tended to find their way to older vehicles sooner or later. *Andrew Jeffreys*

M1343. Three Ms reintroduced the class at Metroline's Willesden just a month after the previous 'final' three had gone, and the wretched state of surviving Potters Bar examples prompted repaints to begin again, M1250 being the first.

Despite a quiet summer in which M numbers held level, a 'route 60' situation broke out when London Easylink collapsed on the afternoon of Wednesday 21 August; Blue Triangle was authorised to abandon the 53 and threw its vehicles into action on the 185 immediately. Over the next few weeks they were joined by Metrobus, First Capital and Metrobus-operating Carousel, Amberlee, Trustline, Red Route Buses and Imperial, while the 42 saw brief Metrobus operation from Ensignbus before settling down under the aegis of East Thames Buses, which was eventually awarded the service. On the 185 a more settled service was instituted from 9 September whereby Blue Triangle, in overall control, sub-contracted London Coaches, a.k.a. Arriva presenting London. This company used closed-top Metrobuses normally employed in the wintertime and since added to at the expense of Arriva London North.

Ms still formed the majority of school-bus stock with their operators, given the reluctance of staff to risk damage to new vehicles; for the new school year (31 August) Mitcham Belle lost the 613, Leaside Travel abandoned the 221 and Stockwell's 77C was renumbered 670, while on 4 September two new Leaside Travel routes were introduced linking North Finchley (683) and Southgate (688) with the new Jews Free School (JFS) in Kingsbury. These latter used three standard-liveried and one red M transferred from

Wood Green, reducing the latter's stock to two. Metropolitan Omnibus took some Thorpe's Metrobuses on loan to bolster its 626, while Thorpe's added an M class code to its four ex-West Midlands machines (rendering them M208, 524, 700 and 875). The M looked threatened at Potters Bar when the 84 and its allocation on the 310A was officially single-decked with EDRs, but none left and indeed continued to turn out on the 82, 84 and 263.

Two Metrobuses were introduced to First Capital's Rainham in September to assist with Dominator replacement (otherwise performed by new Tridents), but the same month saw the replacement of the M on route 184 by new Leaside Travel-dedicated VLW69 on 30 September. Hounslow Heath at London United received the 81 from Hounslow on 5 October, immediately adding its Ms (already busy as guests on the 285, 411 and H23).

Still uses were found for the Metrobus; on 12 October enhancements to the 6 and 98 at Metroline required both extra Ms and extra RMLs; the latter were supplied by Holloway, six Ms thus taking up crew duties on the 10. On this date Willesden's 260 was transferred to Harlesden, M appearances supporting the AVs as early as the first day, but Cricklewood lost the 316 to Thorpe's, precluding any more Ms turning out.

Most unusual extras provided on two occasions a fleetwide strike was held by London Underground were by London Coaches; on 25 September its open-top Metrobuses helped out the 11, 38 and 73, these routes being aided again on 2 October with the addition of the 52.

Above: The London Coaches 'MB' class of former Ms were not too proud of their tourist role to have to revert to stage operation, and the entry into service of tri-axle Metrobuses (EMBs) from Hong Kong made enough of them spare to eventually become the predominant type on the 185, an assignment which ended up lasting over a year. MB710 (KYV 710X) departs Lewisham bus station on 29 October 2002, showing that its livery included a lot more of the secondary Cotswold stone colour than did its stage-service counterpart. *Geoff Rixon*

Above: Defying the final months of Ms in service was Leaside Travel, which conversely went from strength to strength. From 4 September 2002 new routes 683 and 688 linked the Jews Free School (JFS) in Queensbury with some quite distant catchment areas, and required five buses between them. They were generally Ms from the B- and C-registered blocks which had come off service at Wood Green and been seconded for this work in replacement of earlier Leaside Travel examples. In January 2004 M1332 (C332 BUV) and a similarly-liveried colleague sandwich a third M still in Arriva colours. *Tony Wilson*

Two autumn sales affected Metrobuses; that of Sovereign to Transdev on 22 October, following which some spare London United Ms were eventually made available to Edgware (BT) as trainers, and that of Metropolitan Omnibus's operations and vehicles on 1 November to Thorpe's, which continued to use 12 ex-Metropolitan Omnibus Ms (and its own) on the 626, 643, school journeys on the 143, 302 and H12 and occasionally on the 187 and 487. Three more (M468, 693, 809) passed to Blue Triangle.

On 9 November Arriva London North's 24 was transferred to Metroline London Northern, removing the possibility of appearance by Tottenham's small fleet of Ms, three of which went on to quadruple the complement at Clapton. Enfield was reintroduced to the type, however, when it absorbed Palmers Green's allocation on the 121 and took four spare Ms (694, 740/85 and 1252) with which to do so; one (M740) was positively the last Arriva London North repaint. Leaside Travel itself was experimenting with redder liveries, trying out a maroon skirt on M575. Finally for Arriva serving London in November, three of the tri-axle tour-bus Metrobuses (EMB768/70/3) worked shorts on the 38 on 26 and 27 November, the first two days of a subsequent three-day London Underground strike covered once again by London Coaches 'MBs' on the 38, 52 and 73 and this time adding the 8. Finally for 9 November, Blue Triangle began new route 372 to replace the 324 and 348; eventually Ms began to sneak out onto it. A Shepherd's Bush M was also seen on London United's new 148, introduced to exploit the Congestion Charge area.

Merton garage of London General withdrew its last example, M1226 in November, but First CentreWest's Uxbridge replaced the LLW on Buckinghamshire County Council route 335 with one at the end of November so that the Lance SLF could depart. In a curious PR exercise (so to speak), Metroline renamed its Harlesden garage to Park Royal on New Year's Day 2003 and recoded it from HR to PR.

As 2002 rolled into 2003 even the refurbished Metrobuses had shot their bolt; between 28 December and 12 January Arriva East Herts & Essex's Ware-based contingent on the 310 and 310A gave way to Olympians displaced from the 142 by new DAFs. The London United Ms supporting Tellings-Golden Miller's 235 came off on the 11th and by the end of January London General had taken delivery of enough new WVLs to displace the company's last Ms – the withdrawal of Stockwell's last three (M1215, 1337/91) by around 18 February made London General the second post-LBL company to lose the type entirely. Shuffles at Arriva London North at the end of January removed the M from Enfield but put two (M785 and 1402) into Stamford Hill temporarily, to make brief return appearances on the 149, 242 and 253; Enfield very quickly gained back its lost examples. First Capital 178, with two other providing support to Rainham's TNLs on the 123, was repainted red in January, but omitting the broad yellow band.

On 1 February the 76 returned to Arriva London North after five years with First Capital, and Tottenham's M holdouts could soon be counted upon to support the scheduled VLWs. Increases to London United's crew-operated 9 and 94 could not be

accomplished with RMLs, none being available, so nine Ms were repainted and put into Shepherd's Bush garage; a similar situation prevailed with First CentreWest's 7, which began to gather Ms at Westbourne Park. The first OPO conversion in five years, however, was that of the 10, but four of the Holloway Ms supporting it simply switched their remit to new RML-operated route 390 created to cover the Archway-Marble Arch half. The other six swelled numbers at Potters Bar, portending improved fortunes there owing to the withdrawal of the Scanias (Ss) from the 84 and 'real' 242; by April 20 Ms were available for service. Otherwise Metroline touted for drivers by repainting trainers M4 and 1067 turquoise with the appropriate ads. M1 retained its 1978 livery upon repaint at the same time.

The penultimate new garage to be given an allocation of Metrobuses was King's Cross (KX), opened by Metroline London Northern on 29 March for the 390; as well as RMLs and RMs, M1042 went in and lasted until May. Holloway kept the 390 on Sundays (as OPO, meaning its own Ms could visit). This spring the last scheduled M routes were theoretically converted, Metroline's 240 at Edgware receiving cascaded VPLs in April and Arriva London North's 125 at Edmonton taking its DLPs from the middle of the same month. Neither garage lost Ms entirely, of course, and the holdouts were apt to switch back and forth from garage to garage when top-ups were required. The new low-floor DAFs were also officially allocated to prestige school routes 683 and 688.

Above: Despite modernisation in 1996 with ex-MTL DAF single-deckers, the 310A and 310B regained Ms in March 1999 not long after the Merseyside connection was broken, and their second period lasted until 4 September 2002, when EDR-class Darts took over for what would turn out to be one final year. On 7 March 2002 Potters Bar's M1330 (C330 BUV), now in Metroline livery, is at Ponders End bound for Enfield Town. *Author*

Thorpe's effectively stood down its Metrobuses from schoolday work in mid-March, replacing them with the Volvo B10M rebuilds converted by Grey-Green. On 5 April the 185 finally settled with its new operator, East Thames Buses, which took over London Easylink's VPs and allowed Blue Triangle and its supporting sub-contractors to leave; only London Coaches remained, finally coming off in October.

Leaside Travel gained the route 167 school journey on 26 April, but the company's four-speed Ms were finally retired following the move of similarly-souped-up Ls to replace them after 31 May; this was due to the split of the 253 into two routes on that date, which finished off Clapton's Ms finally plus the rogue at Stamford Hill. Leaside Travel's latest livery, pioneered on M1126, was all-red with just a white tape band in the same position as the yellow band on existing Arriva buses.

After 24 years of Metrobus operation, Fulwell lost its last two on or around 21 May; these were M1271 and 1343, while First Capital's withdrawal of M843 left Dagenham with just the three mkIIs.

Conversions to double-deck in the post-Congestion Charge period of breakneck spending involved the 217 and 231 at Potters Bar from 7 June, all of which retained their M support (and made the 231's Leaside Travel journeys redundant), but on the same day the 310A and 310B, by far the most successful of the late-LBL forays into commercial services, were withdrawn. On 28 June another splitting divided the 260 across Golders Green; this route transferred back to Willesden (retaining M wanderings alongside a

mix of AVs and stand-in TPs) and the northern end became new Park Royal-operated 460, again with an element of Ms. School route 643 was transferred from Thorpe's to Metroline (Cricklewood) with Ms, as was the appropriate working of the 143, while the 626's Thorpe's element was also retired.

Some oddments were still possible in the dying days of the M – East Thames Buses' M1010 was restored to traffic in July to serve as the 661's officially-allocated bus from Belvedere (BV), but on 19 July worked an extra on the 108 between North Greenwich and Lewisham together with other double-deckers needed after a concert. Even odder, it performed once on the 150 out of Ash Grove.

The 125 was transferred from Edmonton to Enfield on 19 July, leaving just M718 behind to cover the 34's recently-delivered DLAs. On the 26th Potters Bar's 263 was transferred again, this time to Holloway; the arrival of VPs for the 260 at Willesden released several Ms into this garage, boosting its numbers (mainly used on the 4) to seven, while three went into Perivale (PV) for the first time, assisting on the 297 during an emergency period of double-deck (TP) operation and turning out once each on the 112 and recently-introduced 205. An increase to the 302 from 30 August employed Willesden's three Ms.

London United stripped both Tolworth and Hounslow Heath of Ms during July, just M1243 remaining allocated to Hounslow and eight at Shepherd's Bush supporting RMLs on the 9 and 94.

The last repaint of a First Metrobus was by CentreWest to Uxbridge's M861 during July, this bus still able to visit the 207 and U4 (and more so on the

Above: It was ironic that the class which had played such a part in reducing the numbers of Routemasters when new should finish their careers in crew mode as adjuncts to them. Although withdrawals were looming, there were none left to spread among routes that needed service increases, so Ms had to step in. London United went as far as to repaint nine to help out the 9 and 94 at Shepherd's Bush for the duration of 2003, and that August M1361 (C361 BUV), still able to display a third of its original grille badging, albeit overpainted, waits to make the right turn from Oxford Street into Regent Street. *Geoff Rixon*

Below: Similar Metrobus augmentation was implemented by First (formerly CentreWest, but now officially stripped of any subsidiary physical indication to this end) on routes 7 and 23, allowing the M an Indian summer at Westbourne Park four years after the 18's loss to TNs. At Marble Arch in March 2003 is M1415 (C415 BUV). *Geoff Rixon*

latter since its official double-decking in May). Thirty-two Metrobuses remained available at Metroline's two firms, though Edgware's M306 was the last there in September. Four Potters Bar machines, M1032/76 and 1150, bought some time with repaints; of these M1114 gained a lower-deck repaint only with a shallow blue skirt. Foreshadowing a renewed and this time, final, lurch towards OPO, the 94 was one-manned again during evenings and Sundays on 30 August, while the conversion of the 23 to OPO outright on 15 November removed Westbourne Park's M support, latterly in the person of M859, 1245 and 1415.

The sundry second-hand operators were just about done with their Ms by now, East Thames Buses' M1010 reverting to training use and Thorpe's replacing its Ms with new Darts during the autumn, though not before one got out on the 210! London Coaches finally vacated the 185 on 5 October after a valiant year of help, and at Arriva London North M718 and 1318 were Edmonton's last non-special purposes Metrobuses, lingering into 2004.

Despite the reversion to DLD of the 297 on 2 September the route needed double-deckers and a batch of VPs was ordered for it by Metroline; their arrival in December allowed Perivale's stopgap Ms (1193 and 1403) to leave. At Arriva London North, Enfield ceased M operation in November (M1252 being the last) and Wood Green's once-enormous runout was now down to three, M1276, 1300 and 1323, all based on the 141 and collectively replaced by the transfer of DLA 45-7. The roughest of the three, M1300, escaped to Leaside Travel in September, while on the morning of 8 December M1323 refused to proceed beyond the gates of its home garage while about to take up WN59 on the 141, sealing its fate. M1276 was finally withdrawn by 30 January. That winter saw Tottenham's seven Ms (M665, 1319/22/4, 1402/5/6) drifting from their allotted 73 onto the 243 and 41 for old times' sake; M1402 was the last in red and yellow-striped Cowie livery.

Left: The 23 was to be the third of the final 20 Routemaster routes to go over to OPO, losing its RMLs on 15 November 2003 and enabling Westbourne Park's Metrobus holdouts to be stood down finally. On 17 March M1438 (C438 BUV) is seen in Threadneedle Street by the Bank of England. *Author*

Below: Arriva London North was now rapidly running down its Ms, and of the once-huge allocation at Wood Green, only M1276 (B276 WUL) managed to last into 2004, sticking doggedly to the 141. With a mixed upper- and lower-case blind panel that sits uncomfortably in the ultimate box, it is seen on 18 April at the 141's first southbound stop at Wood Green. *Author*

Above: The First subsidiary formerly known as CentreWest also operated Ms into 2004 - just, leaving small numbers at Uxbridge long after the rest had been swept away by Tridents. M1051 (A751 THV), taken back after spending time at First Capital as 351, helped double-deck the U4 (the route once known as 204) in May 2003 and is seen on the 28th of that month at Hayes. *Geoff Rixon*

Below: Metroline cleared out all its Ms in the space of one week in February 2004; M1034 (A734 THV) survived to become one of Harrow Weald's last examples, which mostly stuck to the 182. With mismatched windows, battered panels, fading paintwork and painful-looking scoring down the side, this bus has definitely had enough and in this shot has mere days left in service. *Haydn Davies*

Finally London United, First and Metroline could undertake a purge of their Ms as 2004 got going. The arrival of TLA-class Dennis Tridents for the 94 released enough RMLs to the 9 to ease out Shepherd's Bush's final Metrobuses (M1344/5/51/6/60/1/3) in advance of the 94's OPO conversion on 24 January, and Hounslow's lone M1243 was finished off by the same means; the survivors were relegated to special purposes only until June, their ticket machines being removed. At First, cascades of vehicles allowed Rainham to stand down M171/2/8 in February, while Alperton's M1258 and 1382, the last two of five, were delicensed on 13 February, leaving just M859 marooned on a Tesco contract. Uxbridge was then whittled down by 27 February, again just a single example surviving out of six; M348, a.k.a First Capital 324 and still wearing that operator's livery, held out on school route 698 until March. Alperton's M859 became the only Metrobus to actually carry one of the quite ludicrous fleetnumbers that had been dreamt up for FirstGroup vehicles the previous November, ending up as WD35859. In February Metroline stood down most of its training fleet and then turned its attention to the service buses; Holloway's final example, M1385, finished that month and in March withdrawals swept through four garages in the space of one week; Park Royal's M1197 and 1342 came off by 13 February, Willesden's M391, 1042, 1181/93 and M1385 (ex-Holloway) last worked on the 16th and Harrow Weald's last was M1032 on the 182 on the 18th. The withdrawal of Cricklewood's three last

examples (M339, 1339 and 1428), latterly used on school routes 611 and 643 only, completed the programme, and other than the nine (M1032/42/76, 1114/50/89/97, 1208/50) now holding out at Potters Bar, safely beyond TfL's iron fist, Metroline's last Metrobus was M1, which continued to serve as a trainer/company representative/preservation piece; in this role it performed guest appearances on three Routemaster finales, the first of which was supporting the last day of conductors on the 6 and 98 (Friday 26 March) at Willesden, then appearing on Stagecoach East London's 8 on 16 May and finally on the infamous Black Friday, 3 September, where it performed a diagram on the 390 (including re-creation of the full extent of the 10) to see off Metroline London Northern's last RMLs of all.

Following one rogue three-day spell by East Thames Buses' M1010 on the 180 on 18-20 August (circumventing, and by its own company at that, TfL's effective ban on non-low-floor buses applying since 24 July!), the honour of being the last Metrobuses on frontline service, scheduled or otherwise, with a company not descended from the old London Transport went to the surviving pair at Mitcham Belle, 048 (M960) and 049 (M1106); in the interim poor 047 (M1039) had fallen to pieces! They lingered on until Mitcham Belle itself fell apart on 27 August, and did not form part of the company's sale to Centra. Even now Blue Triangle was apt to let its Ms creep onto the 248 and 368 when it had absolutely no other choice, but 2004 really was their last year.

Above: As all eyes were on the rapid withdrawal of Routemasters in 2004/05 following Ken Livingstone's infamous turnaround, there still remained the possibility for the M not to be outlived and at the same time pay tribute to its most illustrious of forebears. On 16 May 2004, as part of extensive commemorations surrounding the last weeks of crew operation on the 8 at Stagecoach East London's Bow, M1 (THX 101S) was brought out to join T1 (THX 401S) on a special shortworking of the route from Victoria to St Paul's and back, and here is where we can compare the two contemporary types. M1 had also helped see off Willesden's conductors on the 6 and 98 and would do the same at King's Cross for the 390 on 3 September. It was sold to Ensignbus in 2008. *Author*

Above: Arriva London North's last three Ms finished on 18 June 2004, all on the 41, but their main role for a couple of years had been in support of RMLs on the 73 at Tottenham; ironically they were replaced by extra Routemasters released by the 137's one-manning! On 24 May M1324 (C324 BUV) is travelling westwards down Oxford Street.
Author

In the best tradition of the old London Transport, it was now time to think about a grand finale; and perhaps the only advantage of the great splitting of traditional operations was that Londoners got three of them. The first goodbye by Ms was on scheduled all-day TfL services; Tottenham's seven had been reduced to three at the end of May by the withdrawal of M665 and 1319/22/4, replaced on the 73, ironically, by RMLs, and on Friday 18 June M1402/5/6 all made their final bow on the 41. However, another tube strike forced Tottenham to put M1402 out on the 73 on 29 and 30 June! The second and most significant finale was at Potters Bar, where the 84 and 'real' 242, despite their severing from the network two decades ago, were routes still recognisably descended from the old way of things. Of the seven Ms left in service, M1189 was withdrawn in July, M1208 in August and M1042, 1114/50 in September, leaving just M1076, 1197 and 1250. it was intended to run this trio one last time on Saturday 11 September, helped by M1, but unfortunately all three sat out the festivities, albeit in plain view at the garage gates, due to the refusal of drivers to take them out. M1 did the honours in their stead, helped by a last-minute appearance of Sullivan Buses' M1309, in LR Travel colours, on its local route 398. So after just short of 26 years, the Metrobus bowed out without ceremony, the type never having needed glory or glamour – and even after that, a clutch of school services continued to specify Leaside Travel's Ms.

TfL's rapid and unpopular withdrawal of the Routemaster family during 2005 was part of a policy to make the whole network 'accessible' by the end of that year, and once this was complete a final push was made against the school routes. On Friday 13 January 2006, the last day of Leaside Travel itself, as it transpired, M1124 and 1312 turned out on the 121 and M1320 and 1367 were on the 675, but it was M1312 that stole in to represent the third and last finale, sent out by Enfield on Tuesday 17 January to work the 121.

For two more years trainers continued to ply the streets in gradually diminishing numbers, the most numerous being the white Ms of Arriva's two London chapters (their numbers swelled by Leaside Travel's cast-offs), followed by London United's small band, but successive legislation conspired to thin their numbers; first the requirement from July 2007 that training buses be fitted with ABS and finally the Low Emission Zone. This particularly ill-conceived statute, applying from 8 July 2008, has also had the effect of prohibiting preserved vehicles built after 1973 from visiting anywhere within the M25 unless fitted with expensive emission-reductions equipment. Thus, the appearance of preserved M1 on Routemaster-operated Heritage Route 15H on 29 June and on the 84 on 5 July proved to be the last time any Metrobus carried fare-paying passengers, and after that precious few of the M class can still be seen by the Londoners they served so faithfully – ever unappreciated, yet never ruffled.

Above: Operating as they did principally outside the boundaries of the old GLC area, routes 84 and 242 were early candidates for tendering and both fell under the responsibility of Hertfordshire County Council; in the event the the 84 gained its 'red' buses back after four years and the 242 never lost them. Thus by 2004 Potters Bar Ms were still in charge to see the class out. Coy about its ownership, M1250 (B250 WUL) calls at Potters Bar Station during May. *Dave Brown*

Left: And finally to the last day - or at least as it should have been. The three stars sat out their own party in the doorway of Potters Bar on 11 September 2004 while M1 operated their routes 84 and 242 for them. From left to right they are M1076 (B76 WUL), M1197 (B197 WUL) and M1250 (B250 WUL), the last mentioned with a slightly higher skirt but otherwise repainted comparatively recently. They were kept on the books at Potters Bar until the following May and then sold. *Author*

SEVEN

After Service

The sheer size of the M class meant that the type would be spread far and wide upon exile from London, and to fully explore that scope would require another volume in itself. Where London is concerned, however, large numbers of Metrobuses continued to linger in and around the capital in a variety of roles.

Tour work

Between 1994 and 1998 **London Pride** of Rainham acquired a large number of Metrobuses new to LT, South Yorkshire PTE, West Midlands PTE, Maidstone & District, Hull and Reading. Open-top conversion was the most popular option, with partial open-top buses also used and closed-top buses retained for the slower winter season. A red base colour was broken by silver or gold relief, both lined out in black. Multiple changes of ownership characterised the latter part of the 1990s, but finally the London Pride identity was subsumed within Ensign's City Sightseeing brand and vehicles departed for overseas branches of this successful unit. For many years this company's Metrobuses operated a successful Christmas Day-only commercial network in the absence of any other bus operations on that day.

The Maybury family's **Big Bus Company** took its first Metrobuses in May 2001, giving them the elegant and lovingly-maintained maroon and cream with gold lining-out. However, this ML class was formed of three-axle examples new to China Motor Bus. Former LBL subsidiary **London Coaches** also took ex-CMB tri-axle Metrobuses (EMB class), having otherwise built its Wandsworth-based operation on ex-Arriva London North and South Ms, which it reclassified MB. Again a mix of full / partial open-top and closed-top buses operated from 1995 onwards, their livery evolving from red and white with 'Original London Sightseeing Tour' fleetnames to 'Arriva presenting London' red with a large cream scoop at the front. As well as tour work and rail replacement services, a period of stage service was undertaken on the troubled 185 route between September 2002 and October 2003; otherwise all ex-LBL Ms had been withdrawn by 2007, leaving just the EMBs, adapted for LEZ standards.

Local operators around London

Blue Triangle commenced in September 1996 with ex-Merseybus and GM Buses Metrobuses for rail-replacement work, soon followed by mkIIs new to SYPTE, but the company's place in London bus history was cemented with its valiant emergency stand-ins on routes 53, 60, 127 and 185 between 1998 and 2003, an effort which brought the company a steady trickle of tendering gains on which to use its Metrobuses and Titans. The former, acquired in 1999 mostly from London United, were reclassified into an MCW class and bore two liveries; one of red and cream, followed by a simplified scheme of more red with just cream striping. Operations on what became TfL's school routes dwindled away by late 2004, and since 29 June 2007 the company has been known as **The London Bus Company**.

In spite of its tremendous success as a bus dealership, Ensign still felt it was worth operating bus services, and in May 1998 commenced a second incarnation of its **Ensignbus** identity with the familiar blue and silver livery; Metrobuses from just about every operator ever to have specified the type found their way into this fleet, which was put to work on two commercial routes east of Romford. Another change of mind only eleven months later saw this operation's sale to **Town & Country**, which eventually introduced a dark blue and light blue livery of its own before going out of business itself. Ensignbus's remaining rail-replacement work continued, though only two Metrobuses survived the LEZ; in 2008 M1 was acquired as a working preservation piece.

The dark green livery of Rainham-based **Imperial** was among the best ever on Metrobuses, and from late 2000 it adorned a miscellany from various sources. Rail-replacement work and limited stage operations in Essex kept them busy. Other operators to specify liveries recalling buses' glory days were **Carousel Bus & Coach** of High Wycombe (whose red livery was adorned with a logo recalling London Country's early 'flying Polo' device) and Gravesend-based **Red Route Buses** (with a livery similar to London United's); the latter figured prominently in the saga of route 185. **Nostalgiabus** (later known as **Northdown**) also helped out where London's bus operators fell down, eventually giving its small

Left: London Pride's peak years are epitomised by 260 (EWF 460V), formerly Grey-Green 460 and before that, South Yorkshire PTE 460. In May 1996, not long after its conversion to partial open-top, it is seen crossing London Bridge. A second livery, with a silver midriff sweeping up towards the front, was phased in later before the relaunch as a CitySightseeing franchise. *Tony Wilson*

Left: London Coaches amassed a number of Metrobuses in the mid-to-late-1990s prior to its absorption into the Arriva empire; its former Arriva London North and South Ms became an MB class and received red and white livery for what was still known as the Original London Sightseeing Tour. In March 1996 MB245 (BYX 245V) was one of two converted to open-top, but a year later they were partially re-roofed with awkward-looking front window panels; the result is crossing London Bridge in July 1997. *Tony Wilson*

Left: Ensign's greatest success of recent years has been its CitySightseeing operation of branded tour franchises. Arriva presenting London (begun as London Coaches) eventually sprouted a CitySightseeing arm and repainted many of its ex-service Metrobuses into the red livery with locally-appropriate signwriting. Known in this incarnation as MB509 (GYE 509W) since acquisition in 1998, the former M509 is seen at Marble Arch on 29 March 2002. *Geoff Rixon*

Right: The MCW Metrobus was not only a success in its native Britain, Hong Kong-based CMB and KMB taking a strong liking to the type and indeed probably prolonging its existence in production. Here, however, they were very different beasts, their three-axle bodies capable of cramming in over 100 seated passengers. At the turn of the century it became good business for Ensign to buy them and ship them home as high-capacity tour buses in refutation of accepted wisdom that 12m buses could not negotiate central London. Arriva presenting London called its acquisitions EMBs, while The Big Bus Company took a dozen as an ML class; ML153 (F153 UJN), passing through Marble Arch on 24 May 2008, was formerly known as China Motor Bus ML68. The maroon and cream livery lined out in gold is truly splendid. *Author*

number of acquired Ms a red livery with black and white relief. **White Rose Travel**, part of the Sidney Road Travel group that also spawned **Sullivan Buses**, had a less sucessful innings, running its Ms in 1978 livery with white relief before overstretching itself and collapsing in 2002, but Sullivan Buses survived and itself gave rise to **Griffin Bus**. The remnant of White Rose became **Wiltax**, with a poppy-red livery recalling BTS, with whom the management had connections historically. After helping out in London, **Metrobus**'s ex-LT Ms could be seen further south all the way to Lewes and Brighton.

With regard to smaller companies, it is no exaggeration to say that almost everyone involved in bus operations in the 1990s and 2000s took advantage of the cheap and versatile post-London Transport Metrobus. Going anticlockwise geographically round London, Essex could field **Trimmer Travel** and **Caistors Coaches** of Romford, **Croftpeak** of Rainham, **Barnes Coaches** of Dagenham, **Regal** and **Barker Buses** of Harlow, **SM** (or **S & M**) and **Kingstons** of Benfleet, **Roomes** of Grays, **Stansted Transit** and **Locallink Trave**l of Stansted and **Master Travel** of Brentwood; across the river in Kent one could find

Right: Several operators on the fringes of London acquired second-hand Metrobuses as cheap and versatile stopgaps on which to build their companies. London Traveller was the trading name for a handful of stage services in north-west London, but a provincial component was also operated under the name of County Traveller. GOG 230W was the only one of the company's Metrobuses to receive two shades of green, and on 21 March 1998 is seen bringing it through St John's Wood on a rail replacement service. *Malc McDonald*

Left: Regal Busways' M577 (GYE 577W), when captured behind East Finchley Station on a Northern Line rail job on 30 October 2003, is carrying the livery of previous owner Crawley Luxury Coaches; since withdrawal from Arriva London South at Croydon in April 2000 it had also served at Arriva Scotland West and Carousel. *Author*

Left: As the memory of unified London Transport started to dim, enthusiasts-turned-operators resurrected some of the better aspects of the old organisation for their own small undertakings; one of them, White Rose of Thorpe, added the white upper-deck window surrounds of 1976-79 to its Metrobuses and Titans operating Surrey County Council route 461 from 27 January 2001, like M737 (KYV 737X) at West Molesey. *Geoff Rixon*

Left: White Rose foundered in February 2002, but was reborn as Wiltax, a handful of Metrobuses donning a poppy-red and yellow livery patterned after that of BTS. Almost all of them gained Routemaster registrations during their tenure, exemplified by M429 (VLT 191, ex-GYE 429W) alongside M449 (VLT 177, ex-GYE 449W) at Wisley airfield during the 2005 incarnation of Cobham Open Day. The buses were later reclassified to match their registrations, this particular pair becoming MB91 and MB77. *Author*

Right: Sullivan Buses perpetuated White Rose's retro livery of red with white upper-deck window surrounds. M563 (GYE 563W), transporting Tube passengers away from Euston on 22 October 2003, had achieved earlier fame as the testbed for a new London Northern post-privatisation livery based on that company's route X43 Scanias. It passed on to associated Griffin Bus in 2007 and was scrapped in September 2008. *Author*

Right: Imperial gathered a handful of Metrobuses from a variety of sources, putting them to work on Essex County Council school contracts based around Loughton and then adding commercial services. HM520 (SAG 520W), acquired in January 2002 via London Pride, was former Kingston-upon-Hull 520, and is seen at Loughton later that year on local service H1. *Andrew Jeffreys*

Right: In the early years of the 21st century it started to be good business to bring back British-built double-deckers from Hong Kong following their mass replacement by low-floor buses. Ensign was at the forefront, first taking a handful of Dennis Condors and tri-axle Metrobuses for the Big Bus Company and then snapping up one for itself; the result is the spectacular 484 (F84 UJN), formerly China Motor Bus ML75. On 7 April 2002 it conveys passengers to and from Brooklands airfield on the occasion of Cobham Open Day. *Author*

Nu-Venture (a firm fan of Titans but which did once hire an M), **Griffin Bus** of Polhill and Strood-based **Amberlee**, **Owen's Coaches** and its successor **Mann's Coaches,** and straddling the Surrey border, **Camden Coaches** of variously Swanley and West Kingsdown.

Surrey itself could boast **Leggs Travel** (Weybridge), **Aventa** (Horsham), **Frimley Coaches**, **Crawley Luxury Coaches**, **Anglia Bus Company** (Thorpe), **Atbus** (also Thorpe), **Country Bus** (New Malden), **Southdown PSV** (Horsham), **Clockwork Travel** (Crawley) and the unmemorably short-lived **Driver Express**. **Arriva Southern Counties**, incorporating the former London & Country, Guildford & West Surrey and portions of **Maidstone & District** plus **New Enterprise Travel**, had its Metrobus heyday at the turn of the century, replacing more expensive newer buses with cast-off but refurbished Ms.

Middlesex was home to **Bear Buses** of Feltham and **Thorpe's** (which had an outstation at the Millennium Dome for a service that hardly ever operated), **Imperial Coaches** of Southall and Edgware-based **Able Coaches**. Buckinghamshire could field **Z&S** of Aylesbury, **Abbey Coaches** of High Wycombe and **Motts Travel**, and finally in Hertfordshire were

County Traveller, a green-liveried sibling to London Traveller, and its **Watford & District** operating arm; **Decker Bus**, **Gordon Sexton** and **Dave Lepick Travel** of South Mimms, **Kelly Coaches** and **Shire Coaches** (St Alban's), **Bryan's** of Enfield (in dealership mode), **Falcon Coaches** of Enfield, **London Travel** of Borehamwood, **Crown Line** and **South Mimms Travel**, **On-A-Mission Coaches** (of Letchworth) and **LR Travel**. Very few Metrobuses found their way to **Arriva the Shires** until two of the original Leaside Travel coaches (M1379 and 1437) gravitated to Harlow in 2005 to see out their days. Completing this county were **A to B Bus & Coach** of Tring, **Mullany's** of Watford and **Green Light Travel**.

Largely without fixed abode were **Mediabus** (deriving from Metroline and housed at either Connex's Beddington Cross premises or, later, Northumberland Park of First Capital), Mitcham Belle's replacement **Centra** and untraceable **Andilee Travel**, and deriving from further out but important on London Underground replacement was **Supreme Travel** of Southend and the later ill-fated **Alec Head**. Finally, Alton-based **Alder Valley Travel** has revived that classic bus identity.

Above: From as far away as Southend came Alec Head to rescue the wilting Underground on several occasions before TfL decided that its rail-replacement services would be restricted to its own contractors regardless of the risk of drastically reducing the numbers of buses available for such work. On 15 October 2005 former M274 (BYX 274V) heads north past Warren Street as dusk sets in. The attractive livery thankfully draws attention away from the rusted welt in the offside roof dome. *Author*

Left: By 2008 Metrobuses were thin on the ground indeed, even the smaller operators being obliged to move to low-floor buses or sell up. Only council school buses and non-TfL rail work are where one can see the type today, and even here Atbus is one company to defeat the LEZ by fitting emissions-regulation gear to two otherwise superannuated former London-area Metrobuses; M1100 (B100 WUL) at Wisley Airfield on the occasion of 2008's Cobham open day allows the reader and traveller to experience the angry snarl that only a Cummins L10 engine can emit. *Author*

Training buses

Dedicated training schools over and above companies' own arrangements found the ex-London Transport Metrobus an easy and versatile steed for the novice driver, and the green and cream livery applied by **Thames Valley Training** (trading as **Graham's Training Service**) was superb. Hackney-based John's School of Motoring (or **JSM**) preferred a blue and grey livery and HGV/PCV school **Heavy Load Training** of Cockfosters owned M1392 between August 2004 and August 2006.

Government and utilities

Using Metrobuses for various community-liaison projects have been the London Boroughs of **Enfield, Ealing, Croydon** and **Hounslow** and **Hertfordshire County Council**. Two engineering contractors, **Field Systems Design** of Dartford and **JTS Engineering** of Billericay, used Ms as mobile platforms for maintenance work in the Dartford and Limehouse Link tunnels respectively.

Weird and wonderful

Finally, the humble Metrobus has seen post-service use in the guise of colleges, churches, pubs, drug-treatment centres, hospitality units, election battle buses, after-school clubs, Scout huts, playbuses, paintball targets, hospitals, zoo attractions, convention props, transport for Page 3 girls, Internet cafés and film and TV support vehicles. As for TV adverts, the most outrageous incarnation involved Sullivan Buses' M1069 performing a *Live and Let Die*-style loop-the-loop (thankfully CGI-generated!) on an advert for Channel 4. London Transport-specification Ms have also advertised milk, frozen foods, cinema tickets, banks, building societies, CDs, mobile phones and their ringtones and London bus operations in general.

The final journey and preservation

Inevitably the majority of buses make their way to the scrapyard, the roll of honour (or dishonour) where the M is concerned including Commercial PSV (Maybells) of Dagenham, PVS, Ripley, Wigley, Bus Bits and Erith Commercials, but preservation has thankfully saved several Metrobuses for posterity. Currently to be seen on the British rally circuit in the ownership of museums or private individuals are M1/6/14/38/48/59/67, 278, 394, 781/9, 961, 1000/1/14, 1309 and 1441 in various stages of livery, while M1369 was a former member of this elite club before destruction by fire in 2004. Still, even now the class's service period has not quite ended even as former Ms approach their thirtieth birthday, with scattered examples still able to take passengers for second or third owners.

Left: The fate of the majority of buses — pulled apart unceremoniously in some Barnsley mudheap. This was where M1349 (C349 BUV) finished up after an interesting weekend spent being raised and lowered to a prone position to demonstrate the crash-recovery process to attendees of Routemaster 50 in Finsbury Park on 24/25 July 2004. At the close of that momentous event the sorry-looking remains are being hitched up to the tender one last time. At least some parts will have gone to deserving fellow Metrobuses to keep them operational. *Author*

Left: Preservation has now reached the M class after two and a half decades of service. Resplendent in original condition is preserved M1000 (A700 THV), dressed as a Clapton bus for Showbus 2007. Clapton was its third garage of four during a 16-year service career. *Author*

Below left: Representing the early Metrobuses of London Transport is M6 (WYW 6T), now owned by Cobham Bus Museum but since 2008 effectively marooned there by the imposition of the Low Emission Zone. Everything is just right on this bus — from the unusual numberplates (which managed to survive several repaints during its career) to the reinstated foglights and most interesting of all, the automatic fare-collection machine restored to full functionality during 2007. On 15 June 2008 it is setting off from Hampton Court on the last occasion it was allowed to penetrate London's borders. *Author*

Right and below: Although Ms carried a variety of interiors during their time with London Transport and its successors, the original scheme of what might be called earth tones endured for longest. Upon its acquisition by Cobham Bus Museum, M6 (WYW 6T) was fully restored by Cobham, with graffiti cleaned off, scratched windows replaced and best of all, its automatic fare-collection machine restored, giving enthusiasts unfamiliar with this machinery a look at what it was like. *All: Author*

Appendices

1.   LT FLEET NUMBERS, REGISTRATIONS AND CODES

Order year	Fleet numbers	Registrations	LT code	MCW code	Notes
1977	M1-5	THX 101-5S	1M1	DR101/3	
1978	M6-55	WYW 6-55T	2M2	DR101/8	
1979	M56-95	WYW 56-95T	2M2	DR101/9	
1979	M96-205	BYX 96-205V	2M2	DR101/9	
1980	M206-315	BYX 206-315V	2M2	DR101/12	
1980	M316-45	EYE 316-45V	2M2	DR101/12	
1980	M346-430	GYE 346-430W	2M2	DR101/12	
1980	M431-46	GYE 431-46W	2M3	DR101/12	Airbus batch
1980	M447-505	GYE 447-505W	2M2	DR101/12	
1981	M506-605	GYE 506-605W	2M2	DR101/14	
1981	M606-31	KYO 606-31X	2M2	DR101/14	
1981	M632-805	KYV 632-805X	2M2	DR101/14	
1983	M806-91	OJD 806-91Y	3M4	DR101/16	
1983	M892-955	A892-955 SUL	3M4	DR101/16	
1984	M956-99	A956-99 SYF	3M4	DR101/17	
1984	M1000-5	A700-5 THV	3M4	DR101/17	
1984	M1006-29	A706-29 THV	4M5	DR101/18	Second Airbus batch
1984	M1030-43	A730-43 THV	3M4	DR101/17	
1984	M1044-55	A744-55 THV	1/3M6	DR101/19	RLST, PA fitted
1984	M1056-83	B56-83 WUL	3M4	DR101/17	
1984	M1084-1105	B84-105 WUL	8M4/4	DR134/1	Cummins engines
1985	M1106-1305	B106-305 WUL	3M4	DR101/17	
1985	M1306-1440	C306-440 BUV	3M4	DR101/17	
1984 (AVE)	M1441	A441 UUV	5M7	DR102/45	MkII
1984 (AVE)	M1442	A442 UUV	6M7	DR132/5	MkII, Cummins engine
- (acquired)	M1443-7	GBU 1, 4, 5, 8, 9V	-	DR101/6	Ex-GM Buses 1987
- (acquired)	M1448/9	UWW 518/9X	-	DR101/15	Ex-Yorkshire Rider 1987
- (acquired)	M1450/1	CUB 539/40Y	-	DR102/32	MkII, ex-Yorkshire Rider 1987
- (leased)	M1452-78	E452-78 SON	-	DR102/63	MkII, new 1987
- (leased)	M1479/80	E479/80 UOF	-	DR102/65	MkII, new 1988
- (acquired)	M1481-5	VRG 415-9T	-	DR101/4	Ex-Busways 1988

*Seating: All H43/28D except M6-205 (H43/24D), M431-46, 1006-29 (H43/9D), M1443-7 (H43/30F),
M1448/9 (Alexander RL H43/32F), M1450/1 (H46/30F), M1452-80 (H45/30F), M1481-5 (H40/36F)*
Notes: *M1443-7 new GMPTE 1979, M1481-5 new Tyneside PTE 1979, M1448/9 new WYPTE 1982, M1449/50 new WYPTE 1983*

2.   RE-REGISTRATIONS IN LONDON OWNERSHIP

M151	33 LUG (02.03), BYX 151V (10.08)	M1046	VLT 46 (08.89), A746 THV (08.01)
M188	188 CLT (12.90), BYX 188V (02.98)	M1185	WLT 893 (07.94), B185 WUL (05.01)
M197	197 CLT (12.90), BYX 197V (02.98)	M1236	WLT 646 (04.94), B236 WUL (05.01)
M198	VLT 98 (12.90), SGK 374V (12.95)	M1273	WLT 902 (07.94)
M278	78 CLT (07.91), BYX 278V (12.98)	M1304	304 CLT (08.93)
M284	VLT 284 (05.92), BYX 284V (02.98)	M1315	VLT 15 (08.89), C109 NGH (10.93)
M379	WLT 379 (07.92), GYE 379W (02.98)	M1372	772 DYE (07.93)
M398	398 CLT (08.93)	M1379	VLT 88 (02.88)
M463	WLT 463 (06.91), GYE 463W (02.99)	M1389	89 CLT (04.90)
M479	VLT 179 (02.91), GYE 479W (02.98)	M1429	WLT 826 (04.94), C429 BUV (01.04)
M542	542 CLT (12.91)	M1432	WLT 432 (12.92)
M819	WLT 342 (07.94)	M1434	WLT 434 (07.89), C629 VMX (08.02)
M845	545 CLT (01.91), OGK 708Y (02.93)	M1435	435 CLT (02.93), C637 VMX (09.02)
M853	VLT 53 (09.89), SGC 671Y (01.97)	M1436	VLT 136 (10.89)
M954	WLT 954 (07.92)	M1437	VLT 12 (10.87)

3. DATE OF DELIVERY AND ENTRY INTO SERVICE (LT/LRT/LBL)

Month	Quantity	Delivered	Quantity	Licensed for service and initial allocation (not necessarily garage at which bus first enters service)
04.78	1	M1		
06.78	1	M2		
07.78	1	M3		
08.78	1	M4		
09.78	3	M5-7		
10.78	2	M8, 9		
11.78	4	M10-13	3	M1-3 (**W**)
12.78	2	M14-15		
01.79	4	M16-19		
02.79	10	M20-29		
03.79	17	M30-45/7	25	M4 (**W**), M6-29 (**FW**)
04.79	10	M46/8-53/5/6/8	14	M30-39/41/2/5/7 (**FW**)
05.79	12	M54-7/9-65/7	5	M40/4/6/9/55 (**FW**)
06.79	9	M66/8-72/7/8/83	18	M48/50-4/6-65/7/71 (**FW**)
07.79	12	M73-6/9-82/4-86/9	16	M5 (**W**), M9/43 (**FW**), M66/8/70/2/3/5/7-9/81/3-5 (**NB**)
08.79	14	M87/8/90-101	6	M74/6/80/2/7/9 (**NB**)
09.79	16	M102-13/20/3/5/8	15	M86, 102 (**NB**), M88/90-101 (**HW**)
10.79	24	M114/6-9/21/2/4/6/7/29-36/8/40/1/4/5/6/8/9	15	M104-13/5/9/20/5/8 (**HW**)
11.79	31	M137/9/42-4/7/8/50-70/2/5/7	26	M103/14/6-8/21-4/6/7/9-33/5/7/40/1/5/7/9/51/6/61 (**HW**)
12.79	32	M171/3/4/6/8-205	25	M136/54 (**HW**), M134/8/9/42/3/6/8/52/3/5/7/9/64/6-71/4/7/81/6 (**V**)
01.80			25	M163/76/8/9/83/4/7/9/93/5/98, 201 (**ON**), M175 (**HW**), M182/5/8/90/1/94/6/7/9, 200/2/5 (**AE**)
02.80	10	M206/8-12/4/7/23/4	12	M150/60/92, 203/4 (**AE**), M158 (**V**), M162/5/72/3/80/6 (**ON**)
03.80	17	M207/13/5/6/8/9/22/31/5-9/42/4/6/8	4	M208/10/1 (**FW**), M214 (**NB**)
04.80	9	M230/40/1/5/7/9/51/2		
05.80	29	M220/1/5-29/32/3/43/50/3-6/8-62/4/5/9/72/6/8/83/7/99	1	M222 (**FW**)
06.80	44	M234/57/63/6-8/70/1/3-5/80/2/4-6/8-98, 300-10/2-6/9	69	M206/15/23/4/30/5/6/47/9/52/78/82/6/91/6, 305 (**ON**), M207/88/90 (**FW**), M209/20/5-9/32/3/7/9/41/3/5/8/50/3-6/8-62/4/5/9/72/6/83/7 (**SE**), M216/63/7/74/80/9/92/7, 300 (**AE**), M212/3/8/31/40/2/4 (**AC**), M219 (**W**)
07.80	36	M277/9/81, 311/7/8/20-47/9/53	42	M217/46/51/98, 303/4 (**ON**), M221/34/57/66/8/70/1/5/7/9/81/4/5/93/5, 301/2/8-10/2-4/7-21/3/4/6/7/30/6 (**W**), M340/2 (**HW**)
08.80	30	M348/50-2/4-72/4-8/80/2	30	M311/5/6/25/8/9/32-4/8/41/3-6/9/51/5/8/9/61 (**HW**), M322/9/31/5/9/47/54 (**FW**), M353 (**NB**), M357 (**AC**)
09.80	27	M379/81/3-91/3-8, 400-5/7-9/11	32	M324/37/50/2/6/60/3-5/7-9/78/84/6/7/9 (**FY**), M370-2/4/5/85 (**FW**), M348/81/3 (**AE**), M362/6/77/80/2 (**NB**), M388 (**AC**)
10.80	39	M392/9, 406/10/12-21/3-46/52	37	M273, 307/79/90-5, 400/2/4/7/8/14-6/23 (**FY**), M376 (**NB**), M401/3/6/13/8 (**HW**), M405/9/10/2/7/9-21/4-6/9/30 (**EW**)
11.80	21	M373, 422/47-51/3-64/6/8	36	M299, 396-9 (**FY**), M373, 411/2/8/47-61/3/4/6/8 (**EW**), M306 (**AC**), M431-46 (**V**)
12.80	40	M465/7/9-505	13	M462/5/7/9-78 (**EW**)
01.81			24	M479 (**V**), M480-96/9-502/4/5 (**HL**)
03.81			1	M498 (**HL**)
05.81	28	M506-11/13-21/3-32/4-6		
06.81	29	M512/22/33/7-49/51-63	24	M497, 503 (**HL**), M506-10/3-6/9-21/6/30/1/3/8/42 (**WN**), M511/2/7/8 (**MH**)

Month	Quantity	Delivered	Quantity	Licensed for service and initial allocation (not necessarily garage at which bus first enters service)
07.81	36	M550/64-95/8/9, 602	50	M523/4/9/34-6/40 (**WN**), M532/7/9/45-7/9 (**MH**), M554/6/7/62-84/6-95 (**FY**)
08.81	17	M596/7, 600/1/3-8/10-4/6/8	27	M522/5/7/8/41/4/8 (**WN**), M543/50-2 (**MH**), M553/8/9/88/9 (**FY**), M560/1/96/7, 600/1/3/8/10/1/4 (**AD**)
09.81	25	M609/15/7/9-39/41	4	M601/15 (**AD**), M 622/6 (**WN**)
10.81	31	M640/2-71	29	M585, 602/5-7/12/6/7 (**AD**), M618-21/3-5/7-32/4/5/7/9/41-4 (**WN**)
11.81	29	M672-84/6/8-702	25	M633/6/8/40/5-53/5-60 (**WN**), M664/6/9-71/6 (**PB**)
12.81	28	M685/7, 703-28	26	M604/5/12/65 (**AD**), M654 (**FY**), M661-3/7/8/72-4/7-83/6/8/90 (**PB**), M685/7, 700 (**E**)
01.82	15	M729-42/4	42	M684/9/91 (**PB**), M692-9, 701-19/22-33 (**E**)
02.82	22	M743/5-65	24	M610 (**AD**), M654/98, 734-50/2/3/5/6 (**E**)
03.82	40	M766-805	19	M720/1/30/51/3/4 (**E**), M757-69 (**EM**)
04.82			10	M770/2-8 (**EM**), M789/90 (**SF**)
05.82			18	M780-8 (**SF**), M791-9 (**AR**)
06.82			6	M800-5 (**SP**)
01.83	1	M806		
02.83	7	M807-13	3	M807 (**FW**), M810/1 (**AF**)
03.83	35	M814-47/9	39	M806/8/12/3/5-7/21-44 (**FW**), M814/18-20/45-7/9 (**AF**)
04.83	12	M848/50-60	5	M848/50-4 (**AF**)
05.83	15	M861-75	14	M855-60/5-9 (**B**), M862 (**FW**) M872/3 (**ON**)
06.83	6	M876-81	8	M861 (**X**), M863/70/4/5/8/9 (**NB**), M881 (**AF**)
07.83	13	M882-94	9	M876/7 (**FW**), M882-8 (**X**)
08.83	8	M895-902	1	M892 (**X**)
09.83	11	M903-12/4	21	M809/64/89/90/4-907/11/4 (**S**), M893 (**X**)
10.83	15	M913/5-28	19	M871/80, 912/3/5-8/22 (**S**), M909 (**V**), M910 (**HW**), M920/1/3-8 (**FW**)
11.83	15	M929-42/4	16	M908/35-42/4 (**WD**), M919/29 (**WN**), M930/1/3/4 (**S**)
12.83	12	M943/5-55	9	M943/5/7-54 (**WD**)
01.84	8	M956-63	4	M946/55 (**WD**), M957/9 (**S**)
02.84	35	M964-98	30	M956/8/60-3 (**S**), M964/5 (**NB**), M966 (**HW**), M967 (**AV**), M968 (**ON**), M969-74/7/80/2-5 (**WD**), M975/6/8/9 (**UX**), M986-8 (**HD**)
03.84	7	M999-1005	10	M991/7, 1001 (**GM**), M993, 1003 (**HW**), M995/9, 1002/5 (**FW**), M1000 (**HD**)
04.84	20	M1006-25	19	M981 (**CT**), M1006-13/6-25 (**V**)
05.84	16	M1026-38/40-2	16	M992 (**CT**), M994, 1032-5/8/41/2 (**HT**), M1026-9 (**V**), M1030 (**FW**), M1031 (**HW**), M1036/40 (**AF**)
06.84	11	M1039/43-50, 1441/2	5	M1037 (**HT**), M1039/43 (**NB**), M1044/5 (**GM**)
07.84	5	M1051-55	10	M1046-55 (**GM**)
08.84	7	M1056-62	3	M989/90 (**CF**), M1441 (**SW**)
09.84	10	M1063-72	12	M1057/62 (**CT**), M1058-61 (**HT**), M1064-65/8/9 (**CF**), M1442 (**SW**)
10.84	12	M1073-84	19	M1066/7/71-81 (**CA**), M1070-3/82/3 (**CF**)
11.84	18	M1085-1100/3/6	14	M1084, 1086-97, 1100 (**BN**)
12.84	38	M1101/2/4/5/7-40	10	M1085/98/9, 1101-3 (**BN**), M1106/11/2 (**HT**), M1125 (**AG**)
01.85	22	M1141-61/3	18	M1105 (**BN**), M1107-9 (**AR**), M1113-20 (**HT**), M1121/26-8/31/4 (**WN**)
02.85	24	M1162/4-83/5/6/9	45	M1122-4/9/32/3/5/7/8/40/52/4/5 (**AR**), M1136/41-51/3/56-61/3 (**HT**), M1162 (**B**), M1164/6/7 (**TC**), M1168-71 (**AG**), M1174/81/9 (**W**), M1183 (**ON**)
03.85	37	M1184/7/8/90-1217/20-5	15	M1139, 1201/7/12 (**TC**), M1195/7/8, 1202/4/5/8 (**W**), M1196 (**UX**), M1203/14 (**BN**), M1206 (**AF**)
04.85	27	M1218/9/26-49/52	39	M1177/8 (**EW**), M1179/82, 1209/10/3/20/5 (**N**), M1199, 1200/37-40/2/3 (**TC**), M1211/6/34 (**AG**), M1217/9/21-4/26-33 (**BN**), M1235/6 (**W**), M1245 (**ON**), M1246/7 (**UX**)

Month	Quantity	Delivered	Quantity	Licensed for service and initial allocation (not necessarily garage at which bus first enters service)
05.85	22	M1250/1/53-1272	8	M1251 (**FW**), M1255 (**WN**), M1256/8/60 (**HL**), M1257 (**EW**), M1263 (**AD**), M1265 (**PB**)
06.85	18	M1273-90	12	M1248/9/52-4 (**TC**), M1268-73 (**NB**), M1282 (**UX**)
07.85	15	M1291-1305	8	M1110 (**BN**), M1277-81 (**EM**), M1298, 1300 (**X**)
08.85	18	M1306-23	45	M1165/73/5/6, 1283/5/6/8-91/3-5/7/9, 1303/7-9 (**AR**), M1241/4/61/2/4/6/7 (**NB**), 1275/6 (**EM**), M1284/7/92/6/8, 1300/14 (**HT**), M1301/2/4/5/11/5 (**AF**), M1310/2 (**AD**), M1313 (**WN**)
09.85	25	M1324-48	8	M1318/20-5/7 (**WN**)
10.85	29	M1349-77	21	M1317/9/26/9-34 (**WN**), M1337-47 (**NB**), M1357 (**CT**)
11.85	22	M1378-1408/10	43	M1328/35/6/48/9/74/5/81/3/4 (**NB**), M1350-53/66-71/3/85/6/8-1401 (**SP**), M1354/6/8-63 (**CT**), M1355 (**AE**), M1364/76-8/80/2 (**X**), M1387 (**GM**)
12.85	15	M1409/11-24	19	M1403/6/9 (**BN**), M1404/5/7/8/10-2/20/2 (**HW**), M1413/4/7 (**AR**), M1415/6 (**X**), M1418/9 (**NB**)
01.86	16	M1425-40	17	M1423 (**X**), M1425-40 (**BN**)
02.86			1	M1424 (**AR**)
05.87	9	M1443-51		
06.87			9	M1443-51 (**PB**)
11.87	3	M1452-54	3	M1452-4 (**HD**)
12.87	24	M1455-78	20	M1455-71/3-5 (**HD**)
01.88			4	M1472/6-8 (**HD**)
02.88	2	M1482/3	2	M1482/3 (**PB**)
03.88	1	M1481	1	M1481 (**PB**)
04.88	4	M1479/80/4/5	4	M1479/80 (**HD**), M1484/5 (**PB**)

Above: Where the Metrobus triumphed over the Titan was in the manufacturer's greater willingness to give operators what they wanted, a policy which for enthusiasts produced a greater variety of layouts depending on the roles specified. All the while, continuous modifications were made, both by MCW and LT (and its successors). The most recent two configurations of the frontal radiator-grille treatment are demonstrated by sister Edmonton vehicles M1281 (B281 WUL) and M1277 (B277 WUL), delivered in June 1985 for the 259's aggrandisement on 3 August and captured in Holloway that afternoon. *Malc McDonald*

4. DISPOSITION OF METROBUSES UPON PRIVATISATION OF LBL SUBSIDIARIES, 1994

CentreWest, 2 September 1994 (management):
M192, 222/36/72/4/6/81/5/91, 305/8/11/6/9/24/9/30/2/7-40/3/5/7/9/52/8/60/2/4/8/9-71/3/4/83/90/3/7,
406/13/4/8/21/5/7/34/42/51/2/65/70/86/7/9/94/7-9, 504/5/23/83, 843/51/7/9-61/6/72/4/5/82-7/92/3/8,
901/38/41/3/52/79, 1049/51/4, 1144/99, 1201/44-7/56/8-60/7, 1328/35/8/40/75-8/80/2/4, 1400/12/5/8-22/38
Total 125 (all for service - disposition AT 25, ON 41, X 34, UX 25);
M192, 222/36/72/4/6/81, 324/52/73 owned by London General

Leaside Buses, 29 September 1994 (T. Cowie plc):
M266, 317/36/53/82, 419/22/6/45/50/64/74/8/85/93, 500/7-10/8/9/22/5/8-31/3-6/8/40/3-5/7-9/51/7/9/62/7/9/73/5/81/2/5-7/90/1/3/6, 600/2-5/9-15/7/9/22/4-8/30-2/5-8/41-53/7-61/3-6/9/72/3/5/6/9/81/4/6/8/9/92/4/8-702/7-21/3/6-34/6-8/40/2-54/6-8/61/2/5-8/70-8/80-93/5/6/8, 891, 903/19/29/39/88/96/8, 1000/44/70/4/5,
1109/12/21-4/6-40/52/4/5/62/4/5/9/70/3/5/6/9/82, 2209/10/3/4/6/7/9/21/7-9/31/3/9/48/9/52-5/63/5/75/6/8/9-83/5/6/8-91/3-300/3/7-10/2-4/6-24/6/7/32/62/7/79/98/9, 1401/2/4-6/13/7/24/37/43-7
Total 334 (330 service – disposition AD 59, AR 54, CT 23, E 82, SF 38, WN 74; private-hire 4)

Metroline, 7 October 1994 (management):
M1-5/18/20/41/8/54/7/8/62/70/3/7/83-5/7/8/90/1/4/7, 102/7/9/11/3/9/25/7/8/35-7/40/2/50/1/5/63/6/7/9/72/8/80/4,
238, 300/6/9/13/5/24-6/33/5/42/4/52/61/7/73/6/80/7/91/4, 403/7/9/24/8/9/32/6-8/40/3/4/6/8/9/53/5/9-61/7/8/73/82,
524/50/95, 618/21/83/96, 810/9, 910/1/24/35/7/45/50/5/6/68/74/82/93/5, 1004/31/4/5/43/7/56/7/68/71,
1167/8/74/81/3/5/6/9/92/3/5/7/8, 1202/4/5/8/18/26/73/4, 1339/42/6/8-50/66/83, 1408/9/16/23/5-31
Total 169 (150 service – disposition AC 29, EW 18, HD 43, W 56, loaned to Atlas Bus 4; Commercial Services 18 (trainers 10 (all W), private-hire 8 [HD 2, W 6]), under repair 1)
M325/33/61 owned by London General, M387 owned by London United

London Northern, 26 October 1994 (MTL Trust Holdings):
M9/12/25/7/32/3/5/42/67/72/5/8-82/92/5, 101/3/14/5/7/8/24/6/30/3/9/45/8/60/1/81/9/94/9, 213/43/94, 322/8/41/56,
481, 512/60/1/3-5/70-2/4/6/8/9/88/94, 608/16/20/3/39/40/56/74/7/8/93, 739/55/64/97, 800-2/4/24/9/76/8/9/90/6/9, 912/5-7/21/5/8/34/57/61/4/71/87/9/97, 1032/3/8/40-2/5/52/8-61/3/5-7/72/6-83, 1111/3-5/7-20/41-3/5-51/3/6-61/3, 1234/50/77/92,
1325/9-31/3/4/55/65/9/85/90/2-7, 1403/14
Total 179 (174 service – disposition HT 96, PB 78; trainer 1, private-hire 4 (of which open-top 1))

London General, 2 November 1994 (management):
M11/45/7/55/6/61/76, 120/41/4/53/6/8/64/5/71/4/6/7/88/90/1/6-8, 201/2/7/9/11/2/4-9/24/6/8/31/4/5/7/9/41/2/4/6/7/9/50/2/4-62/5/7-71/3/5/8/9/84/6-9/92/3/5/7, 302/3/7/18/20/1/3/5/31/3/4/48/50/1/4/5/7/9/61/75/9/81/5/6/92,
401/4/5/8/11/2/6/20/3/30/1/3/5/47/57/63/6/71/2/5-7/9/80/3/4/8/90, 502/13/4/6/27/32/42/6/56/66/89/97,
606/7/62/7/8/70/90/5, 706/25/60/3/9/79/94, 806-8/11/2/4/6-8/ 23/6/8/30/3/4/7/8/42/5-9/52-5/62/7/8/70/1/3/7/80/8/97,
900/2/4/5/7-9/12/4/8/22/3/6/31/3/ 40/2/4/6/7/9/53/65/70/5-8/83/91/2, 1002/5/46/55, 1107/8/77/80/96,
1203/6/11/5/20/2-6/30/2/5/7/41/64/8, 1301/2/4-6/11/5/37/47/57/64/70-3/86-9/91, 1410/1/32-6/40
Total 296 (295 service – disposition A 89, AF 28, AL 86, SW 82; private-hire 1, on loan to CentreWest 10)
M192, 222/36/72/4/6/81, 324/52/73 on hire to CentreWest

London United, 5 November 1994 (management):
M8/13/5/7/9/21/2/8-30/1/4/6/9/43/4/6/9/52/9/68/86/9/93/6/9, 100/10/12/22/31/4/8/46/7/54/7/9/62/79/83/6/7/93/5,
203/4/6/21/3/7/64, 327/63/6/87, 415/62, 506/26/54/92/8, 685/7/97, 813/5/31/2/5/6/9/41/4/56/64/81/9, 906/20/32/51/8/60/2/3/6/7/9/72/80/1/5/90/4/9, 1001/3/6-30/7/9/48/50/3/64/9/73, 1106/10/25/66/71/2/8/84/7/8/90/1/4, 1200/7/12/38/40/2/3/51/7/61/2/6/9-72, 1336/41/3-5/51-3/6/8/60/1/3/8/74/81, 1439
Total 177 (164 service – disposition AV 47, FW 46, S 21, V 50 (including 32 Airbus); trainers 9, unlicensed 4)

South London, 8 December 1994 (T. Cowie plc):
M6/7/10/4/24/38/40/9/51/60/3-6/9/74, 121/3/9/32/43/9/68/70/3/5/82/5,
200/5/8/10/20/5/30/2/3/40/5/8/51/63/77/80/2/3/90/6/8/9, 301/4/10/4/46/65/72/8/84/8/9/95/6/8-400/2/10/7/39/41/54/6/8/69/91/2/5/6, 503/11/5/7/20/1/37/9/41/52/3/5/8/68/77/80/4, 601/29/33/4/54/71/80/2/91,
722/4/41/99, 803/5/9/25/7/40/50/8/63/5/9/94/5, 927/30/6/48/54/9/73/84, 1036/62/84-1105/16, 1354/9, 1407/41/2
Total 160 (157 service – disposition BN 36, N 36, TC 62, TH 20; trainers 2, private-hire 1)

TOTAL 1450

5. METROBUSES OPERATED BY NON-LBL COMPANIES ON LT TENDERS OR 3/2 (LLSA) SERVICES

BTS
Acquired from Kelvin Central, 01.90; operated until 03.92):
CKS 385/8X, ULS 614/6/7X (Alexander RL H45/33F, new Alexander (Midland) 1982)
Hired from West Midlands Travel, 12.93:
BOK 46V, GOG 110/3/99W (MCW H43/30F, new 1980/1)

ENSIGNBUS (ENSIGN CITYBUS 29.11.90, CAPITAL CITYBUS 14.10.91, FIRST CAPITAL 03.07.98, FIRST LONDON 25.03.01, FIRST 06.12.03)
Acquired from South Yorkshire Transport, 05.88:
295-9 (JWF 495-9W) (MCW H46/27D, new SYPTE 1980; *rebuilt as H46/30F in 1992/3*)
New, 11.88:
279-94 (F279-94 NHJ) (MCW MkII H46/27D; *rebuilt as H46/31F in 1992/3*)
Acquired from Leicester CityBus, 02.90:
275-8 (FUT 39/6-8V) (MCW H45/27D, new 1980)
Acquired from Derby City Transport, 07.90:
112 (GRA 102V) (MCW H43/30F, new 1980)
Acquired from Kelvin Central, 05.90 (571), 06.90 (570), 10.90 (111):
111[i] (ULS 621X) (Alexander RL H45/33F, new Alexander (Midland) 1982)
570 (UMS 751T) (Alexander AD H46/27F, new Alexander (Midland) 1982)
571 (BLS 671V) (Alexander AD H43/30F, new Alexander (Midland) 1982)
Acquired from South Yorkshire PTE, 11.91:
101-3/6/10/3-20 (JHE 171/2/96/57/78/80/69/2/82/46-150W)
Acquired from Optare, 02.92:
107 (G107 FJW) (MCW MkII H43/30F, new West Midlands Travel 1989)
Acquired from Kirkby Leasing, 02.92:
170/1/8/9 (E470, 461, 478, 472 SON) (MCW MkII H45/30F, new LBL 1987);
179 renumbered 172 in 06.99; 171/2/8 renumbered M171/2/8 in 02.03
Hired from West Midlands Travel, 05.10.92-30.01.93:
BOK 14/39/46/53/9/62V, KJW 281/4W, LOA 419X (MCW H43/30F, new WMPTE 1979-82)
Acquired from Mainline, 09.94:
104 (JHE 194W) (MCW H46/31F, new SYPTE 1981)
Acquired from Stevensons, 09.94:
105 (JHE 138W) (MCW H46/31F, new SYPTE 1981)
Acquired from MTL, 02.96:
100/9/11[ii] (JHE 194/52/6W) (MCW H46/31F, new SYPTE 1981);
175-7 (DAE 510/2/3W) (MCW CH43/30F, new Bristol 1980)
Acquired from London General, 02.98:
301-7/9/15-9 (GYE 379, 479, 546W, BYX 284V, GYE 405W, KYO 606X, BYX 287/49V, GYE 355, 416/57W, KYV 668, 769X)
Hired from London General, 03.98:
100/11[iii], 620 (M274, 260, 246)
Acquired from CentreWest, 01.99-07.99:
310/2/3/8/22-5/7-31/5-7/9/50-4/7/61 (GYE 369W, EYE 339/43V, GYE 498/87W, OJD 843Y, GYE 348, 465W, OJD 872Y, GYE 418W, A898 SUL, EYE 330V, A941 SUL, OJD 884/66/87Y, EYE 319/40V, A751 THV, A952, 892 SUL, OJD 874/57/61Y)
Acquired from Leicester CityBus, 01.99:
330/2/3 (EYE 330/2V, GYE 413W)
Acquired from London General, 02.99:
324/34/8 (GYE 348, 484/8W)
FirstGroup national renumbering 11.03: M1245/8/9, 843, 348, 1051, 859/61, 1376-8/82, 1199, 1415, 416, 1438, 171/2/8 to to 35245/8/9, 35348/51/9/61/76-8/82/99, 35415/16/38/61/72/8 with optional WD class code; only WD35859 (M859) ever carried its number physically.
Most ex-SYT examples sold in 1999, others between 2001 and 2004

COUNTY BUS (ARRIVA EAST HERTS & ESSEX FROM 02.04.98)
Hired from West Midlands Travel, 12.93-06.94:
POG 583Y, A698 UOE (MCW MkII H43/30F, new WMPTE 1983)
Hired from West Midlands Travel, 06.94-01.96:
B781 AOC (MCW MkII H43/30F, new WMPTE 1984)
Acquired from Ensign, 03.94:
M75, 80 (JBO 75, 80W) (MCW H46/31F, new Newport Transport 1981)
M75 delicensed 03.97, sold 05.97; M80 delicensed and sold 04.98
Hired from Capital Citybus, 26.09-07.10.94:
112 (GRA 102V) (MCW H43/30F, new Derby City Transport 1980)
Hired from West Midlands Travel, 07.95:
D959 NDA (MCW MkII CH43/26F, new 1986)

Acquired from Cowie Leaside, 06.97:
M1-5 (GBU 1, 4, 5, 8, 9V) (MCW H43/30F, new GMPTE 1979); *renumbered 5351/4/5/8/9 in 1999*
(5351 re-registered OPP 741V in 05.99 but subsequently restored to GBU 1V by preservationists)
Acquired from Grey-Green, 03.97 (M367/72), 08.97 (M366):
M366/7/72 (DTG 366/7/72V) (MCW H46/31F, new Newport Transport 1980)
M372 sold 1998; M366/7 renumbered 5356/7 01.01.99; 5357 sold 1999, 5356 sold 03.00
Transferred from Leaside with Leaside Travel, 27.10.97:
M170/5, 537/73, 625/49, 1248, 1367/79/98, 1437; (M266, 491, 544 added 1998)
All transferred to Arriva London North, 03.10.98.
Acquired from Arriva London North and Arriva London South, 1998-2000:
5250-7/9/60/2/3/9, 5348/53/60/2-7/9/70 (BYX 240V, KYV 681X, KYO 612X, B283 WUL, C404 BUV, B155 WUL, KYV 756/71X,
B289 WUL, BYX 290V, KYV 782X, BYX 230V, B169 WUL, KYV 786X, GYE 493W, BYX 220/32/3/83/63V, EYE 336V, GYE 508W,
BYX 299V, A988 SYF)

GREY-GREEN (ARRIVA LONDON NORTH EAST from 02.04.98)
Acquired from South Yorkshire Transport, 02.88:
450-7/60/5 (EWF 450-7/60/5V) (MCW H46/27D, new SYPTE 1980)
451 burnt out 01.93; 457/65 sold 1995, 450/2/3/6/60 sold 03.96
Acquired from Newport, 03.93:
466-72 (DTG 366-72V) (MCW H46/31F, new 1980)
468/9 sold 03.96, 467 sold 03.97, 466 sold 08.97
Transferred from Arriva London North as trainers, 12.98:
069, 280, 788 (WYW 69T, BYX 280V, KYV 788X)

METROBUS
Acquired from London General, 09.97:
WYW 76T, BYX 216/28/35/52/9/62V, EYE 320/1V, GYE 447, 527W (ex-M76, 216/28/35/52/9, 320/1, 447/527)
Renumbered 376, 316/28/35/52/9/62, 320/1, 347, 327 in 1998

WESTLINK
Acquired from West Midlands Travel, 11.94 (until 23.09.95):
POG 594Y, B878/9 DOM (MCW MkII H43/30F, new 1982/5)

ARMCHAIR
Acquired from Ensign, 08.01:
E748 SKR, F772 EKM (MCW MkII H46/31F, new East Kent 1988/9)
Renumbered M748/72 02.02, sold 06.02
Hired from Limebourne, 19-21.04.02:
BYX 279V, GYE 476/7W
Hired from CentreWest, 19-21.04.02:
B235/59 WUL, C382 BUV
Hired from Ensign, 24.04-04.05.02:
GYE 461, 517W, KYO 630X, KYV 731/74X, OJD 829Y

LONDON TRAVELLER (incorporating COUNTY TRAVELLER; renamed METROPOLITAN OMNIBUS 09.00)
Acquired from GM Buses South, 08.98:
101-4 (MRJ 47, 54W, ORJ 76W, SND 145X (MCW H43/30F, new GMPTE 1981/2)
Acquired from West Midlands Travel, 01-08.98:
BOK 64V, GOG 228/30/3-5/7/8/45W (MCW H43/30F, new WMPTE 1980/1); *most sold 09.01*
Acquired from Metrobus, 09.99:
M76, 235/59/62, 320, 447, 527 (WYW 76T, BYX 235/59/62V, EYE 320V, GYE 447, 527W)
Acquired from Ensign, 02.00:
M199, 571, 693, 764, 801 (BYX 199V, GYE 571W, KYV 693, 764, 801X)
Acquired from Ensign, 09.01:
M468, 708, 809, 1206 (GYE 468W, KYV 708X, OJD 809Y, B206 WUL)
Acquired from Arriva Southern Counties, 03.02:
M709 (KYV 709X)
Survivors sold to Thorpe's, 01.11.02

THORPE'S
Acquired from London United, 04.00:
M415, 815
Acquired from Travel West Midlands, 06.01:
GOG 208W (MCW H43/30F, new WMPTE 1981)
POG 524Y, A700 UOE, B875 DOM (MCW MkII H43/30F, new WMPTE 1983/5)
Renumbered M208, 524, 700, 875, 09.02
Acquired from Metropolitan Omnibus, 01.11.02:
M76, 292, 444/68, 571, 693, 708/9/64, 801/9, 1206

LIMEBOURNE
Hired from various sources, 1998/9:
M34, 73, 549, 612/31/2/73, 719/76, 1134/52/5
Acquired from various sources, 1999:
M73, 120/88, 237/79, 476/7, 531, 673, 719

CONNEX BUS
Acquired from Ensign, 02.00:
M54, 140, 303, 565, 656, 802
Acquired from West Midlands, 03.00:
MW259/62, 387/95/8 (GOG 259/62W, LOA 387/95/8X) (MCW H43/30F, new 1981/2)
Most sold by April 2001 and all by August

TRAVEL LONDON
Acquired from Limebourne, 19.08.00:
471-3/6/7/9 (KYV 719X, BYX 237V, GYE 473/6/7W, BYX 279V). *Company sold to Connex Bus, 2001.*
Acquired from Travel West Midlands, 06.04 (as trainers):
2922/8/48/51/5/8 (D922/8/48/51/5/8 NDA) (MCW MkII CH43/23F, new WMT 1986)
(Note this is the second Travel London incarnation, formed out of Connex Bus in 2004)

IMPERIAL
Acquired from various sources, 2000-3:
THX 103S, BYX 132, 228/39V, EYE 322V, GYE 433/6W, KYV 802X, C440 BUV;
GOG 259W, LOA 395/8, 409X, (MCW H43/30F, new WMPTE 1981/2),
SAG 520W (MCW H43/30F, new Kingston-upon-Hull City Transport 1981),
A625 BCN, C759/67 OCN (MCW MkII H46/31F, new Northern General 1984/6)

OMNIBUS LONDON
Operated on route 60, 23.01-03.02.99:
CJH 166/70V (MCW H45/27D, new Reading Transport 1980)

SIDNEY ROAD TRAVEL / WHITE ROSE GROUP
Acquired 1998-2001:
M2, 34, 57, 73, 88, 161, 276, 377, 819/21/36/42 (THX 102S, WYW 34, 57, 73, 88T, BYX 161, 276V, GYE 377W, OJD 819/21/36/42Y);
B149 EDP (MCW MkII CH39/27F, new Reading Transport 1984)
Many displaced to spin-off Sullivan Buses, 1999

CAPITAL LOGISTICS
Acquired from Metrobus, 07.99 (*Sold 03.00***):**
BYX 216V

MITCHAM BELLE
Acquired, 17.06.00 (*until 07.04***):** 047-9 (B106 WUL, A960 SYF, A739 THV)

EAST THAMES BUSES
Acquired from Ensign, 2001:
317/8 (OJD 831/2Y) as trainers, M1010 (A710 THV) for service
Acquired from Ensign, 10.02:
BOK 70V (MCW H43/30F, new WMPTE 1980) as trainer

RED ROUTE BUSES
Acquired from Ensign, 2001-3:
M5, 49, 322, 761/71, 820/54, 1071, 1229 (THX 105S, WYW 49T, EYE 322V, KYV 761/71X, OJD 820/54Y, B71, 229 WUL)

BORO'LINE MAIDSTONE
Hired from Maidstone & District, 02.90-03.90:
5204/7/10 (A204/7/10 OKJ) (MCW Mk II H46/31F, new 1984)

BLUE TRIANGLE
Acquired from Ensign, 1998/9:
MCW19, 27/8, 112/46/60/79/95, 270/1, 462/3, 616, 932/81, 1012/33 (WYW 19, 27/8T, BYX 112/46/60/79/95, 270/1V, GYE 462/3W, KYO 616X, A932 SUL, A981 SYF, A712/33 THV); MCW503 (GBU 3V) (MCW H43/30F, new GMPTE 1980), MCW1950/2-5 (C950 HWF, C952-5 LWJ) (MCW MkII CH42/28F, new SYPTE 1985/6) (*sold 05.99*)
Acquired from various sources, 1996/8:
JUM 501/2V (MCW H46/31F, new WYPTE 1980), UKA 20/1V (MCW H43/30F, new Merseyside PTE 1980), DAE 514W (MCW H46/30F, new Bristol 1980), MNC 494/7W, ORJ 73W (MCW H43/30F, new GMPTE 1980/1), PUA 508W (MCW H46/31F, new WYPTE 1980)
Acquired from London United, 08.02:
MCW1190, 1200, 1341 (B190, 200 WUL, C341 BUV)
Acquired from Metropolitan Omnibus, 01.11.02:
MCW468, 693, 809 (GYE 468W, KYV 693, 809X)
Acquired from Ensign, 10.02-01.03:
MCW444, 571, 801 (GYE 444, 571W, KYV 801X)

ARRIVA CROYDON & NORTH SURREY, ARRIVA GUILDFORD & WEST SURREY, ARRIVA WEST SUSSEX
Acquired from Arriva London North and Arriva London South, 1999/2000 (retaining fleet numbers):
M168, 378/88/95, 417/54/92/6, 503/19-22/8/34/6/47/8/51/7/9/86/96, 611/3-5/31/2/48/54/8/60/76/86, 709/17/76, 996, 1134, 1210/63/75/80
Acquired from Arriva Kent & Sussex, 04.99:
5201-10 (A201-10 OKJ) (MCW MkII H46/31F, new Maidstone & District 1984). *Disposed of 2001*

ENSIGNBUS (second incarnation)
Acquired from various sources, 1999-2003 (fleet numbers varying according to use):
BYX 140/2, 243/50/68V, EYE 344V, GYE 401, 570W, GRA 102V, BSN 878V, GOG 138/75, 256/61/5/9/72W, KJW 322W, SAG 525W, ORJ 76/8, 100W, SND 106X, ANA 180Y (MCW MkI); UWW 515/7/9X (Alexander); A638/44 BCN, A144/6 AMO, B147/9 EDP, C779/80 OCN, E747/9/52 SKR, F762/7/73/5EKM, F292 NHJ, F821 YLV (MCW MkII); F84 UJN (MCW MkII tri-axle)
Former Ensignbus 100/6/16/7/22/8/34/8/44/6/7/9/56/8/60/1/5/9/72/4/6/8/80/90, 242-4/70 sold to Town & Country, 11.00
Preserved in museum fleet, 2008: M1

6.   METROBUSES OPERATED BY DEDICATED TOURING FIRMS

THE BIG BUS COMPANY
Three-axle examples acquired from Ensign via New World First Bus, Hong Kong:
ML69, 153/9/64, 326/55, 764, 869/81, 901/49 (F69 SYE, F153/9/64, 326/55 UJN, E764, 869/81, 901/49 JAR)
Re-registrations and reclassifications: ML164 to ML16 (B16 BSS), ML159 to ML20 (B20 DMS) and ML355 to ML15 (B15 BUS)

LONDON COACHES (Arriva presenting London)
Acquired from Arriva London North and Arriva London South, 1998-2000:
M121/43, 245/96, 353/89, 495, 500/9/25/30/3/9/53/5/8, 603/63/72/82, 707/10/24/9/48, 840/63/95, 927, 1152, 1227/39/65, 1310, 1401 (*into MB class; closed-top variants used in service on 185*)
Tri-axle examples acquired from Ensign via New World First Bus, Hong Kong:
EMB 763-5/7-73/5-82/5 (D553 YNO, E964/5, 767-73 JAR, D675 YNO, A737/5 WEV, UAR 776Y, MXT 179, A755/0/49 WEV, WKJ 785)
EMB779 converted to single-door. All full open-top.

LONDON PRIDE SIGHTSEEING (City Sightseeing London)
Acquired from various sources, 1994-2000 (various fleet numbers according to roof status):
WYW 26, 64, 74T, BYX 129/44, 205/55V, EYE 319/25V, KYV 804X
VRG 415-8T, BOK 68/72/5V, EWF 452/4/5/7/60/5V, FKM 266/70V, LAT 505-7/10/1/3-5V, DTG 368/9/71V, SAG 516-8/20/2/4-6/8W, GOG 128, 223/33W, JHE 141/3/63/4W, JWF 490W, MRJ 53W, ORJ 80W, ULS 621X, SND 111/25/32X, ANA 160/79Y
A144/6 AMO, F292 NHJ (MCW Mk II)
UWW518/9X (Alexander)

7A. GARAGES AND ROUTES ALLOCATED METROBUSES

LONDON TRANSPORT GARAGES AND SUCCESSORS

Garage	Start Date	End Date	Routes (unscheduled in italics, (ii) denotes second route of same number)
A (Sutton)	29.09.90	07.02	80, 93, 127, 151, 152, 154, 157, 163, 164, 189(i), 213, 280, 293, *393*, 413, N44, N68, N88, N155
AA (Colliers Wood)	03.06.89	23.02.91	*152, 163*, 200
AC (Willesden)	01.06.80	06.02	**Crew:** 6, 8
			OPO: 6, 52, 98(ii), 172, 226, 260, 266, 297, 302, *316*, N6, N18, N52, N91(i), N98
	07.02	16.02.04	**Crew:** 6, 98
			OPO: *260*, 302
AD (Palmers Green)	19.09.82	10.01	29, 34, 102, 121, 125, 141, 298, 329, W2, N9(i), N29
AE (Hendon)	10.02.80	06.06.87	113, 143, 183, 186, 240, N59
AF (Putney)	25.02.83	05.02	14, 22, 37, 39, 74, 85, *170*, 264(i), 265, *P11*, N14, *N22*, London by Night Tour
AG (Ash Grove)	18.10.84	11.86	35, 106, N56, Touristlink
AK (Streatham)	10.06.87	14.03.92	49, 50, 59(i), 109, 118, 137, 137A, 159, *249*(ii), 250, 349
AL (Merton)	08.89	11.02	19, 22, 44, 49, 77, 152, 155, *156*, 163, 164, 170, 200, *201*, 219, 270, 280, 344, 355, 452
AR (Tottenham)	17.06.82	18.06.04	**Crew:** 41, 73
			OPO: *24*, 41, 67, 73, 76, 149, *168*, 171A, *188*, 243, 243A, 259, ELX, N41, N73, N83
AT (Acton Tram Depot)	27.03.93	12.00	207, E3
AV (Hounslow)	04.09.82	01.04	9, 27, 37, *81*, 91(i), 98(i), 110, 111, 116, 120, 140, 202, 222, 232(i), 235(ii), 237, *257(i)*, 281, 337, *391*, 406, 509, E4, H22, H23, *H25*, H32, *H37*, H91, *H98*, R70, N9(ii), N11, N65, N97
B (Battersea)	06.05.83	02.11.85	39
B (Wood Lane)	05.94	05.94	*9A, 72* (loans from Shepherd's Bush)
BB (Battersea Bridge)	08.06.96	27.06.98	49, 295
BN (Brixton)	19.11.84	21.07.90	**Crew:** *109, 133*
			OPO: 50, 59(i), 95(i), 109, 118, 133, 189(i), N69, N78
	10.02.93	11.01	**Crew:** *137, 159*
			OPO: 19, 59(ii), 109, 118, 137, 137A, 159, 250, 319, 689, N19
CA (Clapham) *(displaying AK code)*	27.10.84	07.02.87	37, 249(i), N60
CF (Chalk Farm)	30.08.84	10.86	**Crew:** 24, *68*
			OPO: 24, 46, 168, 214
	06.09.92	31.07.93	*46*, 135(ii), 139, 274(ii), Z1
CT (Clapton)	14.04.84	22.04.87	22, 22A, 30, 277
	23.11.91	05.00	38, 106, 242(ii), 253, N38, N253
	10.00	05.03	*38*, 242(ii), 253
E (Enfield)	30.12.81	07.02	**Crew:** 279, 279A
			OPO: 107, 121, 135(i), 144A, 149, 191, 192, 217, 217B, 231, 259, 279, 279A, 307, *313*, 317, 359, N90, N149, N279
	11.02	01.03	121, *149, 279*, 307, *313*
	02.03	11.03	121, *149, 279*, 307, *313*
	17.01.06	17.01.06	121
ED (Edmonton)	11.11.95	27.04.96	4, 41, 271
EM (Edmonton)	24.03.82	01.02.86	**Crew:** *149, 279, 279A*
			OPO: 191, 259, W8, N90
EC (Edmonton)	03.10.98	13.01.06	**Leaside Travel:** 34, 121, 167, 184, 231, 232, 313, 616(ii), 617, 629, 667, 675, 679, 683, 688, 699, W13
	01.06.02	07.04	**Service:** 34, 125, *444*
EW (Edgware)	22.10.80	09.03	13, 32, 107, 113, 140, 142, 143, 143A, 186, 204(ii), 205(i), 221, 240, 286, 288, 292, *303*, *305*, N16, N18, N59, N66, N98, *N140*
FW (Fulwell)	19.03.79	21.05.03	**Crew:** 27, 33, 281
			OPO: 27, 33, 57, 71, *85*, 90, 90B, 110, *131*, 202, 267, 270, 281, 281s, 285, 290, 337, *391*, 411, R68, *R69, R70*
FY (Finchley)	25.09.80	04.12.93	**Crew:** *13, 43*
			OPO: 13, 17, 26, 43, 82, 125, 134, 221, 263, W7, N2, N13, N21
G (Greenford)	07.03.98	05.99	282, E1
GM (Victoria)	04.07.84	13.08.93	**Crew:** *2(i), 2B, 11, 19*, 52A, *500*
			OPO: 9, 11A, 14, 19, 22, 39, 52, 52A, 77A, 344, RLST, Night Bus Standby

Garage	Start Date	End Date	Routes (unscheduled in italics, (ii) denotes second route of same number)
HD (Harrow Weald)	14.04.83	18.02.04	**Crew:** 140 **OPO:** 114, 136, 140, 182, 183, 186, 209, 245, 258, 340, N17, N59, *H12, H14*
HH (Hounslow Heath)	06.03.99	07.03	*81, 216,* 235, *285, 411,* H23, H91, *R70*
HL (Hanwell)	17.01.81	27.03.93	**Crew:** 207 **OPO:** 92, 105, 195, 207, 274(i), 282, 607, E1, E2, E3, N89
HR (Harlesden) *(recoded and renamed **PR** (Park Royal), 01.01.03)*	23.09.00	13.02.04	*95*(ii), 260, 266, *460*
HT (Holloway)	08.05.84	02.04	**Crew:** 10, *74, 390,* N93 **OPO:** 4, 10, 13, 14, 14A, 17, 17A, 19, 27, 41, 43, 46, 74, 91(ii), 104, 134, 135(ii), 139, 143, 153, 214, *263,* 263A, 271, 274(ii), 390, *C11,* W7, *X43,* N1, N2, N5, N6, N13, N20, N43, N65, N91(ii), N92, N93, N134
HW (Southall)	17.09.79	09.08.86	92, 105, 120, 195, 232, 273, 274(i), 282, N89
K (Kingston)	29.10.94	23.09.95	411, *468*(i)
	28.06.97	12.97	57
(13-27.05.02 at outstation)	13.03.98	27.05.02	411, 467, 568
KX (King's Cross)	29.03.03	05.03	**Crew:** *390*
MH (Muswell Hill)	11.06.81	11.88	**Crew:** *43,* 134 **OPO:** 43, 134, 244, W7, N2, N59 *(2 Ms till 21.07.90)*
N (Norwood)	27.04.85	07.02.87	2(i), 68, 196
	21.07.90	25.05.91	**Crew:** *2B* **OPO:** 2(i), 2A, 3A, 68, *X68*
	28.11.92	27.01.96	2(ii), 2A, 68, 137A, *249*(ii), *X68*
NB (Norbiton)	15.07.79	07.09.91	**Crew:** 65 **OPO:** 57, 65, 71, 72, 85, 131, *200,* 211(i), 213, 213A, *216,* 285, X71
ON (Alperton)	24.01.80	05.12.98	**Crew:** 18, 83 **OPO:** 79, 79A, 83, *91*(ii), 92, *95*(ii), 105, 112, 182, 187, *205*(iii), 224(ii), 226, 258, 282, 297, E1, N89, N98, N207
	17.05.99	13.02.04	79, 83, 92, *258*
PB (Potters Bar)	19.11.81	11.09.04	**Crew:** *134* **OPO:** 82, 84, 84A, 107, 217, 231, 232(ii), 234(ii), 242(i), 263, 298, 310A, 310B, 313, 317, 326s, 634, 699, W8, *X43,* N13, N20, N21, N80, N92
PV (Perivale)	26.06.03	12.03	*95*(ii), *205*(iii), *297*
RA (Waterloo)	09.98	25.05.02	**Crew:** *11* **OPO:** 77A
S (Shepherd's Bush)	31.08.83	01.04	**Crew:** *9, 10, 12, 94* **OPO:** 9, *9A,* 10, 27, 49, 72, 73, 88, 94, 148, 220, 255(i), 283, 295, H91, N50, N51, N65, N92, N93, N94(ii), N97
SE (Stonebridge Park)	02.06.80	15.08.81	**Crew:** 18, *260,* 266 **OPO:** *112*
SF (Stamford Hill)	03.06.82	13.05.95	**Crew:** *149, 253* **OPO:** 67, 73, 106, 149, 243, 253, N83 **Leaside Travel:** 617, 629
	04.03.96	27.10.97	617, 629 (**Leaside Travel**)
	01.03	31.05.03	*149,* 242(ii), *253*
SJ (Swanley) *(known internally as **Y**)*	01.12.95	02.96	*61*
SP (Sidcup)	12.07.82	21.06.86	**Crew:** 21, 161 **OPO:** 21, 21A, 51, 161, 228, 229, 233, 299(i)
SW (Stockwell)	28.08.84	08.86	170 *(AVE trials; plus very occasional loans of standard Ms from Victoria)*
	27.01.91	18.02.03	11, 37, 49, 52, 77A, 77C, 88, 133, 156, 170, *188,* 189(i), *196,* 295, 337, 344, 345, 670, P11, N11, N19, N37, N44, N77, N87
TC (Croydon)	14.02.85	15.03.87	**Crew:** 68 **OPO:** 68, 127, 127A, 130, 130B, 157, 166, 190(i), 197, *234*(i)
	14.03.92	04.01	50, 59(i), 64, 68, 68A, 109, 130, 197, 255(ii), 264(ii), 312, *403, 407,* 409, 412, 466, 468(ii), 612, *TL1,* X30

Garage	Start Date	End Date	Routes (unscheduled in italics, (ii) denotes second route of same number)
TH (Thornton Heath)	10.93	05.04.96	*60*, 109, *250*, 264(ii), *312*, N69, N78
TV (Tolworth)	03.11.01	07.03	*57*, 406, 418, 467
UX (Uxbridge)	15.07.81	03.04	**Crew:** 207
(new location from 03.12.81)			**OPO:** 98(i), 98A, 204(i), 207, 207A, 222, 223, 224(i), 607, 622, 697, 698, *U1*, *U4*, *X767*, N89, N207
V (Turnham Green)	19.12.79	10.05.80	91(i), 267, N97
V (Stamford Brook)	10.05.80	06.01.90	**Crew:** 27
			OPO: 9, 27, 91(i), 267, A1, A2, A3, E3, E4
	07.09.91	09.11.96	9, 27, 94, 190(ii), 609, A1, A2, E3, E4, H91, N9(ii), N27, *N67*, N97
	30.10.97	25.05.02	27, 94, 283, *391*, H91
W (Cricklewood)	c11.11.78	02.04	**Crew:** 16, 16A, 266, N94(i)
			OPO: 16, 16A, 32, 112, 113, *139*, 143A, *189*(ii), 205(ii), 240, 245, 266, 316, 611, 616(i), 634, 643, N16, N59, N66, N94(i)
WD (Wandsworth)	23.11.83	11.07.87	**Crew:** *28*, N68, N88
			OPO: 39, 44, 220, 295, N68, N88
WN (Wood Green)	04.06.81	30.01.04	**Crew:** 29, 41, *141*, N29
			OPO: 29, 34, 41, 67, 84A, 102, 141, 144(i), *144*(ii), 144A, *184*, 221, *263*, 298, 329, 617, 629, 644, 684, W2, W3, N29
WR (West Ramp)	03.09.94	08.96	A1, A2
X (Westbourne Park)	27.06.83	12.03	**Crew:** 7, 18, *23*, *28*
			OPO: 7, 18, 23, 27, 28, *31*, 52A, 295, *328*, N18, N23, N27, *N31*, N50, N56, N59, N99, N139
Y (St Mary Cray)	27.03.00	28.04.00	1
	21.12.01	04.02	61

INDEPENDENT GARAGES

Company	Garage	Start Date	End Date	Routes (unscheduled in italics) - all OPO
Ensignbus	**PT** (Purfleet)	16.07.88	18.08.90	62, 62A, 145, 165, 246, 248, 252, 348, 365, 446, 550
(Ensign Citybus,	**DM** (Dagenham)	02.12.89	23.03.02	1, 62, 62A, *86B*, 97A, 123, 145, 165, 215, 248, 252, 277, 296, 323, 348, 365, *396*, 550, 552, 645, 650, 652, 674, 678, D5, D6, N99
Capital Citybus,				
First Capital,				
First London,	**H** (Hackney)	19.10.96	28.06.97	1, 158, 215, 257, 678, *D5*, *D6*, ELX
First)		21.03.98	23.02.02	*20*, *158*, 257, *678*, *D5*, *D6*
	NP (Northumberland Park)	30.11.91	07.02	*19*, 20, *22B*, *67*, *76*, *91*(ii), *97*, 97A, *153*, 158, *191*, 212, 215, 257, *259*, *263*, *298*, 299(ii), 357, 616(ii), 678, ELX, W8, N1, N20, N50, *N91*(ii)
	R (Rainham)	23.02.02	02.04	123, *179*, 369
Ensignbus	**PT** (Purfleet)	08.02	08.02	42
(second incarnation)				
Armchair	**AH** (Brentford)	08.01	29.06.02	65
Blue Triangle	**FL** (Ferry Lane)	29.08.08	12.05	60, 127, 185, 248, *368*, 474, *492*
London Traveller	**NE** (Neasden)	27.06.98	mid-1999	*42*, 143, 187, 302, 487, 626, 643
(Metropolitan Omnibus)	**HN** (Harlesden)	mid-1999	01.11.02	143, 187, 302, 487, 626, 643, H12, N18, N98
Driver Express	Beddington	23.01.99	03.02.99	60
Connex Bus	**QB** (Battersea)	15.03.00	17.03.00	156
		07.07.01	07.01	156 (*as Excalibur Travel*)
	BC (Beddington Cross)	05.02.00	07.01	*3*, 156, N3
Capital Logistics	West Drayton	23.01.99	04.99	60 (*Hired from London General*)
		07.99	04.03.00	60 (*M216*)
BTS	**BT** (Borehamwood)	01.90	03.91	*292 (ex-Kelvin Scottish examples from route 355)*
		11.93	04.12.93	*292 (hired ex-West Midlands examples)*
County Bus	**GY** (Grays)	03.96	19.03.03	324, 348, 370, 373, 383
(Arriva East Herts	**WE** (Ware)	04.96	12.01.03	310, 310A, 311, 395, 510
& Essex)				

INDEPENDENT GARAGES continued

Company	Garage	Start Date	End Date	Routes (unscheduled in italics) - all OPO
Grey-Green	DX (Barking)	22.02.88	07.96	20, *103*, 125, 173, 235, 313, 275, 473, W13
	SH (Stamford Hill)	22.02.88	03.96	125, *141*, *168*, 298, 313
Metrobus	MB (Green Street Green)	30.08.97	10.97	261
		29.08.98	10.98	*161*, 261
		06.99	06.99	*119 (once)*
		19.03.01	05.05.01	*196*
Nostalgiabus	Mitcham	17.05.97	23.04.01	60, 127, 156, 196, 613
East Thames Buses	BV (Belvedere)	02.02	20.08.04	*108, 132, 180*, 661 *(just M1010)*
	AG (Ash Grove)	07.03	07.03	150 *(once, by M1010)*
MTL London Suburban (MTL London)	ED (Edmonton)	26.05.95	11.11.95	4, 41, 271, N6
				*Thereafter see **ED** (Edmonton) and **EC** (Edmonton) in Appendix 7A*
Amberlee	Strood	08.02	04.03	185
Carousel Buses	High Wycombe	08.02	11.01.03	185
Trustline	South Mimms	07.09.02	04.03	185
London Coaches (Arriva presenting London)	WD (Wandsworth)	09.09.02	05.10.03	185
Limebourne	Battersea	20.10.98	19.08.00	1, 42, 156, *211*, 344, *C3*
Travel London	QB (Battersea)	19.08.00	07.07.01	156, 344
Thorpes	Wembley	01.11.02	10.03	143, *187*, *210*, 302, *487*, 626, 643, H12
Westlink	K (Kingston)	29.10.94	23.09.95	*131*, 411, *468*, 661
				*Thereafter see **K** (Kingston) in Appendix 7A*

8.   COMMERCIAL AND COUNTY COUNCIL ROUTES OPERATED BY METROBUSES

LBL
310, 310A (commercial), 84, 242, 360 (Hertfordshire CC)

London United
402, 416, 555, 556, 557, 681 (Surrey CC)

MTL London / Metroline London Northern
360, 840, 841, 842 (Hertfordshire CC), Z1 (commercial)

Metroline
716, 732 (Christmas Day commercial services),
812, 832A, 832B, 832C, 833, 834 (Hertfordshire CC)

Westlink
402, 416, 661, 681 (Surrey CC)

CentreWest
335 (Buckinghamshire CC), 618 (commercial)

Capital Citybus / First Capital
323, 324, 347, 348, 349, 510, 511, 623, 648 (commercial)

Arriva Croydon & North Surrey / Arriva Guildford & West Surrey / Arriva West Sussex
405, 406, 408, 409, 420, 422, 440 (Surrey CC)

London General
70, 70D (commercial open-top),
420, 440, 520, 522, 540, 668 (Surrey CC)

Arriva East Herts & Essex
310, 311, *331*, *333*, 370, 373 (Hertfordshire CC),
310A (commercial, joint with MTL London Northern / Metroline London Northern), 324, 348 (commercial)

Nostalgiabus
306, 755 (commercial)

Town & Country
324, 348 (commercial)

Ensignbus (second incarnation)
324, 325, 348 (commercial)

Cowie Leaside / Leaside Travel
318, 327, 333 (tourist), *DSS* (government)

BTS
355 (Hertfordshire CC)

Above: The only duties on which Metrobuses can be seen nowadays in London are those carrying tourists round at a leisurely pace. London Coaches, known since 1998 as Arriva presenting London, was the recipient of several of CMB's 12-metre tri-axle mkII Metrobuses at the same time as The Big Bus Company was taking examples. Twelve are now operated, including EMB773 (E773 JAR), which began life in November 1987 as ML52 (DU 8341). On 17 September 2006 it is wrenching its not inconsiderable bulk round the revamped Trafalgar Square. *Author*

Bibliography

Books

The London Bus Review of … (1975-1992), LOTS, 1975-1992
London Transport Buses / London Bus Handbook, Lawrie Bowles / Nicholas King *et al*,
    Capital Transport 1977-2002
London Transport Scrapbook for 1977, 1979, Jim Whiting, Capital Transport 1978, 1980
British Bus Fleet Survey: Rear-Engined Double-Deckers, Gavin Booth, Ian Allan 1987.
The London Bus Diary 1991/92, R. J. Waterhouse, TPC 1992.

Magazines, supplements, articles and periodicals

The London Bus, LOTS, monthly 1974-present
London Bus Magazine, LOTS, quarterly 1975-present;
    (notably No 119, 'Modern Workhorses 2: MCW Metrobuses' by Matthew Wharmby, Spring 2002)
BUSES magazine, Ian Allan monthly;
    (notably 'Unsung Metropolitan Heroes' by Matthew Wharmby, August 2004)
SUP-43A London Bus Disposals – The Ms, Ts and Ls, Where are they Now? November 2000, LOTS, 2000.
SUP-44A London Bus Disposals – Where are they Now? March 2008, LOTS, 2008.
Metrobus Dispersal, Keith Jenkinson, Autobus Review Publications, 2005.

Websites and Groups

Bus Lists on the Web (www.buslistsontheweb.co.uk)
Ian's Bus Stop – MCW Metrobus (http://www.countrybus.org/Metro/metro.htm)
The Old Bus Garage's Modern London Transport Classes in Preservation
    (http://www.self-preservation-society.co.uk/jotter/history/other.shtml)
mcw-metrobus Yahoogroup (http://autos.groups.yahoo.com/group/Mcw-Metrobus)